Divided States of America

The Slash and Burn Politics
of the 2004
Presidential Election

D0029364

Divided States of America

The Slash and Burn Politics of the 2004 Presidential Election

Edited by

LARRY J. SABATO

UNIVERSITY OF VIRGINIA CENTER FOR POLITICS

New York · Boston · San Francisco
London · Toronto · Sydney · Tokyo · Singapore · Madrid
Mexico City · Munich · Paris · Cape Town · Hong Kong · Montreal

Executive Editor:	Eric Stano
Senior Marketing Manager:	Elizabeth Fogarty
Cover Design Manager:	Wendy Ann Fredericks
Cover Designer:	Base Art Company
Cover Photos:	John Kerry: ©Jim Young/Reuters/Landov and George W. Bush: ©JimYoung/Reuters/Corbis
Senior Manufacturing Buyer:	Alfred C. Dorsey
Printer and Binder:	Courier Westford
Cover Printer:	Phoenix Color Corp.

Library of Congress Cataloging-in-Publication Data
Divided states of America : the slash and burn politics of the 2004 presidential election / edited by Larry J. Sabato.—1st ed.
    p. cm.
Includes bibliographical references and index.
ISBN 0-321-27764-3 (alk. paper)
    1. Presidents—United States—Election—2004.   2. Political campaigns—United States.
I. Sabato, Larry.
JK5262004.D58 2006
324.973'0931—dc22
                                    2005011696

Visit our Web site at www.ablongman.com

ISBN: 0-321-27764-3

2 3 4 5 6 7 8 9 10 – CRS – 08 07 06 05

Table of Contents

✣

✢

✢

✢

✢

✢

Introduction

Larry J. Sabato

UNIVERSITY OF VIRGINIA CENTER FOR POLITICS

What an election year! The country may be deeply divided about the results of the 2004 presidential contest, but everyone can agree that the Bush-Kerry clash was about as good as it gets in American politics.

The photo-finish recount dispute put 2000 in the history books, even though the actual Bush-Gore campaign was dull and undistinguished, fought over micro-issues and blurred visions of the future. Not 2004. Bush and Kerry were opposites, fighting about macro-issues of war and peace, recession and prosperity, irreconcilable cultural values. Most campaigns have lulls, sometimes lengthy ones. Not 2004. Most observers cannot recall even a long weekend without attacks, big events, and intrigue in this intense political war. Virtually every modern race involving an incumbent President is either a runaway reelection victory or a death watch for an unpopular Chief Executive. Not 2004. George W. Bush never truly seemed out of harm's way, nor did he appear mortally wounded at any point. Voters usually see the major-party candidates in shades of gray, both men a muddled mixture of attractive qualities and notice-able flaws. Not 2004. The match-up between Bush and John F. Kerry was a battle of Good versus Evil, or Evil versus Good, depending on one's party and ideological affiliations. Almost no one was neutral, most everyone was passionate—and a kind of biblical Armageddon was the result.

Blood was not literally spilled, but figuratively, the map of the United States was sharply divided between the clashing colors of Bush Red and Kerry Blue. It took little imagination to see the hues as by-products of the rivers of blood, sweat, and tears shed by the hundreds of thousands of hard-working volunteers on each side of this nasty party war.

Along with many of the contributors to this volume, I spent my election year traveling to several dozen states, crisscrossing the Red and Blue boundaries and visiting some battlegrounds so often I could have established residency. Some academics and political practitioners have attempted to downplay the differences among the peoples of the various American regions, but to me those differences were stark in 2004, a great gulf separating the average audience one would encounter in the Northeast or California from those of the South or Midwestern breadbasket states.

In this book, my colleagues and I will try to explain this amazing election, looking at the nonviolent civil war between Red and Blue, Republican and Democrat, Bush and Kerry. We will cover everything from the mechanics of the party campaigns to the quasi-reliable election-day exit polls, looking at the big picture while taking care to bore into the often contradictory data generated by survey and voting results. Sometimes we will disagree, as political aficionados are inclined to do, and leave the resolution of the disputes to you, dear readers. But we all approach this election with the respect a historic encounter deserves.

The book begins with a look at the ups and downs of the nominations and conventions by Brooke Brower, a member of ABC News's political unit during the hectic election season.

Next, *The Hotline's* Editor-in-Chief, Chuck Todd, looks at the impact of small events on the presidential race. Claude Marx of the *Eagle-Tribune* takes a close look at the ups and downs of Howard Dean's candidacy.

The next two chapters take an in-depth look at both the present-day and historical significance of the 2004 presidential race first by the editor and then by Rhodes Cook of *The Rhodes Cook Letter*. Next, Susan MacManus of the University of South Florida considers the impact of Senator Kerry's campaign strategies within the Red States.

Two writers tackle the role of the media in the 2004 election. My colleague at the University of Virginia, Paul Freedman, examines campaign advertisements and the Swift Boat Veterans for Truth, while *The Hotline* editor Vaughn Ververs considers the impact of everything from bloggers to the Dean Scream.

Commissioner Michael Toner from the Federal Election Commission explores the impact of campaign finance on the 2004 race, while Dr. Michael Cornfield of PEW Internet and American Life Project looks at the role of the Internet. Russell Muirhead, Nancy L. Rosenblum, Daniel Schlozman, and Francis X. Shen from Harvard University provide an in-depth examination of the role of religion in politics in their chapter.

William Saletan of slate.com and Charlie Cook of the *Cook Political Report* provide two different synopses of the 2004 election through their highly interesting, but varying looks at the presidential race in their concluding chapters.

I would like to pay special thanks to Molly Clancy at the University of Virginia Center for Politics for her dedication in assembling a fantastic group of authors. I would also like to thank Matt Smyth, Peter Jackson, and David Wasserman for the editorial and graphic talents they provide for my Crystal Ball. Through their editorial support, Joshua Scott and Ken Stroupe were essential to the book's compilation, title, and success. The staff, Board of Advisors, and interns (particularly Samantha Silverberg and Rishi Roy) at the Center for Politics deserve recognition for their tireless work on behalf of the Center. The team at Allyn & Bacon/Longman—especially Eric Stano, Kara Wylie, and Elizabeth Fogarty—have been essential throughout the publication process. Also, thank you to Lorraine Patsco from Big Color Systems, Inc. for her resolve in producing this book.

Undoubtedly, the biggest influence in producing this book has been my Crystal Ball (http://www.centerforpolitics.org/crystalball) where more information can be found on the 2004 election as well as up-to-date analyses of the upcoming 2006 and 2008 races.

When you have finished our work, we hope that you will have not just a greater understanding of the 2004 presidential campaign, but also a deeper appreciation for the precedent-setting nature of this remarkable contest. As always, the future is unknowable, and 2008 may or may not bring another election of comparable drama. Yet after reviewing the highways and byways of 2004, it is nearly impossible to believe that the next time will be less exciting. Given the precedents of 2000 and 2004, and the unquestionable polarization that exists among the regions of the United States, the 2008 election is much more likely to see more slash and burn politics than the necessarily sleepy accounts written of the Reagan-Mondale and Clinton-Dole match-ups of, respectively, 1984 and 1996.[1] And for that, we scribblers of politics will be grateful.

Larry J. Sabato
Director, Center for Politics
University of Virginia
Charlottesville, Virginia
February 2005

NOTES

1. For example, see Jack Germond and Jules Witcover, *Wake Us When It's Over: Presidential Politics of 1984* (New York: Macmillan Publishing, 1985); and Larry J. Sabato, *Toward the Millennium: The Elections of 1996* (Boston: Allyn and Bacon, 1997).

CHAPTER ONE

Nominations and Conventions

Brooke Brower
FORMERLY OF THE ABC NEWS POLITICAL UNIT

INTRODUCTION: POST-9/11 NOMINEES

The 2004 presidential election will hold the rights to the claims of "most expensive" and "highest turnout" for at least a couple of years until the 2008 election likely shatters those records. The election's more lasting legacy could very well be the stories of the two nominees: how one man became the nominee against seemingly insurmountable odds and how the other man won reelection against seemingly insurmountable odds.

President Bush had no major opposition to getting the GOP's nomination for a second term. This was in contrast to the experience that his father, President George H. W. Bush, had had in 1992 when conservative commentator Pat Buchanan challenged him. This President Bush had a much different experience as the party (and much of the country) had rallied around him since 9/11, and a vast majority of Republicans only strengthened their embrace for the president with the war in Iraq and continuing efforts to prevent future terrorist attacks.

So, with the Republican nomination a foregone conclusion, Democrats received much of the media's attention and scrutiny during 2003 and the early part of 2004. National security dominated the debate, intertwined with the war in Iraq and often overshadowing the economy and other domestic issues. A large Democratic field of candidates further enhanced the media's attention to the nomination process—that was at least until a certain New Englander ran away with it after another New Englander appeared to have already run away with it and lost it spectacularly.

Once the Democrats settled on their ticket and the conventions arrived, the Bush-Cheney and Kerry-Edwards campaigns seemed to engage in a tug-of-war over the same message. Both parties used their conventions to assure America that they would keep the country safe and secure. The conventions would mark the beginning of the general campaign sprint to Election Day, but the road to those conventions had a number of major turns, especially for the Democrats.

THE INVISIBLE PRIMARY: THE AUTUMN OF KERRY'S CAMPAIGN

It's a wonder that Republicans—and even some Democrats—never seized upon the theme of "Dead Man Walking" to describe the presidential campaign of Sen. John Kerry. Perhaps it would have been too morbid, too extreme, and dare I suggest even too negative for the ever-sinking tastes and sense of decorum in political discourse displayed on television. But in the fall of 2003, Kerry was exactly that—a floundering candidate with an unclear message and a campaign that many Democrats, Beltway pundits, and primary voters viewed as dead on arrival.

And to all of their credit, things were terrible for Kerry. After months and months of forgettable sound-bite producing multi-candidate debates only the press, Iowans, New Hampshirites, and the writers of *Saturday Night Live* cared about, even less interesting cattle-call forums hosted by interest groups, countless appearances on television, and weeks-on-end of glad-handing in the Hawkeye and Granite States, Kerry had failed to emerge as a strong candidate to even ride in the wake of the uber-hype machine of a fellow New Englander.

The "Dean Machine" consumed all of the political press corps' attention in the summer and fall of 2003 (of course with the slightly distracting and made-for-television spectacle of Gov. Gray Davis' ouster and Arnold Schwarzenegger's ascension to power in California). Indeed, former Vermont Gov. Howard Dean's campaign seemed worthy of all of the hype with his clear anti-Bush and anti-war message, the curious success of his campaign's Internet fundraising efforts, and his ever-growing embrace by a coalition of labor groups, Democratic Party leaders past and present, minority and women's groups, passionate college students, and, to be sure, the national political press corps.

For a Democrat whom Republicans lampooned as someone who had plotted to run for the presidency since the days of the Nixon White House, Kerry didn't look so good. His decades-long route to a presidential campaign seemed completely derailed by a doctor who had only attained the title of governor initially because his predecessor died in office.

Nonetheless, that's where things stood by the fall of 2003. Dean was on a roll. He had already landed on the cover of *Newsweek* and *Time* at the beginning of August. By October, he had healthy leads in both New Hampshire and Iowa, which prompted all of the reporters to remind themselves (and the country) that 13 out of the previous 14 Democratic presidential nominees had won either or both of those states, with Bill Clinton being the only exception in 1992. Revered soothsayer Charlie Cook said at the beginning of October, "This nomination is going to Howard Dean unless and until someone takes it away from him."[1]

Dean had raised a record amount of money during the late summer and early fall (roughly $15 million). In November, Dean landed the support of an impressive labor coalition of the American Federation of State, County, and Municipal Employees (AFSCME), the Service Employees International Union (SEIU), and the International Union of Painters and Allied Trades (IUPAT)—who combined represented roughly three million American workers whose leadership pledged to provide invaluable support on the ground in Iowa, New Hampshire, and other key primary states. There was even talk that Dean might decline federal matching funds for his campaign if he secured the nomination—a bold and cocksure move that only further enhanced the Dean campaign's appearance of a self-assured machine of political passion inevitably on its way to the nomination. Dean confidently boiled it down to a very simple equation: all they needed to do was find two million people to donate $100 each—or some permutation of that math.[2] The national political press corps nodded with eyebrows raised at this confidently cruising campaign, wondering, as Cook suggested, if it was possible for any candidate to take the nomination from Dean. And this was all before, unbeknownst even to his campaign manager, Dean was set to grab the very high profile endorsement of former Vice President Al Gore in early December, which was described as "huge"—but not necessarily a clincher—by Steve Rosenthal, the head of the 527 group America Coming Together.[3]

At the same time, in a completely different place in terms of success (moderate) and outlook (cloudy), Kerry stood on the brink of collapse. He trailed Dean in polls, fundraising, and hype. Meanwhile, Kerry's home state was in the news constantly because the Massachusetts Superior Court had said the commonwealth could not stop same-sex marriages. On the flip side, President Bush was calling for a constitutional amendment to define marriage as only a union between a man and a woman. While Kerry openly disagreed with the Bay State court's decision, he did endorse civil unions.

Perhaps most distracting, Kerry was continually dogged by his fellow candidates and the press as being unclear in his stance on the war in Iraq and the war on terror. Kerry had voted in the fall of 2002 to give President Bush the authority to use military force in Iraq, but by the fall of 2003 had taken to criticizing the president and saying Bush had done the right thing in the wrong way—which is a relatively (and generously) concise way of stating his position. Kerry also voted against $87 billion in additional military funding that fall, which opened him up to attacks of not supporting the troops.

Two major decisions shook things up and would later be credited with turning things around for the Kerry campaign. The first decision was literally a shake-up when, amidst rumors swirled about internal campaign strife and competing campaign influences, Kerry made the decision in November 2003 to fire campaign manager Jim Jordan. Kerry replaced Jordan with Mary Beth Cahill, the former chief of staff to Sen. Ted Kennedy, Kerry's longtime Bay

State colleague. The move surprised some Democrats because Jordan was a longtime and loyal aide to Kerry, but Kerry was dissatisfied with some of Jordan's decisions, statements, and management of the campaign. It reportedly pained Kerry to let him go. Nonetheless, Kerry felt, according to advisers, that a change needed to be made to reinvigorate the public's perception of the campaign.[4] The leadership change also had the effect of perpetuating discussions among pundits and politicians about who was running Kerry's campaign and who was to blame for their failure to live up to the high expectations many had months earlier.[5]

Kerry's other major decision at the end of 2003 was to take it directly upon himself to improve his campaign's coffers. In the shadows of the seemingly incessant consideration by the press over his ability to tap into the fortune of his wife, which he could not, Kerry arranged in December a $6.4 million mortgage for his home in Boston. He invested the money into his campaign to show that he had not given up on his campaign and in hopes that the show of confidence would improve fundraising efforts.[6]

In retrospect, these personnel and staffing decisions were credited as having a central part in turning things around for Kerry. At that time though, the effects were still to be seen and national polls at the end of 2003 showed Kerry still lagging behind Dean and others in the polls. Kerry was still having trouble with voters, regardless of what criticisms the media had for him. Polls and pundits indicated that Kerry still had a long way to go to battle the lingering perception that he was some bad combination of the following traits: aloof, elitist, liberal, wavering, and not up to the task of being president in a post-9/11 America.

THE NOMINATION FIGHT:
HAPPY NEW YEAR, SENATOR!

At the end of a long 2003, a better staffed and better financed Kerry was busily stumping in Iowa when a supporter asked him if he had a resolution for the New Year. His response was quite simply: "To win."[7]

The buzz in Iowa the week before the Iowa caucuses had a puzzling and almost apocalyptic quality to it. Observers harrumphing to know the mindset of Iowans talked themselves silly with an endless number of scenarios and what amounted at times to hypothetical babbling. Missouri Rep. Dick Gephardt's campaign and the Dean campaign were really taking it to each other. Most caucus watchers, Gephardt campaign staff included, felt that the former House leader had to either win or pull a very strong second for his campaign to go on after the first contest. Hailing from a neighboring state and having won the Iowa caucuses back in 1988, Gephardt, according to conventional wisdom, really had no excuse not to do well. Dean and Gephardt regarded each other as the main threat to winning Iowa, and each would soon invest heavily in tearing the other down.[8]

The rest of the field for the caucuses actually wasn't that big. Florida Sen. Bob Graham's campaign had long since dropped out by the time of the caucuses. The campaigns of Connecticut Sen. Joe Lieberman and Gen. Wes Clark (Ret.) had made the decision not to invest any time or money in Iowa—a move that would only be viewed as successful if either achieved a string of successes starting in New Hampshire (which ultimately neither man did).[9] Former

Ambassador Carol Moseley Braun dropped out of the race the
Thursday before the caucuses and endorsed Dean, but her supporters were few in number in Iowa and not expected to have much of
an impact for either her or Dean. No one expected much of a showing for Rev. Al Sharpton, who had not spent much time or money in
Iowa, but there was talk that Ohio Rep. Dennis Kucinich could be
a minor spoiler in Iowa, appealing to the laborers and farmers with
his populist rhetoric and stealing support from one of the other
contenders. Most observers agreed that the real caucus clash came
down to four men: Kerry, Dean, Gephardt, and North Carolina
Sen. John Edwards.

Dean had invested an amazing amount of his campaign in Iowa,
benefiting from, among other things, the vocal support from labor
groups and college students across the state as well as a much publicized and successful effort to visit all of Iowa's 99 counties. The
final hours leading up to the caucuses were no different. Armies of
supporters came in from across the country to reinforce the so-
called "Deaniacs" on the ground in Iowa. Orange knit-capped volunteers combed the state to encourage participation in the caucuses
and support for Dean. All the while, Dean played it cool, even slipping off to Georgia to sit down with former President Jimmy Carter,
who asserted to the endlessly curious press that he was not making
an endorsement, but certainly pleased to meet with the governor
and discuss how the campaign was going and the state of the
Democratic Party.

As the handicapping and hypothesizing continued among the
press at the Polk County Convention Center in Des Moines and at
various candidate events around Iowa, the growing story undoubtedly was Kerry. Many reporters were focused on Dean's orange-

headed kids running around the state, but another organizational story in the works was the leadership of strategist Michael Whouley, who had been brought in months earlier to lead Kerry's ground game. Whouley had a deserved reputation of being a master in turning out voters. The challenge of the caucuses, as compared to a primary, was that rather than just having to swing by the polling place for a few minutes at any point on one day, caucus goers had to show up at 7:00 p.m. and stay there possibly for as long as a few hours. Whouley had achieved Iowa success before for Michael Dukakis in 1988 and Gore in 2000. Kerry called him "magical."[10] In short, more and more Iowans and veteran caucus observers were beginning to believe that Whouley's strategy could pay off huge. Another Iowa factor for Kerry was the unplanned, public support of a Vietnam crewmate named Jim Rassman, who hadn't spoken to Kerry since 1969. In an emotional reunion in Iowa, Rassman said that Kerry had saved his life in Vietnam and now he saw that Kerry needed his help in another battle.

The *Des Moines Register* poll on Jan. 17, 2004, showed that Kerry and Edwards had vaulted past both Dean and Gephardt, who had been in the first two slots just two months earlier. The caucus battle was still considered close with only eight percentage points separating Kerry in first at 26% and Gephardt in fourth at 18%, but the bigger story (and buzz!) going into the caucuses was how Kerry and Edwards had leapfrogged the other two, who, as mentioned before, had spent their final weeks tearing each other down. *Register* pollster J. Anne Selzer said in their report, "The luster has faded from Dean's campaign and Gephardt has stumbled down the stretch as well."[11] Two days later, the outcome of the caucuses matched that latest poll.

Kerry won Iowa convincingly. Post-mortem analysis showed that Kerry's record as a legislator and veteran appealed to Iowa's largely senior and middle-class Democratic electorate.[12] Dean's ground game apparently didn't do the job. Anecdotes from around Iowa showed that the campaign was ultimately unable to sell its anti-war message and many reports were that the orange-capped and eager Deaniacs simply rubbed Iowans the wrong way. The phrase "Dated Dean, Married Kerry" was tossed about with reckless abandon.

The other surprise in Iowa was Edwards' close second place finish, a 32% share compared to Kerry's winning 38%. Dean and Gephardt's vicious warfare did both of them in, and Edwards' sunny message shone through and appealed to more Iowans on caucus night. Dean came in third with 18 percent, and Gephardt finished fourth with a devastating 11 percent.

The day after the caucuses, Gephardt tearfully dropped out of the race in a press conference in his native St. Louis, telling supporters and reporters, "I gave this campaign everything I had in me." He would soon endorse Kerry. Dean, on the other hand, adamantly and quite infamously vowed to fight on. This is of course where the now notorious "Yeargh!" scream occurred, a political moment that has been deconstructed countless times. The collective reaction by the press watching on television at the Polk County Convention Center in Des Moines was one of puzzled intrigue.[13] It wasn't as though they were waiting for Dean to melt down, but he didn't do much to make them stop thinking about it. For months, it seemed that Dean's determination and confidence would will him to the nomination. But now, as the press had long contemplated, Dean actually needed voters to win, and he had failed tremendously in the first major test to do that.

The adage persisted that New Hampshire didn't want Iowa to tell it what to do. Dean still maintained a lead in the state that bordered his own home state. The USA TODAY/CNN/Gallup Poll conducted in New Hampshire prior to the results of the Iowa caucuses showed Dean leading at 31% with Kerry close behind at 24% and Clark in a solid third with 20%.[14] After a final week of bounding around New Hampshire that included one last New Hampshire debate at St. Anselm's College in Manchester, the remaining seven candidates hunkered down for the primary. Despite Kerry's convincing win in Iowa and acknowledged momentum, the dynamics in the Granite State were different, not only because Lieberman and Clark were actively competing this time or because it was Dean's next-door neighbor, but also because the primary ground game was different with independents able to vote in the New Hampshire primary.[15]

In the end, the tide of Kerry's Iowa victory did seem to push through into New Hampshire. Kerry won handily with 39% and Dean came in second with 26%. Clark and Edwards essentially tied for third at about 12% each. Lieberman came in a dismal fifth at 9%, but he optimistically assured supporters on primary night that they had secured a "three-way split decision" with Clark and Edwards. Lieberman's campaign, which had never really gained much steam in the first place, was quickly unraveling and some urged him to exit the race.[16] But Lieberman and the others, minus the high-riding Kerry, vowed to march on to the geographically diverse primaries between Feb. 3 and March 2, otherwise known as Super Tuesday.

After much drama and build-up in Iowa and New Hampshire, the rest of Kerry's ride to the nomination happened without much incident. DNC Chairman Terry McAuliffe had promoted and successfully instituted a frontloaded nomination calendar so that his party's nominee would be determined early and able to compete financially with the president's campaign, and it seemed that Kerry's path could not have been more perfectly tailored to McAuliffe's vision.[17]

On Feb. 3, Kerry proved himself capable of winning nationwide with victories in Missouri, Arizona, North Dakota, New Mexico, and Delaware. Edwards won South Carolina and Clark won Oklahoma on that same day, but those would be their only victories. Lieberman dropped out after pinning his hopes on success in Delaware, where he finished tied for second with Edwards at 11%, far behind Kerry's winning 50%. He would later endorse Kerry. A few days later, Kerry continued to win another diverse sampling in Michigan, Washington, and Maine. On Feb. 10, Kerry won in Tennessee and Virginia, asserting that he had appeal in southern states and moving Clark to drop out as he could no longer campaign on claims of southern and moderate appeal. Clark soon thereafter endorsed Kerry.

It was truly an ironic reversal of fortune for Kerry and Dean. Dean, who seemed to have everything going for him before the nomination contests began, had yet to win a contest. He proclaimed that the Feb. 17 Wisconsin primary would be do-or-die for his campaign; it would prove to be death. Dean finished third in Wisconsin and unceremoniously ended his campaign two days later. While he would no longer actively campaign for the nomination, he said he would still welcome the support of delegates so that he could help shape the party's platform in their convention.[18] He eventually endorsed Kerry and actively campaigned for him.

As Super Tuesday approached, Kerry won low-profile contests in Idaho, Hawaii, and Utah. Edwards' campaign, encouraged by some polls showing him beating President Bush in a one-on-one match-up,[19] geared up to make one last stand against Kerry in the 10 states on March 2, but success would elude them nationwide. Kerry won in Massachusetts, California, New York, Ohio, Minnesota, Rhode Island, Maryland, Connecticut, and Georgia, the one state where Edwards came in a close second. Kerry lost only Vermont, where the no-longer-campaigning Dean scored his one and only victory in his home state.

Edwards bowed out the next day, saying that Kerry had "what it takes to be president." Kerry, in kind, said that Edwards was a "valiant champion of the values for which our party stands." Kerry had won 27 of the first 30 nomination contests. Edwards had won just one, but talk of a Kerry-Edwards ticket was non-stop among many Democrats and media. Many saw Edwards' gracious exit as a step to endearing himself to the possibility of becoming Kerry's running mate, though Edwards had spent weeks and months dismissing the notion that he was running to be vice president.[20] With Edwards' departure, amassing the rest of those delegates would be a mere formality. Only Sharpton and Kucinich remained as active campaigners, but they would pose no threat. Both eventually withdrew and endorsed him.

VEEPSTAKES: SOMETIMES THE INEVITABLE IS INEVITABLE

After months of speculation and a much ballyhooed overture to Republican Sen. John McCain of Arizona to form a bipartisan ticket, Kerry's shortlist for a running mate was reportedly down to three men: Edwards, Gephardt, and Gov. Tom Vilsack of Iowa. While the latter two each offered a home state considered to be a battleground state, Edwards offered a national following from his own campaign and potential appeal in southern states to balance Kerry's northeast roots. The question of whom Kerry would pick occupied pundits and supporters alike for most of the spring and early summer. All the while, Edwards was intensely campaigning on Kerry's behalf at fundraisers around the country. There were also still some murmurs that Kerry could pick from a few dark horse candidates who offered other electoral qualities: Florida Sen. Bob Graham, who had appeal in the most infamous of battleground states, Delaware Sen. Joe Biden, a strong Democratic voice on foreign affairs and the war, and Sen. Hillary Rodham Clinton, consistently shown, for better or worse, to be one of the most nationally known Democrats.

The press loved to report on the relationship between Kerry and McCain, and indeed there were conversations between the two veteran politicians in which Kerry floated the idea of a bipartisan "unity" ticket, but never formally offered him the job. As late as mid-June 2004, the *Washington Post* reported that the idea had gone nowhere because McCain reportedly felt that the concept might not work and that it could weaken the presidency if they were to win on such a bipartisan ticket.[21]

It should be noted briefly here that McCain had the dubious distinction of having his name tossed about as a possible running mate for both Kerry and Bush. There was some speculation that the president might replace Vice President Dick Cheney on the ticket with McCain, allegedly to assuage concerns about Cheney's viability as a running mate because of questions concerning his health and nagging charges of sinister corporate dealings.[22] One of the most high profile "dump Cheney" calls came from the always opinionated former Sen. Alphonse D'Amato of New York, but most of the chatter was underground and treated merely as rampant speculation by the media. Ultimately, of course, President Bush asserted to supporters that Cheney would be his running mate again.

In the end, the secrecy surrounding Kerry's choice was well-guarded. In the first week of July, the press caught wind of a late-night meeting that reportedly sealed the deal at former Sec. of State Madeline Albright's house, which just happened to be on the block in between Kerry's house and Edwards' house in the Georgetown neighborhood of Washington, D.C.[23] However, Edwards was reportedly in Florida vacationing with his family at Disney World and Vilsack was in Iowa, and so much of the speculation concluded that the meeting was with Gephardt. But a day later, Gephardt told ABC News that he had never been to Albright's house in his life.[24]

On July 6, the nation waited to see whose name would join Kerry's on the side of his campaign plane. The campaign had maintained extreme secrecy and pretty successfully milked the choice speculation for all that it was worth.[25] The press would learn that the meeting at Albright's house was with Edwards, who flew from Orlando to Washington and back to meet with Kerry and then return to his vacation. The two Johns enjoyed a nice media honeymoon with their photogenic families. The addition of Edwards showed no major boost in the polls, but some polls prior to the pick showed that none of Kerry's possible choices were expected to do very much of that.[26] The long-anticipated unveiling had some comic moments too.

The *New York Post* famously splashed an "exclusive" headline that Kerry had picked Gephardt. Leaks from the company that painted Kerry's campaign plane indicated that Kerry had ordered a couple different names to be ready. Later, after the announcement, television cameras caught site of Kerry-Graham signs in the crowd which had been mistakenly passed out to supporters.[27]

THE DEMOCRATIC CONVENTION: AN UNPLANNED HOMECOMING

The 2004 Democratic National Convention took place from July 26 to July 29 at the FleetCenter in Boston. The theme of the convention was "Stronger at Home, Respected in the World." While eager to get their digs in at the president, Democrats wanted more explicitly to offer Kerry's vision and alternatives to dealing with the problems and challenges the country faced.[28] The decision to hold the convention in Boston was made in November 2002, about a month before Kerry initially declared his candidacy, so it was a coincidence that Kerry ended up being nominated in his hometown. Kerry's colleague Kennedy intensely lobbied DNC Chairman Terry McAuliffe and other officials until just before the official announcement. Kennedy reportedly asked McAuliffe, "What more does the Kennedy family have to do for the Democratic Party?"[29]

New York City, Detroit, and Miami were the other leading contenders to host the convention. The competition among cities to host a convention had much less to do with any perceived electoral impact and much more to do with how good of a host a city would be in terms of finances, facilities, and entertainment. However, it is reasonable to speculate that having it in Miami would have at the very least complicated the Democrats' message. It was no secret that Democrats were very intent on crafting a positive and largely uncontroversial theme for their convention. By the summer of 2004, Democratic furor over the 2000 election results in Florida had calmed down just a little bit compared to where it had been a year or two before, despite Michael Moore's film *Fahrenheit 9/11* reigniting those Florida passions. Democrats wanted to harness the Florida rage without dwelling on it, welcoming it as a motivational tool for registering and voting, but cautious to not seem as though their 2004 mission was to avenge their 2000 loss. Boston proved to be a good venue for the Democrats' pitch, despite the fact that it was home to iconic liberals like Kennedy, 1988 nominee Michael Dukakis, the late Tip O'Neill, and even the infamous Big Dig, a decades-long, billions-costing federal project to put Boston highways underground that the GOP loved to use as a prime example of Democratic fiscal irresponsibility. Incidentally, Dukakis was not invited to address the convention, though he was on the convention floor and took part in a number of events and tributes around town.[30]

The primetime slate of speakers included party luminaries and rising stars, with most of them sticking to the convention's carefully crafted tone of optimism and Kerry's vision. Monday featured former Presidents Carter and Clinton, along with Gore and New York Sen. Hillary Rodham Clinton. The two ex-presidents touted Kerry's leadership abilities, with Carter focusing more on international affairs and Clinton on domestic. On Tuesday, Kennedy, Teresa Heinz Kerry, and Barack Obama, the U.S. Senate candidate from Illinois, were the headliners. Obama electrified the crowd in the role of the convention's keynote speaker, but only cable television and PBS audiences saw it because ABC, CBS, NBC, and FOX chose to not air anything that night. Edwards was the main speaker on Wednesday night, and Kerry wrapped things up on Thursday night when he officially took the nomination. Kerry began his acceptance speech by announcing he was "reporting for duty" (a line that embodied his campaign and the convention's theme) and delivered what network political analysts like CBS' Bob Schieffer and ABC's Mark Halperin called his "best speech" ever.[31]

There were no major surprises. The convention was largely a made-for-television event, and ironically, as alluded to above, the broadcast networks decided to air only a few of the 12 hours of primetime speakers lined up across four days.[32] For the Democratic convention, the four networks aired President Clinton, Sen. Edwards, and Sen. Kerry's speeches—and entirely skipped the program on Tuesday. Critics cried that the networks were too concerned with ratings and failing their civic duty (as publicly controlled airwaves) to facilitate the democratic process. Nonetheless, the networks stuck to their limited broadcast and viewers turned to PBS, C-SPAN, and the cable news channels for the rest of the convention.

For all the talk of massive anti-war protests, organizers and city officials were pleasantly comfortable with a relatively small and peaceful showing near the FleetCenter, at least partly attributable to the intense security perimeter and the designated "free speech area" outside of the arena, which the vast majority of protesters said resembled a prison yard and subsequently boycotted. Most political and media folks—and the protestors themselves—predicted that the large-scale anti-Bush/anti-war protests expected at the Republican convention in New York City would dwarf what happened in Boston.[33] That notion would prove true a month later.

THE REPUBLICAN NATIONAL CONVENTION:
IF THEY CAN MAKE IT HERE...

The 2004 Republican National Convention took place from Aug. 30 to Sept. 2 at Madison Square Garden in New York City. It was the first time that Republicans had ever held their convention in New York City. The theme of the convention was "A Safer World, A More Hopeful America." New York City Mayor Michael Bloomberg spent a good bit of energy in 2002 pitching his city as capable of hosting both the Democratic and Republican conventions. Bloomberg argued that hosting one or both conventions would further strengthen Manhattan's—and the nation's—recovery from the 9/11 attacks.[34] In 2002, strategists in both parties were cautiously gauging how voters felt about 9/11. They knew of course that the memories and images of the attacks would be central to voters' thoughts on the security of the country in the upcoming election, but many were still pondering how much of that imagery voters could take before being upset or turned off by it. So, pundits and politicians alike agreed and discussed at length that a New York City convention had its inherent advantages and challenges in 2004.

The selection of New York City over the other contenders, New Orleans and Tampa–St. Petersburg, indicated that Republicans were ready to embrace the central role that New York City had in the Bush presidency. In the aftermath of 9/11, President Bush's visits to New York City, most notably his bullhorn-aided words of encouragement to workers at Ground Zero and his ceremonial first pitch for the World Series at Yankee Stadium, were some of the images that had defined his presidency. Whereas the Democrats' decision to hold theirs in Boston had little impact on the message that they would convey in their sales pitch, the Republicans' message would very much be intertwined with their location.

As was the case at the Democrats' convention, the networks only aired a few hours in prime time of the Republicans' convention. On Monday night, Arizona Sen. John McCain and former NYC mayor Rudy Giuliani were the featured speakers, but only cable and PBS audiences saw them because the networks decided to not air anything that night. On Tuesday night, First Lady Laura Bush and California Gov. Arnold Schwarzenegger were the headliners. The buzz before and after Schwarzenegger's speech rivaled that of Obama's speech in Boston a month earlier, but the difference this time was that the broadcast networks decided to air it, apparently feeling that the former international movie star had more potential to draw viewers than the former state senator. On Wednesday night, Democratic Sen. Zell Miller of Georgia delivered the keynote address, a fiery condemnation of Kerry as unfit for the presidency. This speech would also not be shown on the networks, but many saw and heard reports of it, including lampoons on late night comedy shows. Vice President Cheney also headlined Wednesday night's program.

President Bush accepted the GOP nomination on Thursday night, bringing the convention to a close. The president's speech, a laundry list of issues and topics, was pegged by many pundits as sounding more like a State of the Union speech than a nomination acceptance speech. However, most agreed that it didn't matter because all anyone would remember would be the closing paragraphs in which he spoke about the aftermath of 9/11 and even appeared to tear up in front of a nationwide audience. Just as

Kerry's "reporting for duty" opening to his acceptance speech embodied his campaign, the president's closing embodied his own when he said in part, "My fellow Americans, for as long as our country stands, people will look to the resurrection of New York City and they will say: Here buildings fell, and here a nation rose."

The story outside of the Republican convention started out somewhat intensely with massive and largely peaceful protests on the Sunday before the convention. More than 100,000 protestors marched through midtown to show their opposition to the president and to the war in Iraq. Enormous security forces made a number of arrests and there were minor incidents of violence, but some demonstrators professed that the protest was more subdued than they would have liked.[35]

CONCLUSION: THE BEGINNING
OF THE END

If Kerry's clinching of the Democratic nomination marked the end of the beginning of the 2004 presidential contest, then the conventions marked the end of the middle of the race. The roughly 60 days between the Republican's convention and Election Day would be the shortest or longest experience ever imagined, depending on whom you asked and on which day in that span you asked. Both presidential nominees and their running mates would embark on nonstop barnstorming efforts in the so-called battle-ground states of the Southwest, Midwest, and Great Lakes region. For both campaigns, the much overanalyzed success or lack thereof of a bounce in the polls after their respective conventions proved to be meaningless by September as the polls routinely showed the race fairly even with each candidate ticking up or down only slightly day to day.

Just one year earlier, the Kerry campaign was considered done for, but then Kerry, the so-called "closer" in previous political contests, finished strong and won the nomination. Now, Kerry was running even with the president and all attention turned to the upcoming debates, where many speculated that strong performances by Kerry could help him close strong once again and beat the incumbent president.

Brooke Brower is a former member of the ABC News political unit.

NOTES

1. Marlantes, Liz, "Dean sets a record pace for cash," *Christian Science Monitor*, 10/2/03
2. Curry, Tom, "Unions push Dean closer to triumph," MSNBC.com, 11/12/03
3. Lawrence, Jill, "Dean gains Gore's support," *USA Today*, 12/10/03
4. Healy, Patrick, "Kerry replaces his campaign manager," *Boston Globe*, 11/11/03
5. Nagourney, Adam, "Kerry fires his campaign manager," *New York Times*, 11/10/03
6. Healy, Patrick, "Kerry mortgage to help fund race," *Boston Globe*, 12/19/03
7. Chaggaris, Steve, "Kerry's New Year's resolution," CBSNEWS.com, 1/5/04
8. Yepsen, David, "Debate-winner Dean is back on top in Iowa," *Des Moines Register*, 11/25/03
9. Mishra, Raja and Joanna Weiss, "Clark, Lieberman decide to skip Iowa caucuses," *Boston Globe*, 10/20/03
10. Johnson, Glen, "Dewey Square quietly flexes its political muscle," *Boston Globe*, 7/28/04
11. Roos, Jonathan, "Iowa Poll finds surge by Kerry, Edwards," *Des Moines Register*, 1/17/04
12. Stone, Andrea and Jim Drinkard, "Race crosses into N.H. at full tilt," *USA Today*, 1/19/04
13. The author's personal experience at the Polk County Convention Center in Des Moines, Iowa on 1/19/04
14. Stone, Andrea and Jim Drinkard, "Race crosses into N.H. at full tilt," *USA Today*, 1/19/04
15. Fournier, Ron, "Strategy changes in N.H.," Associated Press, 1/22/04
16. Fournier, Ron, "Kerry scores solid win in New Hampshire," Associated Press, 1/28/04
17. Armas, Genaro, "Primary calendar slowly winds to a close as interest among voters declines," Asso-

ciated Press, 4/26/04

18. Johnson, Glen, "Dean ends campaign," *Boston Globe*, 2/19/04

19. "Kerry, Edwards both top Bush in poll," CNN.com, 2/18/04

20. Barabak, Mark and Scott Martelle, "Kerry wins 9 of 10 states, lauds rival as a champion of values," *Los Angeles Times*, 3/3/04

21. Balz, Dan and Jim VandeHei, "McCain's resistance doesn't stop talk of Kerry dream ticket," *Washington Post*, 6/12/04

22. Froomkin, Dan, "The Cheney Question," WashingtonPost.com, 7/7/04

23. Halperin, Mark and Marc Ambinder and others, "The Note: Doubles partner for a love match," ABCNEWS.com, 7/4/04

24. Halperin, Mark and Anne Chiappetta and others, "The Note: Georgetown alley cat," ABCNEWS.com, 7/5/04

25. Johnson, Glen, "Decision made amid extraordinary secrecy," *Boston Globe*, 7/7/04

26. "Poll shows Edwards favored among Kerry's VP choices," Associated Press, 6/12/04

27. Twedt, Steve, "Kerry gave no sign early of his pick for running mate," *Pittsburgh Post-Gazette*, 7/7/04

28. Balz, Dan, "In Boston, Democrats seek a positive sign," *Washington Post*, 7/26/04

29. Johnson, Glen, "Kennedy compound seen as 'Holy Grail'," *Boston Globe*, 7/26/04

30. Finer, Jonathan, "Where does Michael Dukakis fit in?," *Washington Post*, 7/25/04

31. Associated Press reports, 7/29/04

32. Anderson, Nick, "Networks limit convention time," *Los Angeles Times*, 7/13/04

33. Bayles, Fred, "Protestors plan bigger showing in New York," *USA Today*, 7/29/04

34. Smith, Chris, "The elephant in the room," *New York Magazine*, 9/6/04

35. McRoberts, Flynn and Jeff Zeleny, "At least 100,000 in NYC protest Bush, Iraq war," *Chicago Tribune*, 8/30/04

CHAPTER TWO

Campaign 2004:
The Hidden Story

Chuck Todd
THE HOTLINE

LITTLE MOVES, BIG RESULTS

The "what if" game is very popular with losing political candidates. John Kerry supporters have been pining for a simple switch of 60,000 more votes in Ohio as, of course, that would have swung the electoral college from Bush to Kerry. Never mind that a switch of a few thousand votes in Pennsylvania would have switched that state from Kerry to Bush, ditto in New Hampshire and Wisconsin.

Basically, it's a pointless game since one can "what if" to death any campaign. But what the "what if" game does do for political candidates is remind them that decisions that seem little or less than gigantic can matter more than they realize.

Decisions made months and years in advance can have a trickle-down effect so that the campaign takes on a whole other form.

This presidential campaign saw hundreds of key decisions made by nearly a dozen candidates that ultimately got us to the point of what became a very close and hotly contested election won by the incumbent over Kerry. If just one of these hundreds of decisions had gone in another direction, the chain of events could have easily created a different result, or at least a different Democratic nominee.

Let's browse through some of the bigger, little decisions.

BUSH SIGNS McCAIN-FEINGOLD INTO LAW

One of the most significant decisions Bush made as president which directly impacted how presidential campaigns were set up and ultimately how the general election campaign took shape was signing the McCain-Feingold campaign finance legislation.

Regardless of what the authors intended the legislation to do, the practical facts are the bill accomplished two things:

1. It allowed Bush to double the financial advantage he already enjoyed by increasing the contribution limit to his campaign from $1,000 to $2,000.
2. It convinced the Democratic Party and its supporters that they would have to decentralize some of their operatives if they hoped to stay competitive financially.

Without the creation of McCain-Feingold, the now-hated 527 groups would never have seen the light of day. And the Democratic Party in coordination with the Kerry campaign would have controlled the massive field and get out the vote operation that was largely outsourced through a 527 called Americans Coming Together (ACT).

As any of the operatives in both the Kerry campaign and ACT will tell you, the inability for the two groups to coordinate their activities, from scheduling to precinct targeting, proved to be a bigger disadvantage than they realized. The Republican Party, as run by Team Bush, was never as reliant on soft money in the past and they set up their '04 operations under the assumption the increased contribution limits would give them enough money to keep everything in-house. The right hand of the RNC always knew what the left hand of the Bush campaign was doing. The Democratic Party, ACT and Kerry were essentially three left hands.

Another side effect of the McCain-Feingold provision that increased the individual limits is that it made not accepting presidential primary matching funds from the federal government a realistic option for a campaign, particularly as the Democrats realized the eventual nominee would be facing an unopposed Republican nominee in Bush with $200 million plus to spend BEFORE the Republican convention.

As will be detailed later, the campaigns that chose to accept matching funds ended up running out of cash too quickly.

THE CONVENTION SITE/ DATE SELECTIONS

One of the more interesting games of chicken the political parties played during the four-year long presidential campaign was the timing of the convention.

Worried about the financial advantage Bush was going to have over his eventual nominee, DNC Chair Terry McAuliffe threatened very seriously to hold the Democratic convention either simultaneously with that of the Republicans or just days before. For those who don't realize, there's no law that governs when parties hold their convention, but a gentlemen's agreement exists between the two parties that the incumbent party holds their convention last.

As detailed above, the supposed money problem the Democrats were going to be facing in the dreaded summer months of the presidential campaign had McAuliffe and other Democrats scheming up a ton of ways to get around this issue.

With Team Bush making the decision to hold their convention the very last week of August (which actually bled into September), starting just one day after the end of the Olympics, the Democrats were in a huge bind.

They could either schedule their convention for the same time as the Olympics (not a real option), schedule the convention before the Olympics, but leaving at least a week or so before the Olympics to attempt to create momentum out of the convention, or, shrewdly, as McAuliffe proposed, at the same time (even in the same city) as the Republicans.

McAuliffe was worried that the approximately $75 million each official presidential nominee would receive to spend would put the Democrats at a distinct disadvantage if they had to spread out their government money over 13 weeks versus Bush having just eight weeks.

How serious McAuliffe was about holding the Democratic convention at the same time as the Republicans is not known; but it appears to have been a threat that was designed to get the Republicans to re-think the timing of their convention for before the Olympics.

Ultimately, of course, McAuliffe backed down on his threat for the simultaneous conventions as many leaders of the prospective Democratic presidential candidates in the fall of '02 urged McAuliffe to schedule an earlier convention so that in case the Democratic nominee was broke going into June and July, the campaign could get an infusion of cash earlier, rather than have to wait until Labor Day for their money.

Remember, in '02, Democrats had no idea how much money was out there for them to raise; at this point, Howard Dean hadn't even raised $100,000.

Considering that cash was not a problem for Kerry (after all, he STILL has leftover funds from his primary account), imagine how August could have been completely different for Kerry had his convention not been held until the same week as Bush's convention.

IRAQ WAR RESOLUTION

Any vote that authorizes a president to go to war is a big deal in political circles and is remembered for years to come. Appropriations omnibus votes come and go, but war votes linger forever in the political biography of a politician.

Five of the major Democratic presidential candidates-to-be cast votes on the Iraq war resolution and four of them voted for the resolution: Kerry, John Edwards, Joe Lieberman and Dick Gephardt. The lone major candidate (sorry Dennis Kucinich) to vote against the war resolution was Florida's Bob Graham.

Of this group, the two surprises, in a way, were Graham and Kerry. Graham, a supporter of the 1st Gulf War, seemed to be a typical Southern Democrat when it came to foreign policy; i.e., he was a hawk. And actually, Graham's reasoning for voting against the Iraq war was that the resolution didn't go far enough to deal with countries that were supposedly helping al Qaeda.

Kerry, who voted against the 1st Gulf War, would have been seen as being consistent with his reticent record of sending troops in harm's way. And as a Vietnam vet, it never usually was an issue to him. But post-9/11, Kerry also had to realize that being seen as tough on the enemies of the U.S. was going to be a pre-requisite to being a commander-in-chief.

This author will go to his grave believing Kerry's gut told him to vote against the resolution and that his political advisers talked him into voting for it, with the theory being in the general election, they could take Iraq off the table.

Of course, this Iraq war vote would come to define the presidential primary, which in turn led to Kerry voting against the now-famous $87 billion Iraq war supplemental bill which led to perhaps the defining moment of the general election campaign when Kerry uttered, "I actually voted for the $87 billion before I voted against it."

Had Kerry voted against the original Iraq war resolution, would Dean have gotten the same traction in the primaries? Would Kerry end up voting against the $87 billion? Remember, many of the senators who voted against the original war resolution voted FOR the $87 billion. After all, gotta support the troops!

DEMOCRATS FRONTLOAD THE
PRIMARY CALENDAR

For the first time since both parties moved to the primary system to nominate their presidential candidates, the Democratic Party chose to create essentially a short six-week window for a majority of their convention delegates to be rewarded.

This was an initiative pushed by DNC Chairman McAuliffe as a way to get the primary out of the way as quickly as possible so the eventual nominee could have plenty of time to heal the intra-party wounds.

It was also thought that the frontloading of the calendar would decrease the importance of Iowa and New Hampshire as there would be no dead time between New Hampshire and the next set of primaries.

Of course, the opposite turned out to be true and the front-loading made Iowa and New Hampshire more important than they had ever been. The frontloading also did little to showcase the Democrats in some of the eventual fall battleground states. In fact, of the 13 states that both held a primary or caucus BEFORE March 1 and also doubled as a general election battleground (at least for a time), Democrats lost eight of those states, including Iowa and New Mexico, two states that Al Gore carried in 2000.

Primaries may serve the purpose of separating the strong from the weak but they can showcase a political party at its worst for the host primary/caucus state, not at its best, and that can turn off more voters come November than turn on.

WESLEY CLARK SKIPS IOWA

There's no more-overlooked decision in terms of its importance to Kerry's eventual victory than General Wesley Clark's decision to skip the Iowa caucuses and focus on being the "Stop-Dean" in New Hampshire and beyond.

When Clark entered the race, Dean was nearing his peak and officially claiming frontrunner status among the media elite. Simultaneously, the campaigns of Kerry and Edwards were foundering with both candidates drawing smaller and smaller crowds.

Given his late start, Clark was worried about what kind of campaign he could mount in Iowa. Remember, the assumption was that organization was everything in Iowa and Clark's opponents had a two-year head start (or in the case of Gephardt, a 15-year head start) at finding caucus precinct captains. So, thanks to the advice of the Clinton crowd (a group of Democrats who never had to compete in Iowa), they mistakenly assumed they could make New Hampshire their breakout state.

Well, there are a number of chains of events this decision set off. First, Clark's decision to skip Iowa convinced the influential labor leader of AFSCME, Gerald McEntee, to back Dean. Many a knowledgeable labor source believes McEntee would have endorsed Clark had he decided to campaign in Iowa as McEntee believed his troops could be a real help in that labor-dominated state, more so than the less labor-friendly New Hampshire.

Clark's decision also helped convince the Kerry campaign that they had to focus all their energies on Iowa if they were ever going to recover in New Hampshire. Clark gave breathing room for Kerry at a time when there was very little air in the room left for Kerry to breathe. If Clark goes to Iowa, the Clark versus Dean dynamic is engaged immediately and who knows if the media ever decides to go in search of the comeback Kerry and comeback Edwards storylines that both were born out of the Iowa results.

JOHN EDWARDS ACCEPTS
MATCHING FUNDS

As December 2003 was drawing to a close, Edwards and Kerry were both in some major financial difficulties. Their difficulties were compounded by the fact that the then-Democratic frontrunner, Dean, had raised more than $50 million and decided to bust the spending caps that are in place for candidates who accept matching funds. By not accepting matching funds, the law allowed Dean to spend as much as he wanted for the entire campaign and in any individual state.

Mindful of this spending advantage, candidates Kerry and Edwards had major decisions to make—should they dip into their own personal fortunes to make up the short-term difference they needed for Iowa, in turn keeping them competitive should they strike gold and end up the nominee? Kerry decided to loan himself the necessary money he needed for Iowa and bow out of taking matching funds, allowing him to raise and spend whatever he wanted as a candidate up until he was the official nominee.

Edwards chose not to dip into his fortune and relied on matching funds as the short-term cash infusion to help him in Iowa.

Both moves worked in the short term for both candidates as both got surprising shots in the arm out of Iowa. But Kerry had the ability to continue raising and spending as much money as necessary. Edwards was running up against a primary spending limit that eventually would force him to cherry pick primary states throughout February and make him come across as a regional candidate.

Money wasn't the only mistake Team Edwards made; the most glaring, in hindsight, was the campaign's decision to spend so much of 2003 in New Hampshire, rather than Iowa. It's hard not to believe that a few more days in Iowa, rounding up a precinct captain in every precinct (rather than the 3/4s they had on caucus night) might have allowed Edwards to eke out a win over Kerry and catapulting him into a better position in New Hampshire.

KERRY'S WASTED SPRING

For a challenger, Kerry had an unprecedented amount of time as the unofficial nominee and looking back, it was not memorable time well spent.

There were no trips to Iraq, no unique 50-state campaign swings and no presidential administration creating. It's this final point that we believe future nominees running in a wartime atmosphere ought to consider. With the country at war, there was a sector of the electorate who despite their misgivings for the incumbent was reticent at changing horses in midstream.

What if Kerry had named a war cabinet in-waiting (not dissimilar to how the out parties are shaped in Parliamentary systems)? What if Kerry had used each week of, say, a six-to-eight week span in the late spring and early summer to name a major cabinet member? Kerry would have had more control of each news cycle and likely forced the Bush campaign to be more reactive instead of always proactive.

Still, short of something that out-of-the-box, Kerry didn't do much with his spring outside of raising money, a need which wasn't as great as many in the campaign thought.

ASSUMING ECONOMY OVER NATIONAL SECURITY

The day Kerry picked Edwards as his running mate instead of someone with national security credentials was the day the campaign signaled it believed domestic issues, like jobs, would be the deciding factor for undecided voters instead of national security.

The VP pick, at a minimum, underscores either a strength or fills in a gap in the presidential nominee's résumé. Kerry's folks believed they had a domestic touchy-feely gap that Edwards could fill while they'd handle the national security issue. Anyone believe that Kerry secretly would have liked to war game the presidential result or how a-pure-on-Iraq Bob Graham would have fared (particularly in Florida)? What about Wesley my first name is "General" Clark?

None of these decisions can be called the single most critical of the presidential campaign, but all of them, had they gone another direction, would have changed the course of the campaign—maybe not the outcome, but the path. It should serve as a reminder to future candidates and strategists that no decision should be made in a vacuum.

Chuck Todd is Editor-in-Chief of *The Hotline*.

CHAPTER THREE

The Rise and Fall of Howard Dean

Claude R. Marx

THE EAGLE-TRIBUNE

The scream did not kill him.

Even before Howard Dean gave his now famous concession speech on the night of January 19, 2004, following a third-place finish in the Iowa caucuses he was, politically speaking, a dead man walking.

By then, the former Vermont governor had squandered much of the political and financial capital he had amassed during his transformation from a moderate chief executive of an obscure state to becoming the front runner for the Democratic nomination for president and a hero to many of his party's liberals.

Jimmy Carter and Bill Clinton, the last two Democrats to win the White House, had in fact been governors with limited experience on the national stage. While that was also an apt description of

Dean, he was not destined to follow in their footsteps.

What went wrong?

In the months leading up to Iowa, he had the Midas touch. A nationwide "Sleepless Summer" tour had helped cement his rock-star status among younger voters and his campaign coffers were bulging. During the first nine months of 2003 he raised $25 million, the most ever for a non-incumbent. If, as the late California Treasurer Jesse Unruh said, "money is the mother's milk of politics," then no one on the Dean team had any worries about a calcium deficiency.[1]

Unfortunately for the man from one of the country's biggest dairy-producing states, there was less there than met the eye.

He was unable to overcome three obstacles: massive power struggles within his campaign, inability of voters to see him as presidential, and John Kerry's return to front-runner status among the candidates.

Dean's early surge—in part the result of his well-timed criticisms of the war in Iraq and many other Democrats' unwillingness to attack a popular president—took many by surprise. Though he had had some contact with national party leaders through his earlier chairmanship of the Democratic Governors' Association, to most of them he still was "Howard Who?"

That began to change in earnest on February 21, 2003, when Dean addressed the winter meeting of the Democratic National Committee in Washington, D.C. After his advance team distributed gift baskets of Vermont cheese and maple syrup, he entered the room to deliver fairly standard lines about the situation in Iraq and the overall state of the Democratic Party. His remarks were met with some initial applause.

He received a resounding ovation, however, when he declared "I am Howard Dean. And I am here to represent the Democratic wing of the Democratic Party." *New Yorker* writer Mark Singer described it as a "pivotal moment in the campaign—the transition from 'Dean who' to 'Dean whoa.'"[2]

In the months that followed, Dean harnessed the Internet as a fund-raising vehicle in a way that his rivals would soon emulate. He also became the darling of much of the college crowd, the so-called "brie and Chablis set" of yuppies, while also amassing a smattering of labor support.

This coalition surprised even Dean, especially when it vaulted him to the front of the polls among the candidates for president.

He said the size and enthusiasm of an overflow crowd at a summer rally in Seattle left him "momentarily struck dumb with emotion."[3]

It all started because after 10 years as governor of Vermont, Howard Dean was restless.

He had been an innovative and generally well-liked leader who presided during a time of national prosperity that had trickled down even to states like Vermont, which often lagged behind the rest of the country economically. As a moderate from a suburb of Burlington—the state's largest city—he had worked in a bipartisan manner on many issues. In fact, he often clashed with those on his party's left, over his reluctance to use the budget surplus for new social spending. At the same time, the one-time practicing internist warmed liberals' hearts by acts such as the expansion of health insurance for children.[4]

While he was governor, the Vermont Supreme Court forced the legislature to give some type of legal recognition to homosexual unions. After a grueling debate, the state's lawmakers passed a measure allowing for civil unions, which give many of the benefits of marriage but is less offensive to some conservatives. Dean signed the law behind closed doors and said that doing anything more public would rub salt in the wound of his foes.[5]

Vermont became a role model—albeit a moderate one—for the rest of the country. At the same time, Dean gained the gratitude of the politically active gay community, which provided crucial early financial backing for his presidential campaign.[6]

One of his obstacles to higher office would be his adopted home state. The physically beautiful, sparsely populated place that has had perennial economic problems, is geographically and culturally out of the nation's mainstream. Further, Vermont's unusual political culture—stemming from its reputation as both a playground for the rich and a haven for economic populists—makes it an unlikely launching pad for national office. The last Vermonter to win the White House—Calvin Coolidge—spent his political career in Massachusetts.

Dean, who hoped to end the state's 74-year absence from the Oval Office, was in many ways an unlikely public servant. In contrast to many other successful politicians, he was not an outwardly warm person and rarely expressed public empathy for the problems of others. Further, he had the arrogance that came from being both a physician and a scion of a wealthy New York investment banking family.

But he pursued politics with the same precision he used to diagnose a patient. He climbed the political ladder in Vermont after balancing the demands of a medical residency with volunteer work as community activist on a project to build a bicycle path around

Lake Champlain. He was a state representative and lieutenant governor before serving as governor from 1991 to 2003.

He left office if not beloved, then certainly respected. Along with other transplants to Vermont, he helped continue the transformation of this once solidly Republican bastion into a two-party state. In 2004, Democratic presidential nominee John Kerry won the state by 20 percentage points, while the state's Republican governor, Jim Douglas was re-elected by the same margin.

Dean wanted to see how his act would play on a national stage. In the last year of his governorship, he and his long-time aide, Kate O'Connor, began traveling the country to talk up his vision for America and lay the groundwork for a White House run. She set up a small political office in Montpelier, Vermont's quaint capital city and the only one in the country without a McDonald's. When his term as governor expired in January 2003 and he began campaigning full time, his campaign headquarters moved to Burlington. He then had seven full-time employees working in a 1,000-foot space above a bar and $157, 000 in the bank.[7]

O'Connor, who had worked for Dean since 1989, was both his political alter-ego and protector. She was devoted to his political well-being and ran interference with national advisers and others whom she suspected did not have his best interests at heart. She was never far from his side and often had a hand-held video camera to record his speeches and subsequent encounters with the crowd.

Joe Trippi, Dean's high-strung and occasionally abrasive campaign manager for much of his quest for the presidency, described his conflicts with O'Connor and another long-time aide, Deputy Campaign Manager Robert Rogan.

"If I represented the governor's wild-eyed idealist side, perched on his shoulder, telling him the only way to win was to burn down the old corrupt system, then Kate O'Connor and Bob Rogan were the pragmatic voices, constantly reminding him that if he burned down the castle, he'd have no place to rule," Trippi wrote in his campaign memoir.[8]

When all went well, however, such conflicts seemed meaningless. In the summer and fall of 2003, Dean was the man to beat in the fight for the Democratic nomination.

He brought crowds to their feet not by promising to deliver a laundry list of new programs but by imploring his audience to become involved so that government will no longer be controlled by special interests.

"The biggest lie people like me tell you from stages like this at election time is that if you vote for me I am going to solve all your problems....The truth is, the power to change this country is in your hands, not mine. You have the power to take this country back," he said at the end of every speech.

The crowds went crazy, mobbing him afterwards and prompting him to be perennially late. Though some of Dean's habits caused his aides concern, including a short temper that reared its head after hostile questions from voters as well as a tendency to shoot from the hip, they seemed to have little effect on the campaign's momentum.

He and his staff were considered political geniuses and acted the part; and in retrospect, they seemed all-too-willing to believe everything that was written about them.

Trippi at times appeared to be in a running battle with his candidate for television face time. His stock was so high that he was profiled on the front page of *The New York Times*,[9] a treatment usually reserved for elected officials or top White House staffers.

The Dean team's relationship with the press was highly selective. Major newspapers and broadcast outlets were given relatively frequent access to the candidate and senior staffers. Reporters from less visible media organizations, including those in Dean's home state, usually were relegated to dealing with junior staff members and had little direct access to the candidate or his key people.

During that time, Trippi further promoted himself by regularly holding conference calls to brag about the latest campaign contribution report and to crow about use of the Internet to raise money and thus create a virtual political community.

The fund-raising success prompted the campaign to forego federal matching funds—and the spending limits that came with them. Kerry subsequently followed suit.

Dean's success was driving his opponents crazy. He was competing against, and running ahead of, several prominent individuals including retired Gen. Wesley Clark, Sen. John Edwards (D-N.C.), House Minority Leader Richard Gephardt, Kerry, and former Vice Presidential nominee Joseph Lieberman.

At the debates that seemed to occur almost every week, the other candidates took great delight in aiming rhetorical shots at the former Vermont governor.

During a Nov. 4 debate in Boston's Faneuil Hall, Kerry criticized Dean for "having been endorsed more often by the NRA (National Rifle Association) than the NEA (National Education Association)."[10]

Dean's comment a few days earlier that he "wanted to be the candidate for guys with Confederate flags in their pickup trucks,"[11] prompted a strong rebuke from Edwards.

"The last thing we need in the South is someone like you telling them what to do. It is wrong, it is condescending." Edwards said.[12]

Amidst all the criticism, Dean quipped that "I know I am the front runner because I keep taking buck shots out of my rear end."[13]

If Dean thought he was under attack however, then, he hadn't seen anything yet. About a month later, he received an endorsement that instead of pushing him closer to the nomination, marked the start of his political demise.

On Dec. 9, at events in Harlem and in Iowa, former Vice President Al Gore announced his support for Dean, citing among other things his strong opposition to the war.

Dean, who had been holding regular policy and strategy discussions with Gore, worked out the terms and locations of the endorsements and kept his own staff in the dark until almost the last possible moment.

Trippi, though pleased that the campaign had Gore's support, sensed a downside as well.

"To their (Dean's and Gore's) credit, it was a great day; it really did feel like a coronation of some kind. Still, it turned out to be the beginning of the end for us, the moment our insurgent campaign ended and our short, uncomfortable stint as the front runner began—with a target squarely between Howard's shoulder blades," Trippi wrote.[14]

Dean's campaign hit choppy waters at a time when his main rival, Kerry, was showing renewed signs of life. Though Kerry had been written off by many—and had so much trouble raising money that he had to take out a second mortgage on his Beacon Hill mansion—he seemed to begin a comeback after a Nov. 8 staff shakeup. Among the changes was the hiring of a new manager, Mary Beth

Cahill, the top aide to Sen. Edward M. Kennedy (D-Mass.).

Kerry's speaking style never became as animated as Dean's and he did not excite crowds the way Dean did. Kerry was able, however, to rid his speeches of some of the Washington jargon that had hampered it before. Those changes, coupled with his reassuring, if somewhat stiff demeanor, and his detailed knowledge of foreign policy, made Kerry appear to be more reasonable and electable than Dean.

A popular bumper sticker described people's changing opinions of the candidates: "Dated Dean, but married Kerry."

Furthermore, Dean continued to suffer self-inflicted wounds. On Dec. 15, one day after Iraqi dictator Saddam Hussein was captured by American troops, Dean said in a speech that the event "has not made America safer."

Dean was also hurt by his campaign's approach to Iowa, the site of the first delegate-selection contest. According to the *Des Moines Register*'s Web site, he spent 76 days there before the caucuses, the most of any candidate. Though many Democrats in the Hawkeye State shared Dean's anti-war sentiment and liberal economic views, they bitterly resented being approached en masse by out-of-staters.

So how did the Dean team contact these voters? By sending as many as 14 pieces of campaign literature to some homes and using legions of college kids to get out the vote. Many of Dean's orange hat-wearing volunteers had long hair and body piercings. This image clashed sharply with the state's reputation as a haven for the values depicted in Norman Rockwell's paintings.

"When they get so much (mail), they begin thinking, 'something must be wrong with this guy,'" said former Iowa Democratic Chairman Rob Tully, who co-chaired Edwards' campaign there.[15]

Dean continued to draw large crowds, although polls indicated that his lead was slipping. The endorsement of U.S. Sen. Tom Harkin, the state's most powerful Democrat, and the eventual appearance of Dean's wife, Judith, on the campaign did not stop his fall.

On the night of the caucuses, as he and his supporters gathered in a dance hall in a suburb of Des Moines, Dean was transformed from being a serious candidate to a punchline.

It started innocently enough. Dean used the speech following his third-place finish (behind Kerry and Edwards) not to congratulate his opponents—he barely mentioned them—but to comfort his supporters. The combination, however, of his animated demeanor and a faulty sound system created an instant pop culture phenomenon.

To those in the room, it was just Dean being Dean. This writer noted that "[T]hough his voice was a bit hoarse, Dean retained the charismatic tone that has been the hallmark of his campaign speeches."[16]

In the days ahead, the national media had a different idea. His speech was replayed repeatedly on cable television and analyzed extensively in the media. During the lead up to the New Hampshire primary the following Tuesday, almost every story about Dean included a reference to the scream. Eventually, Dean would be able to joke about it in venues such as "The Late Show with David Letterman" in which Dean described the speech as a "crazy, red-faced rant."

That bad press, coupled with Kerry's momentum after winning Iowa, pushed Dean further downward. Though he still drew large crowds wherever he went, in many respects he became yesterday's story.

After a second-place finish in the January 27 New Hampshire balloting, he shuffled his staff. Trippi was succeeded by Roy Neel, a long-time aide to Al Gore. Neel in some ways symbolized the Washington establishment that Dean was supposed to be running against.

Campaigns do not generally turn on staff changes; such turnover, however, is generally symptomatic of bigger problems. Unfortunately for Dean, the shakeup was too late to rescue his campaign.

Dean had a series of second- and third-place finishes in subsequent primaries and caucuses. He suspended his candidacy on February 18, a day after a third-place finish in the Wisconsin primary. His sole victory would come two weeks later in the primary of his home state.

Though Dean was no longer a candidate, his presence was felt in the speeches of his opponents. Kerry regularly boasted about his fund-raising success over the Internet, something he never did before Dean caught fire. Edwards' speeches regularly included the line "you have the power to break the grip of the powerful special interests in this country and put the people in charge."[17]

Dean would go on to form a political action committee, Democracy for America, and he campaigned tirelessly for Kerry and other Democratic candidates. He urged those on his donor list to give money to several dozen state and federal candidates.

His efforts were rewarded with a prime-time speaking slot on the second night of the Democratic National Convention in Boston. He received tumultuous applause for lines such as: "We're not going to be afraid to stand up for what we believe. We're not going to let those who disagree with us shout us down under the banner of patriotism."

Perhaps feeling nostalgic, many in the crowd cheered more enthusiastically for Dean than they would two nights later during

Kerry's acceptance speech.

One Dean supporter from Tennessee wore a hand-made button that summed up the sentiments of many: "In an arranged marriage with John Kerry. Still in love with Howard Dean."

Defying F. Scott Fitzgerald's contention that there are no second acts in American life, Dean won political redemption—and a continued presence on the national stage—when on February 12 he was elected Democratic National Committee chairman by acclamation.

By emphasizing his affinity for grassroots organizing and prowess in fund-raising, Dean won over party leaders of all ideologies. His supporters included Rep. John Murtha, D-Pa., a cantankerous and hawkish Vietnam veteran, and Phil Johnston, the state chairman of Massachusetts, which has become the modern-day Mecca of liberalism.

Dean's problems with the party establishment were not over. The Democratic leaders of both the House and the Senate, as well as former President Clinton, worked behind-the-scenes to try to elect other candidates. The former Vermont governor won because the Anyone But Dean camp—like many factions of the party—had a better idea about what they were against than what they were for.

Claude R. Marx covered the Dean campaign while a reporter for the Vermont Press Bureau, the State house bureau for the *Rutland Herald*, and the *Barre-Montpelier Times Argus*. He now covers the Massachusetts State house for *The Eagle-Tribune*.

NOTES

1. Claude R. Marx, "Money is no object so far in Dean bid." *Rutland Herald*, Oct. 25, 2003, p. A1.

2. Mark Singer, "Running on instinct," *New Yorker*, Jan. 12, 2004, p. 67.

3. Howard Dean, *You Have The Power*. New York: Simon & Schuster, 2004, p. 18.

4. The best account of Dean's gubernatorial years can be found in a book published by the *Rutland Herald* and the *Barre-Montpelier Times Argus*: Dirk Van Susteren, Editor, *Howard Dean: A Citizen's Guide to the Man Who Would Be President*. South Royalton, Vt.: Steerforth Press, 2003.

5. The most comprehensive account of this battle is by *Rutland Herald* Editorial Page Editor David Moats, who won a Pulitzer Prize for his editorials on the subject: David Moats, *Civil Unions*. New York: Harcourt, 2004.

6. Nedra Pickler, "Some predict backlash for gay support," Associated Press, May 19, 2003.

7. Singer, p. 67.

8. Joe Trippi, *The Revolution Will Not Be Televised*, New York: Regan Books, 2004, p. 122.

9. Jodi Wilgoren, "Dean's manager: Insider savvy, outsider's edge," *New York Times*, Dec. 13, 2003, p. A1.

10. Claude R. Marx, "Aiming at Dean," *Rutland Herald*, Nov. 4, 2003, p. 1A.

11. Thomas Beaumont, "Kerry criticizes Dean's gun views," *Des Moines Register*, Nov. 1, 2003, p. A1.

12. Ibid., Marx.

13. Ibid., Marx.

14. Ibid., Trippi, p. 175.

15. Claude R. Marx, "Reporter's notebook: On the press bus, it's all about access," *Rutland Herald*, Jan. 24, 2004, p. A1.

16. Claude R. Marx, "Loss is big blow," *Rutland Herald*, Jan. 20, 2004, p. A1.

17. Claude R. Marx, "Dean campaign likely to echo throughout the race," *Rutland Herald*, Feb. 7, 2004, p. A1.

CHAPTER FOUR

The Election That
Broke the Rules

Larry J. Sabato

UNIVERSITY OF VIRGINIA CENTER FOR POLITICS

Some would say that politics operates only by the law of the jungle, that there are no rules of the game. In many respects this is true: Just think about the tactics we have seen employed by both parties in recent elections, from vicious negative ads to rumor-mongering of all sorts. Still, there are useful historical precedents that serve as rules, or guideposts, for electoral analysis and prediction. For example, incumbent Presidents tend to be reelected by large margins—or not at all. A bad economy and an unpopular war are poisonous for Presidents and good omens for a challenger. Presidents who fall behind during the election year are very likely to lose. Large turnouts tend to help Democratic candidates, especially in years when the incumbent has become polarizing and controversial. Presidents who first gain office without winning the popular vote serve only one term. A minimal margin in a presidential reelection will not be able to help the President's party gain seats in Congress.

All of these are useful historical benchmarks, and all proved misleading—actually, dead wrong—in 2004. Did this year's presidential election re-write the rules, or was it simply an exception to them? It will take decades to know for sure, but an examination of 2004's fascinating White House contest will offer us some tantalizing clues.

REAL VOTES

Given the embarrassing failure of many pre-election and Election Day exit polls, one can immediately make a helpful observation. Polls are often misleading approximations of reality—true lies. Americans have a love affair with polls because the allegedly precise nature of the numbers generated in the survey process gives powerful meaning to amorphous public opinion. Yet the flaws and misinterpretations of the polling process loom so large that we would do far better to look carefully at real votes, the ballots actually cast by citizens in an election. Yes, after 2000, everyone realizes that there is a small margin of error attached to voting, not just polling. But surely, even cynics would admit that the margin is far smaller with vote totals. Votes are democracy distilled, and those glorious numbers, broken down by region and state and demographic subdivision tell us so much about ourselves and our political choices.

First, please take a long look at Table 1 (see Appendix), which summarizes the official 2004 presidential vote *by states*. The national totals are well known, but let's slice and dice the returns in some revealing ways.

- *Bush and the Electoral College.* George W. Bush won 31 states and 286 electoral votes, just 16 more than the 270 required to win. He gained two states from 2000 (Iowa and New Mexico), while losing New Hampshire. His 286 votes in the Electoral College were an improvement over the near-minimum 271 he secured in 2000, once the 537-popular vote margin in Florida was finally certified. At the same time, this was one of the closest electoral margins in American history—the sixth closest, after 1800, 1824, 1876, 1916, and 2000. The only other incumbent President who had a tighter reelection was Democrat Woodrow Wilson in 1916, who garnered 277 electoral votes to Republican Charles Evans Hughes' 254.

- *Kerry and the Electoral College.* John F. Kerry triumphed in 19 states, including six of the ten most populous states (California, Illinois, Michigan, New Jersey, New York, and Pennsylvania). The Democrats' states accounted for 252 electoral votes, though Kerry officially received just 251 votes due to a "faithless elector" in Minnesota, who cast a presidential ballot for vice presidential nominee John Edwards instead of Kerry.[1]

- *The Popular Vote.* Having lost the popular vote by approximately 539,000 in 2000, Bush managed to do what the other three popular vote losers in American history (John Quincy Adams, Rutherford B. Hayes, and Benjamin Harrison) failed to do: win a second term, and with a substantial popular majority of close to 3 million votes.[2] Bush won 62,025,554 votes (50.7%) to 59,026,013 votes (48.3%), with all third-party and independent candidates together getting 1,214,518 votes (1.0%). Ralph Nader, who had almost certainly cost Al Gore the presidency in 2000[3] dropped drastically from 2.7% of the national vote in 2000 to a mere 0.37% in 2004—barely more than the 2004 Libertarian party nominee, Michael Badnarik, at 0.32%.[4] Nader's decline helped Kerry for sure, though not enough.

- *Historically Close Election.* It is worth noting that Bush's popular-vote margin, in percentage terms, was the slimmest ever for a reelected President. Bush's majority of 2.4% compares unfavorably to the large reelection margins of most modern Presidents and even to the other narrowly reelected Chief Executives: Grover Cleveland in 1892 (3.0%), Woodrow Wilson in 1916 (3.2%), and Harry S Truman in 1948 (4.5%).[5] To the contrary, though, Bush fared much better than the nine incumbent Presidents defeated for election or reelection (Adams Sr., J.Q. Adams, Van Buren, Cleveland, B. Harrison, Taft, Hoover, Ford, and Bush Sr.).[6] And Bush achieved an absolute majority of the popular vote for his second term, unlike reelected Presidents Cleveland (1892), Wilson (1916), Truman (1948), and Clinton (1996). Bush's 50.7% was the first majority vote for President since his father had won 53.4% to win his single term in 1988.

- *Skyrocketing Voter Turnout.* Perhaps the most startling statistic from the 2004 election is the voter turnout. Fully 122,266,085 Americans cast a ballot in the general election of 2004 for President. This is an absolute increase of almost 17 million over 2000's total of 105,402,138. With about 206 million Americans of voting age in 2004, this amounted to 59.4% of the eligible citizens going to the polls.[7] For three of the past four presidential elections, turnout had hovered around 50% of the eligible citizens: in 1988, 50.3%, in 1996, 48.9%, and in 2000, despite the perceived closeness of the election, 51.2%. Ross Perot had stirred passions in the electorate in 1992, helping to boost turnout to 55.2%. But not since the 1960s had turnout approached the 60% mark (1960: 63%, 1964: 62%, 1968: 61%).

Voter Turnout as a Percentage of the Adult Population, Presidential Elections

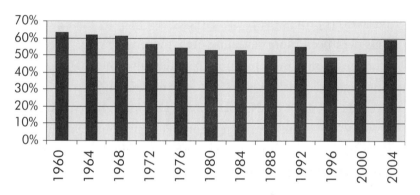

Thus, the 2004 election represented an encouraging leap forward, and backward—the highest turnout since the 1968 election. We will discuss some of the reasons for this heightened public interest later on.[8] But early research has already indicated that turnout was usually higher in the key battleground states where money and media attention were lavished; in states that featured the controversial gay marriage amendments; and in states where high-profile U.S. Senate elections were being held.[9] Also of note is the lesson learned about high turnout in 2004: It doesn't necessarily favor Democrats, as the common wisdom has suggested for generations. Overall, Bush, not Kerry, was helped more by the increase in turnout, though one researcher has concluded that vigorous Democratic turnout efforts cut the expected Republican vote share in major battleground states.[10]

- *The Polarized Map.* The United States of America is homogenized by commerce—there are McDonald's and Marriott's everywhere—but still remarkably distinct, state by state and region by region. The Electoral College both reflects this fact, and reinforces this reality. Just a glance at the dramatic vote variations proves the point. No election map in a close contest has ever been more revealing. Yes, there were only three state changes from 2000, but not coincidentally, the changes made the regional patterns starker. (See Figure 3: Electoral College Results 2004.) With New Hampshire's shift to Kerry, the entire Northeast is Democratic territory. Pennsylvania remained the only competitive large Northeastern state, with Bush losing it by just two and a half percentage points. For the fourth presidential election in a row, most of the Northeast was simply a disaster area for the Republicans, with Democratic majorities ranging up to 18% in New York, 21% in Rhode Island, and 25% in Massachusetts. The other great area of Democratic strength is the West Coast, the culmination of demographic and ideological trends stretching back a couple of decades. California provides a bountiful harvest of 55 electoral votes for virtually any Democrat today, and Oregon and Washington state, while marginally competitive, clearly lean Democratic. Despite a few misleading polls toward the end of the 2004 election, Hawaii ended up Democratic blue, as it nearly always does. The Democrats' only other regional foothold is in the upper

Midwest. Illinois is impregnable now, the Land of Lincoln having converted to Lincoln's partisan nemesis. Michigan and Minnesota are usually Democratic, and Wisconsin has a slight Democratic tilt. Sure enough, Kerry captured every one of these states—but no more.

- *The Inland Sea of Red.* While Iowa, Nevada, and New Mexico are on the knife's edge, all three went to Bush, the former and the latter representing a shift from 2000. Arizona and Colorado, like Oregon and Washington, are marginally competitive, but almost always end up in the GOP electoral column. An inland sea of red—conveniently contiguous for the coloring of schoolchildren—covers the rest of the United States. Bush's margins in states such as Oklahoma (65.6%), Idaho (68.4%), Wyoming (68.9%), and Utah (71.5%) are phenomenal. Democratic presidential candidates are not even remotely competitive in most of the Rocky Mountain West, the Farm Belt (save Iowa), the Border South states (save liberal Maryland), and the vast expanse of the growing South. Florida 2000 looks like an aberration, with Republicans naturally favored there. Bill Clinton's Arkansas remains a possible Democratic target, but only for a moderate candidate. Missouri, the great Midwestern swing state, is now usually Republican. Incredibly, even once heavily Democratic West Virginia has taken on a medium-red hue, as social and environmental issues have driven a wedge between Mountain State voters and the party of Franklin Roosevelt and Robert Byrd. Bush's massive margins in the Deep South (Georgia: 58%, Alabama: 63%, Mississippi: 59%, and so forth) were almost matched by states once considered open to a Democratic candidate, such as Tennessee (57%), Louisiana (57%), Kentucky (60%), and North Carolina (56%). The Tar Heel State was a special slap in the face for Democrats, since native U.S. Senator John Edwards could barely move the needle in John Kerry's direction as the vice presidential nominee. Finally, it is the overwhelming GOP strength in Indiana (60% for Bush) and the marginal Republican tilt of Ohio (50.8% for Bush, a 3.1% margin for the President) that created the Red Electoral majority, as narrow as it was.

- *Every State Mattered, Especially Ohio.* For the second consecutive election, almost every state mattered in a close result. Bush's states in 2000 had gained seven additional electoral votes on account of the Census, an edge that more than doubled the net six additional votes he won via Iowa and New Mexico (minus New Hampshire).[11] Interestingly, just as advertised throughout the election year, the Electoral College decision came down to the Buckeye State and its swing 20 electoral votes. In 2000 Bush managed only a 166,000-vote plurality out of over 4.6 million votes cast, despite the fact that Al Gore had abandoned the state weeks ahead of the election as unwinnable. During Bush's term, tens of thousands of Ohio jobs were lost to a stubborn recession, and Democrats focused millions of dollars and many thousands of volunteers on Ohio's voters as the election year heated up. The Republicans responded in kind, and sure enough, a million more citizens showed up to vote just in this one state. The news media had lavished attention on the Democratic GOTV operations in Ohio, in part because the Democrats were proudly boasting of their alleged superiority on the ground. Yet an age-old principle of politics was at work: *Mobilization begets counter-mobilization.* Alerted to the massive Democratic organizational efforts, national and Ohio Republicans generated their own, equally impressive (if quieter) GOTV program.[12] Bush's margin shrank in 2004, but his 118,000-vote triumph was not terribly close, and the Ohio proportions received by Bush and Kerry closely mirrored the national result. More significantly, the voter turnout in the Ohio counties that went for Bush averaged 71.8%, exceeding the 68.0% voter turnout in the Ohio counties that Kerry won. This at least suggests the Republican campaign effort neutralized or exceeded the success enjoyed by the Democrats.[13] At the same time, it is worth remembering that a shift of just under 60,000 votes would have given Kerry 272 electoral votes, and the Presidency. Of course, his term would have been dogged by the fact that he had lost the overall national popular vote by *nearly six times* the margin Bush lost it in 2000. A three million-vote deficit would not have been an auspicious start to Kerry's stay in the White House.

- *Diversity in a Status Quo Election.* Nationally, Bush's overall margin in the popular vote increased 2.8%, from 47.9% in 2000 to 50.7% in 2004. In yet another measure of federalism, and in contrast to the virtually unchanged Electoral College map, Bush's vote actually varied fairly widely from state to state in his two presidential elections. As Table 2 displays (see Appendix), Bush gained percentage points in 32 states, lost some in 15 states, and his vote proportion was essentially unchanged in just 3 states (plus the District of Columbia). So much for a supposedly "status quo" election! Interestingly, the President's largest increases often came in states he lost, such as Hawaii, New Jersey, and Rhode Island, where Bush posted 5% gains. Why did this happen? In 2000 Bush was buried in a Democratic landslide in those states, and he secured an unusually low percentage of the vote, even for a Republican in heavily Democratic states. Four years later, Bush rebounded to normal, if still losing, vote levels. The President also surged about 5% in some of his strongholds, such as Alabama, Oklahoma, and Tennessee—in the latter case, Bush was no longer running against a Volunteer State native. The mirror image was also true in many states. In 2000 Bush had won nine of the fifteen states where he lost some ground in 2004; his 2000 proportion simply represented a high water mark for a Republican that could not be matched again. However, the state that generated the most sizable vote decline for Bush was liberal Vermont, where Bush tumbled from almost 45% in 2000 to *under 40%* in 2004. Four years ago in the Green Mountain State, George W. Bush was viewed as a moderate, "compassionate conservative," more like his father. By 2004 Bush was seen as far-right in the home state of liberal Democratic presidential candidate Howard Dean, Independent-Democratic U.S. Senator Jim Jeffords (who turned the Senate over to Democratic control in May 2001), socialist U.S. Representative Bernie Sanders, and Democratic U.S. Senator Patrick Leahy (the bête noire of Vice President Dick Cheney).

• *The Tug of Regionalism.* Ohio and a few other very close states aside, the 2004 presidential contest appeared to be more a regional battle than a state-by-state tussle, as vote compilations by analyst Rhodes Cook show. The South went for Bush in a 57.3% to 42% landslide. The margin in the Rocky Mountain West (including Alaska) was nearly identical: 56.9% for Bush, 41.7% for Kerry. The four Great Plains states (Kansas, Nebraska, and the Dakotas) gave Bush an even larger 62.9% to 35.6% for Kerry. Switching columns, Kerry smashed Bush in the Northeast, 55.5% to 43.4%, and the Pacific West, 53.8% to 44.9%. The most competitive region by far—and the likely site of the decisive contests in future close presidential races— was the Industrial Midwest. While the electoral vote there swung to Kerry by 58 to 49, *the popular vote was an exact tie, 49.6% to 49.6%*. Both parties may want to look for presidential and vice presidential nominees in the crucial Midwest for future elections.

THE POLITICAL MAP OF AMERICA

Four years ago in my book, *Overtime: The Election 2000 Thriller*[14] I introduced the concept of the "Political Map of America," ably executed by Joshua J. Scott of the University of Virginia Center for Politics. As noted there, this exercise in cartography is based on the essential notion that 'people vote, not trees or rocks or acres.' The Electoral College has a certain small-state bias, for sure, driven by the two senatorial bonus votes added to every state, whether a lightly populated state such as Wyoming or a behemoth such as California. Yet, the electoral vote result is driven by the *popular vote* in each state; the candidate who wins one more popular vote than the other in each state gets all the electoral votes that state has to offer.

Therefore, the Political Map, based on the population figures in the 2000 Census, is "what politicians, their staffs, and political consultants actually see when they look at our nation." The Northeast has lost millions of residents in recent decades, but notice how large politically the geographically compact region still looms (see Figure 1). The Northeast is more than matched by the South, whose volume on this map has *doubled* since the 1950s, led by Florida and Texas. California is the ultimate mega-state, more than twice its geographical size in the Political Map. The large, swing Midwestern states are, like the Northeast, considerably reduced in size from what they were just a half-century ago, but their importance is clear on the Political Map. Finally, many of our readers will be distressed to see their states shrunk to a volume so small that a postage stamp could cover most of them. These are the states that should be very grateful for the Electoral College, and those bonus votes! As consolation, it should be stressed that many of these states in the West are growing by leaps and bounds, and the next Political Map of America, to be drawn in 2011, will show progress. In any event, when it comes to the Political Map, as in so many other areas of life, size matters, and there is just no getting around that. Poor Alaska: It is a massive piece of territory, but in the Political Map, it is *smaller than Rhode Island!*

So what does the Political Map add to our understanding of the 2004 presidential election? Let's compare the 2000 Bush-Gore map with the 2004 Bush-Kerry map (see Figures 2 and 3).

Both maps put the election into proper perspective. The geographical maps would suggest to a visitor from another galaxy that Bush had scored a landslide in both elections. The Political Maps indicate otherwise, that Bush simply carried the large-acreage,

FIGURE 1
The Political Map of the United States

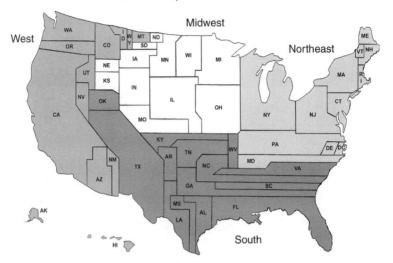

Center for Politics

The Political Map of the United States, 2000: Bush vs. Gore

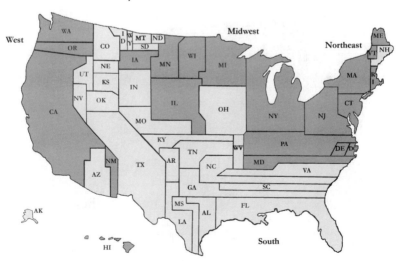

Center for Politics

The Political Map of the United States, 2004: Bush vs. Kerry

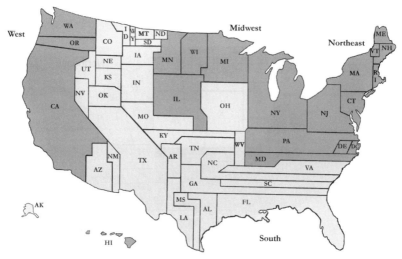

Center for Politics

FIGURE 2
Electoral College Results 2000

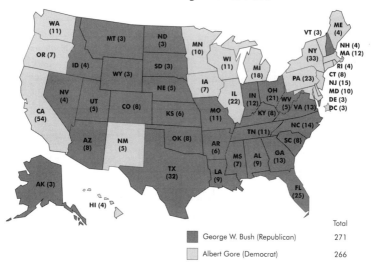

	Total
George W. Bush (Republican)	271
Albert Gore (Democrat)	266

Center for Politics

FIGURE 3
Electoral College Results 2004

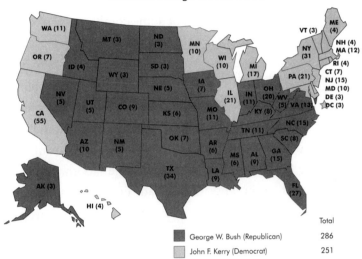

	Total
George W. Bush (Republican)	286
John F. Kerry (Democrat)	251

Center for Politics

small-population states in both elections, and that the actual partisan balance was quite close in both years. Moreover, the subtle changes from 2000 to 2004, with a mere three-state swap, help to clarify our picture of modern American politics. Despite the rough edges necessitated by state boundaries, the 2004 map is a thing of contiguous beauty—with determinative Ohio, quite by accident, near dead-center, as the 'great exception' to regional alignments. Lucky for George W. Bush that it was!

EXIT POLLS: THE CAUTIONS, AND SOME INSIGHTS

One must approach the subject of the 2004 exit polls with some trepidation. Just as in 2000 and 2002[15] the news media's big Election-Day production caused intense controversy and consternation. Perhaps because of poor sampling, or the refusal of many Republicans to participate in a media poll, or some combination of defects, the first waves of the exit polls in 2004 showed John Kerry winning the national popular vote, and tying or capturing virtually all the key battleground states. In mid-afternoon, the National Election Pool (NEP) had Kerry up 19 percentage points in Pennsylvania; he carried the state by three points. The Democrat appeared to be leading in Ohio and Florida, both of which he lost. And a raft of Southern states were "too close to call," despite the fact that Bush was destined to win them in landslides. I had direct access to the Virginia exit poll from NEP, and even in early evening, Bush was barely leading Kerry, about within the margin of error, according to their data. Among many obvious demographic problems with the Virginia exit poll, there were far too many Democratic-leaning women in the sample, and solidly Democratic African-Americans were allocated a sky-high 21% of the sample even though their proportion of the electorate was no more than 15% to 16%. (Blacks have never topped 17% of the electorate in any modern Virginia election.) Unsurprisingly, Bush defeated Kerry by 8% in Virginia, and by even more in other Southern states deemed "close." As for the national popular vote, the NEP exit pollsters *as late as 7:33 p.m. on election night* were sending data to their media clients showing Kerry defeating Bush by nine points among women and losing men by only four points—results that, if true, would have guaranteed Kerry's election. A senior editor at the *Washington Post* revealed that the *final* wave of exit polls "showed Kerry winning the popular vote by 51% to 48%," exactly the opposite of the reality. This editor termed the exit polls "badly flawed" and said they caused "a real problem in our newsroom" on election night. The three-point Kerry lead was not changed until 1:33 a.m. on November 3, and even then, the exit poll had Bush leading by just a single point despite an enormous sample size of over 13,000.[16]

In any event, the national data were widely disseminated by journalists at the networks and major newspapers to their frequent sources, and these sources sent out the information to literally tens of thousands of others via e-mail and blogs. Virtually the entire political community was buzzing by late afternoon of Election Day about the imminent demise of the Bush Presidency and the ascendancy of John Kerry. President Bush himself was informed while on Air Force One, and some of his staff were physically sick and mentally anguished upon receipt of the pseudo-news. Meanwhile, John Kerry was being greeted as "Mr. President" by his Svengali, political consultant Bob Shrum.[17] Most disturbingly, some in the television media were hinting broadly to their national audience *before all the polls had closed* what they *thought* they knew. Some Kerry backers, such as Senator Ted Kennedy, were virtually crowing on CNN in what was later described in a liberal blog as "The 7-Hour Presidency of JFK2."[18] This is not just a matter of some analysts, TV uber-anchors, and exit pollsters having egg on their face. There is always at least the potential for coverage tilted toward a supposed winner having some kind of bandwagon effect on voters who have not yet cast their ballots. Recklessness in exit poll coverage can exact a terrible price. While the pollsters cannot be held *directly* responsible for the November 2nd coverage, they had primary accountability for the embarrassing mistakes that led to the meltdown. Without ever acknowledging any culpability, the NEP and their hired guns have announced significant restrictions on the release of their data in future elections—though one wonders if the changes will be enough.[19]

Sadly, the 2004 mishap was just "déjà vu all over again." Among other problems, the Voter News Service exit poll of 2000 had mis-called Florida in the presidential race, and before all the Florida polls had closed to boot, helping to set in motion the international embarrassment that soon ensued. In the 2002 midterm elections, VNS (a consortium of the five major TV networks plus the Associated Press) collapsed entirely on Election Day itself. Now came VNS's successor, the National Election Pool with the same media participants, which contracted with Edison Media Research and Mitofsky International to conduct interviews with 13,360 voters at polling places scattered across the United States on November 2. (The Election Day interviews were supplemented with telephone surveys of voters who had cast absentee, early voting, or mail-in ballots well ahead of November 2—a group that comprised at least a fifth of all voters in 2004.)

The unfortunate fact is that post-election analysis necessarily depends upon the NEP exit poll. Only the *Los Angeles Times* conducted a "rival" exit poll, and its sample was tiny: 5,154 voters in just 136 locations across the United States, of whom a massive 3,357 voters were Californians at 50 in-state polling sites. Of course, there are literally hundreds of pre- and post-election surveys, but their samples are of projected, "probable" voters, not of the actual voters who showed up on Election Day. So like everyone else in the field, this author will use the NEP data, however flawed, in the analysis that follows. However, it is vital that you, dear reader, keep in mind that the numbers you see are only *approximations of voting reality*—and that may be a kind interpretation, given what we know about the exit poll system. As we will mention, there have already been hot disputes about some of the exit data, even after the information has been refined and re-sifted.

Gender Wars, Racial Divisions

The exit poll claimed that the national electorate was 54% female, an increase from 52% female in 2000. Assuming this shift is accurately portrayed, one might think it represented bad news for Republican Bush, since women almost always tilt to the Democrats in close contests. Sure enough, women favored Kerry over Bush by a 51% to 48% margin, but women had preferred Al Gore to Bush in 2000 by a much wider 54% to 43%. The net gain of 5% for Bush here was critical, and almost certainly it was due to a belief that the President was better able to deal with national security issues than his challenger. Among men, Bush also increased his support, from 53% to 55%—though we should note that the gain with men was less than with women. When race is factored into this equation, Bush's strength among white men becomes apparent. Bush overwhelmed Kerry, 62% to 37%, among white men; Bush captured white women by the lesser but still substantial majority of 55% to 44%. Four years earlier, Bush had barely won white women, 49% to 48% for Gore. *Here is where the election was won by Bush.* While other shifts, discussed in the pages that follow, were also significant, nothing mattered as much as Bush's ability to expand his appeal among female voters. If analysts are looking for "the post-September 11th effect" that delivered a second term to Bush, this is it.

As always, race was a key determinant of the 2004 vote. Whites, fully 77% of the total electorate, gave Bush a landslide, 58% to

41%—a 4% increase for Bush from 2000. Not surprisingly, in many Southern states, Bush's white percentage climbed above 70%: Alabama (80%), Georgia (76%), Louisiana (75%), North Carolina (73%), Oklahoma (71%), South Carolina (78%), Texas (74%), and Bush's national zenith, Mississippi, at 85%. Bush carried a majority of whites in almost all the states, but in the District of Columbia, where even whites are heavily Democratic, he received a paltry 19%. The 11% of the electorate that was African-American voted heavily *against* Bush, 88% to 11%. The needle hardly moved from 2000, when about 9% of blacks cast ballots for Bush. Naturally, this overall national percentage hides considerable variation in the states.[20] Bush's support among blacks ranged from a low of 3% in D.C. to a high of 28% in Oklahoma. In the critical state of Ohio, Bush secured about 16% of African-Americans.

Hispanic voters may well have been one of the keys to Bush's reelection, though there is considerable dispute about this. The NEP exit poll measured Hispanic/Latino support for Bush at 44% in 2004, a giant leap forward from the 35% Bush secured in 2000. At least one major Hispanic group has hotly disputed that finding, insisting that its data show Bush did *worse* in 2004 than 2000, receiving just 32% of the Latino vote.[21] Recent 'refinements' in the NEP exit poll have suggested that the President may have won 40% to 41% of the Hispanic/Latino vote in 2004—a 5% to 6% gain among this critical, swing constituency that constitutes about 8% of the national vote.[22] Most of Bush's Hispanic gains appear to have come among men, and those Latinos who are married. The National Annenberg Election Survey claimed that Bush's share of Hispanic males climbed from 34% in 2000 to 46% in 2004, with married Hispanics backing Bush by 16 full percentage points more than the non-married.[23] We'll never really know the correct answer, but it seems likely that Bush registered some increase among Hispanics, a group his White House shrewdly targeted throughout Bush's first term. Finally, to the extent that a sample of 2% of the whole is valid, Asian-Americans voted for John Kerry by a margin of 56% to 44% for Bush. This indicates a slight gain for the President from four years earlier.

The Youth Vote: Hope for a Democratic Future?

A ray of hope for the Democrats can be seen in the vote cast by the youngest citizens, aged 18 to 29. Kerry won them, 54% to 45%, whereas they were statistically evenly divided in 2000. Again, this suggestion assumes that the poll is correct, and that young people maintain their Democratic leaning in future elections—neither of which is anything approaching a certainty. Despite tremendous efforts aimed at the young to increase voter turnout, the 18 to 29 age cohort comprised exactly the same proportion of the vote in 2004 (17%) as it had in 2000. On the other hand, because of the dramatic increase in voter turnout, it was something of a miracle that the youthful portion of the electorate did not decline, given the highly mobile, distracted nature of life for college-age people and young professionals. By contrast, Bush showed added strength with all the other age cohorts in Table 3 (see Appendix), especially the highest-turnout, eldest voters, aged 60 and up. Bush apparently lost the 60+ group in 2000 by a few points, but the NEP poll claimed that Bush won them by a healthy 54% to 46% margin in 2004. Incidentally, about 11% of the voters said they had never voted before, and these first-time voters (of all ages) went for Kerry by a small margin, 53% to 46%. The first-time voters in the 2000 election were also Democratic-leaning by about the same margin (52% to 43%).

Another perceptive slant on age as a factor in the 2004 election has been provided by pollster J. Brad Coker and marketing executive Jonathan Pontell.[24] Coker and Pontell contend that "Generation Jones," born between 1954 and 1965 (roughly 35 to 49 years of age in 2004), elected Bush. The "Jones" group, claim the researchers, is the most persuadable age cohort because of their "time of life," as many seek new careers, move to new places, and shift lifestyles. The women of the Jones generation—many of them the so-called "national security Moms" swayed to the Republicans by September 11th—backed Bush, while women from all other age cohorts supported Kerry. Both male and female "Jones'ers" were 5% to 10% more likely to end up in Bush's column, at least in the fifteen key battleground states surveyed for the study. Whether this age group has the cohesion and self-awareness to be a major factor in future elections is unknown, but worth reexamination come 2008.

Income, Education, and Party Identification

Much as in 2000, a person's family income was a dead-on indicator of presidential choice. Generally, the higher the income, the more likely Bush was to win an individual's vote. About 45% of the electorate had an income of under $50,000, and Kerry was a 55% to 44% favorite among this broad grouping. For the 55% of the electorate making $50,000 or more, Bush won a 56% to 43% landslide. At the top of the income scale ($200,000+), Bush smashed Kerry by 63% to 35%. Union members and their households, about a quarter of the overall electorate, gave Kerry 59% of their votes—the exact percentage won by Al Gore in 2000.

Looking to educational levels, the normal pattern prevailed, with one notable exception. High school graduates and those with some college training, including a degree, favored Bush by modest margins. Also as usual, people with post-graduate education or degrees tilted Democratic, by 55% to 44%. The change came among the small portion of voters with less than a high school degree. While the exit poll in 2000 had shown them favoring Al Gore by 20 percentage points, the 2004 exit poll showed Bush and Kerry tied in this category.

A person's party identification is usually a powerful predictor of the vote for President, and that was rarely as true as in 2004. The intensity of the Bush-Kerry contest was red-hot and unmistakably heartfelt on both sides. The division in the electorate fell along partisan lines, a fact that surprises many observers who incorrectly have come to believe that political parties no longer matter much. While Americans love to call themselves "independent," three-quarters have a discernible partisan identification. (Actually, political scientists have long shown that 85% or more of Americans have some form of party ID, even if it is weak and latent.) As expected, 74% of the voters in 2004 identified themselves as either Democrats or Republicans. The Democrats cast 89% of their ballots for Kerry, just 11% for Bush. The President did even better with Republicans, with a phenomenal 93% of GOP identifiers voting for him, and only 6% for Kerry. The quarter of the electorate that claimed independent status split their votes evenly between the two major-party candidates. The 2004 results were very similar to the 2000 breakdown by party. What changed in four years was the turnout pattern. In 2000 Democrats outnumbered Republicans in the Election-Day electorate by 39% to 35%. But in 2004, for the first time since exit polling began in the 1970s, Democrats and Republicans were peg-equal, at 37% of the electorate each. These numbers, if valid, are a testament to the relatively hidden Republican turnout operation in 2004. The Democratic efforts, star-studded with Hollywood celebrities and rockers, received far more media attention, but the GOP "machine"—using churches and telephones and mail—was more effective.[25]

Not surprisingly, a voter's outlook on politics and policy, often termed *ideology*, is impressively correlated with the vote for President in modern times. Liberals, only about a fifth of the electorate, went for Kerry over Bush by 85% to 13%. Moderates, who are just shy of a majority of the voters, preferred Kerry by a comfortable 54% to 45%. But conservatives—the remaining third of the electorate—held sway because of their overwhelming commitment to Bush, 84% to 15%. Again, there was little change here from 2000, though Bush appeared to attract slightly more conservatives; the "compassionate conservative" of 2000 had assumed a more firmly pure conservative image after his first term.

Unification of Church and State in the Polling Booth

Religion has played a significant role in American politics since the beginning of the Republic, and in the last couple of presidential elections, it has received considerable attention. We often forget that in the 1960 presidential election, religion was probably as important as party identification in the results of the Kennedy-Nixon contest. JFK, only the second major-party Roman Catholic nominee (after Democrat Al Smith in 1928), won the popular vote narrowly on the strength of 80% backing from his co-religionists. By contrast, Richard Nixon secured nearly 70% support from Protestant voters, who worried about papal influence on the White House. Interestingly, Roman Catholics chose Protestant Bush over Catholic Kerry in the 2004 election—a remarkable shift from 2000, not to mention 1960. Bush captured 52% of the Catholic vote to Kerry's 47%, quite different from Gore's 50% and his 47% in 2000. Catholics were 27% of the electorate in 2004, but Protestants, as usual, were over half (54%), and Bush won them going away (59% to 40%). The Jewish vote provided more good news for Republicans. While Jews are only 3% of the electorate, they are located disproportionately in electoral vote-rich states, and Bush gained 6% overall in this heavily Democratic religious denomination. After a miserable 19% of the Jewish vote in 2000, Bush moved up to 25% four years later.[26] The only religious categories where John Kerry showed strength were "other religions," 7% of the electorate where he beat Bush by three-to-one, and the 10% of the electorate that rejects religion, which voted for Kerry in a 67% to 31% landslide. Obviously, in a heavily religious country such as the United States, the Democrats' profile of backing mainly among non-traditional denominations and the "un-churched" cannot be encouraging to the party. (Gore carried Catholics, but displayed the same a-religious base as Kerry.)

A couple of other intriguing aspects of religion as applied to the 2004 results should be mentioned. For the almost quarter of the electorate that described itself as "white, evangelical, or 'born-again' Christians," Bush was the clear choice, 78% to 21%.[27] Kerry easily won the rest of the electorate, 56% to 43%. Nothing much changed here from the 2000 election. Similarly, just as in 2000, the frequency of church attendance revealed partisan choices. The more often one attends religious services, the more likely one was to vote Bush. Over four in ten Americans go to church once a week *or more,* and these voters chose Bush by 61% to 39%. Occasional churchgoers (monthly or a few times a year) were about as numerous as the weekly+ attendees, and here, Kerry edged Bush 53% to 47%. The 15% of Americans who *never* darken the doors of a chapel were solidly in the Kerry camp, 62% to 36%. It is important to stress the obverse of these findings, that is, *about a third of those who go to church weekly or more often favored Kerry, and about a third of those who never go to church voted for Bush.* Church attendance is a suggestive voting indicator, not a perfect correlation or explanation.

Military, Marriage, and M-16s

If there was one biographical fact emphasized during the 2004 campaign, it was military service. Both President Bush's time in the National Guard during the Vietnam War and John Kerry's tour of duty in the Vietnam War, and Kerry's anti-War activities once he returned to the States became major issues in the paid advertising and news media coverage. The anti-Kerry "Swift Boat Veterans for Truth" became a critical turning point in the campaign when the 527 group began to attack Kerry in early August, using hard-hitting TV ads questioning Kerry's behavior during and after his Vietnam service. In retrospect, Kerry campaign aides said their failure to respond quickly to these attacks was a serious, if not fatal, error since the attacks reversed the post-Democratic convention Kerry momentum. While it is difficult to measure the exact effect of the "Swifties" ads, they may have contributed to a crucial exit poll finding. Close to one in five Americans reported that they had served in some branch of the military during their lifetimes, and these active duty personnel and veterans gave their Commander-in-Chief a strong vote of confidence, 57% to 41%. Those who had never been in the military were equally divided between Bush and Kerry.

Naturally, voters' political outlooks are shaped in part by the family arrangements they choose for themselves. So much of one's life—culturally and economically—is affected by whether one is married or single, whether one has children or not, and so on. For example, marrieds and singles were mirror voting images of each other in 2004. Bush received 57% of the married vote, Kerry 58% of the single vote. (Marrieds outnumbered singles at the polls by 63% to 37%.) People who were married *with children* were even more likely to vote Bush, by 59% to 40%. Despite the President's emphasis on opposition to gay marriage, Bush still received nearly a quarter of the 4% of Americans who said they were gay, lesbian, or bisexual—not far off Bush's 2000 "compassionate conservative" pace of 25%. Still, John Kerry proved again that gays have become a fundamental constituency group of the Democratic party, as he took 77% of this relatively small vote. Gore had secured "only" 70%, so one would assume that Ralph Nader's approximately 5% from 2000 went solidly to Kerry's column, along with a few gay defections from Bush.

According to internal National Rifle Association surveys, NRA members were overwhelmingly in Bush's corner, not surprisingly. The exit poll asked a broader question, whether people's household included a gun owner. Of the 41% who answered in the affirmative, Bush carried 63% to Kerry's 36%.

Timing of the Voter's Decision

One question political scientists and others always ask is: When did voters make up their minds for whom to vote? The answer is unavoidably "squishy" statistically, since we must rely on voters' self-reported memory. Nonetheless, it is obvious that strong partisans would have known all year long for whom they would cast their ballot. The 2004 election was so polarized and intense that relatively few truly undecided voters existed, and also a surprisingly small group of semi-decided voters who were "persuadable" to vote for the other side. Almost all public and private surveys in September and October indicated that the undecideds were numbered in the single digits (some private polls had it as low as 3% to 5%), and certainly not more than another 10% were actually persuadable. The 2004 exit poll inquired of respondents about the timing of their voting decision, and fully 89% claimed their minds were made up before the campaign's concluding days, with nearly eight in ten voters saying they knew well before the last month of the campaign. About one in ten insisted that they decided in the last week (though it was probable most of these voters were clearly leaning one way or the other well before then). Of this group, Kerry won 53% to 44% for Bush. Does this mean there was a last-minute surge to Kerry? That is highly doubtful. In 2000 Al Gore also won the late-deciders, 48% to 45%, but in both cases the data may argue that the Democrats had not adequately sold themselves to their partisan identifiers as quickly or as thoroughly as had the Republicans for Bush. Without any doubt, the enthusiasm levels *for* Kerry (and Gore) were not as high as for Bush. In both years many voters indicated they were voting more *against* Bush than *for* the Democratic nominee. In 2004, by a margin of 59% to 40%, Bush supporters said their vote was mostly *for* Bush rather than against Kerry, but by a massive 70% to 30%, the Kerry voters admitted they were mainly voting *against* Bush.

What Also Matters: Issues, Presidential Job Approval, and Optimism

This may be the age of personality politics, thanks to television in good part, but most Americans really do cast their ballot on the basis of party identification and *issues*. Party ID certainly affects many voters' perceptions of the issues and sets their priorities. For example, Republicans for years have stressed national security and defense, taxes, and moral values, while Democrats have put the most emphasis on domestic issues such as education, health care, and jobs. Sure enough, the exit poll data confirm these policy preferences as a function of the presidential vote. Those concerned about terrorism (19% of the electorate), moral values (22%), and taxes (5%) voted for Bush by, respectively, 86%, 80%, and 57%. By contrast, voters worried about the economy and jobs (20%), Iraq (15%), health care (8%), and education (4%) cast their lot with Kerry by, respectively, 80%, 73%, 77%, and 73%. There are no surprises here, though a poorly worded exit poll phrase about "moral values," combined with an overreaction by the news media, created a gigantic stir in the days following the election. Suddenly, Americans were concerned first and foremost with moral issues, and supposedly, this was the key to Bush's reelection. In fact, simply by combining terrorism and Iraq as voter concerns, one could see that far more voters were focused on these foreign policy challenges than "moral values." Additionally, there is precious little evidence that the social and cultural issues—or the voting blocs arrayed around them—have changed very much at all. While precise comparisons are not possible because of the wording differences in past exit poll questions, our examination of the churched versus un-churched voters (above) gives a clear indication of the partisan alignments of those who are most concerned about value matters. For decades now, the GOP has attracted the lion's share of pro-life and anti-gay rights voters, the Democrats winning most of the pro-choice and pro-gay rights supporters. President Clinton's moral foibles in the late 1990s reinforced the sharp party divisions on morals. So the more things change, the more they remain the same...Except someone forgot to tell the exit pollsters and the news media.[28]

For decades political scientists and pollsters have pointed to a President's job approval numbers as perhaps the best indicator of his ability to get reelected. Approval over 50% among the actual Election-Day voters yields a second term; approval below that probably guarantees defeat. On Election Day among the voters, George W. Bush had about a 53% approval level, and 90% of those who approved of his job performance cast a ballot for him. Of the 46% who disapproved of Bush's performance, 93% voted for Kerry. By the way, a few answers by voters to this basic question are revealing in another way: There is no accounting for tastes, or votes. About 5% of those who "*strongly* approved" of Bush nonetheless voted for Kerry, and 2% of those who "*strongly dis*approved" of Bush still voted for the President. How and why? Who knows? Perhaps the tug of party affiliation was enough to pull some voters back into their partisan column despite their intense views of Bush. Or maybe they just liked or disliked the other candidate more!

Two other dead giveaways of voter intent are usually the "right track/wrong track" question, and the pocketbook issue. The "track" query is simply, "Do you think the U.S. is going in the right direction, or is it seriously off on the wrong track?" This has been a pollster's favorite for many years since it is a powerful summary question, that is, voters can see what they want to see in the wording, and thus can reveal their overall mood about the nation. Respondents were about as closely divided on this dichotomy as they were in the final presidential vote in 2004. Of the 49% who chose "right direction," 89% voted for Bush; Kerry received 86% of the votes of those who said "wrong direction." What about the age-old pocketbook issue? In times of war such as 2004, the economy can be relegated to second fiddle, but the fiddle still plays music that matters on Election Day. At the end of Bush's first term, the national economy was so-so, and one could make almost equally good arguments that the glass was half-full or half-empty. Those convinced it was half-full, and who reported their family's financial situation had become better (32% of the electorate), voted 80% for Bush. Those who saw the glass as half-empty since their family's financial situation was worse (28%) picked Kerry 79% of the time. The largest group of Americans saw the glass as unchanged, their family's financial situation essentially unchanged in Bush's term, and they split their votes evenly between the candidates. The 2004 Bush victory negated a standard economic guidepost about presidential elections. Since 1960, with only one exception, if job growth has been weak in the months preceding the November election, the incumbent has lost, while above average job growth has signaled the incumbent party's reelection. In 2004, job growth was sub-par, yet Bush triumphed, because of national security concerns primarily. Interestingly, the lone exception before 2004 was 1968, when robust job growth could not help Democrat Hubert Humphrey overcome deep voter misgivings about another foreign policy issue, the Vietnam War.[29] Notice the difference four years, and a change of White House administrations, makes. In 2000, when Democrats were the incumbent party, voters who saw their family finances as better voted for Gore in a landslide, and those who thought their finances were worse picked Bush by about the same large margin! As always in politics, where you stand depends on where you sit—and who's in charge.

Hot-Button Topics and Candidate Qualities

Specific hot-button topics can have an impact on a presidential election, too. The intense social and cultural issues that we have mentioned before are certainly among them. At the top of the list for 2004 was gay marriage and its milder cousin, civil unions for gays. A plurality of Americans (37%) wanted no legal recognition of these relationships, of any sort, and they favored Bush over Kerry, 70% to 29%. The quarter of the voters who supported full legal marriage for gays chose Kerry, by 77% to 22%. Slightly more than a third (35%) said they backed "civil unions" as a middle way around the controversy, and the votes were closely divided, 52% for Bush and 47% for Kerry. It must be noted that, throughout polling history, compromise-loving Americans have been inclined to choose the most moderate of three alternatives (the middle choice) as a way of splitting the difference between warring camps. Whether respondents even fully understood the distinctions between marriage and civil unions is a subject worth investigation by public opinion experts. Another, durable cultural controversy centers on abortion, and the political parties could not have been more polarized on it in 2004. The results followed the pattern of the Bush-Gore contest, with close to 70% of those identifying with the pro-choice position in Kerry's column, and 74% of the voters who were essentially pro-life in Bush's column.

Personal qualities also play a role in all presidential elections, though in 2004, one suspects that feelings about Bush, pro or con, plus views on the divisive issues of the day were more indicative of most people's voting decisions. Moreover, personal qualities are seen through partisan eyes in polarized times. Look, for instance, at the voters' evaluations of Bush and Kerry on some personal dimensions. Above all, George Bush was seen as a strong leader, honest and trustworthy, with clear stands on the issues. On the other hand, John Kerry was the "change agent" who was intelligent and cared about people. These images played into both long-standing partisan stereotypes and short-term creations of the candidates' TV advertising. Bush targeted Kerry as "wishy-washy," and some of Kerry's statements had reinforced it. ("I actually voted for the $87 billion [in Iraq troop support] before I voted against it," said Kerry in an infamous clip from a spring campaign forum.) Citizens who cast ballots for Kerry desperately hoped he would change Bush's policies, especially on Iraq and the economy; thus, the Democrat was an automatic "change agent." Kerry was never able to crack Bush's greatest advantage, the intense impression left from the days after 9/11 that the President was a strong leader, and that single, vital personal characteristic alone can explain Bush's margin of victory.

The twin, and more substantive, sentiment that cemented Bush's dominant position was the belief among a majority (54%) that the nation was safer from terrorism than before: eight in ten voters who agreed cast Bush ballots. The 41% of Americans who felt "less safe" were overwhelmingly for Kerry (85%). Similarly, the decision to go to war in Iraq was an accurate predictor of the presidential vote. The 51% who approved that decision voted for Bush by 85% to 14%, while those who disapproved chose Kerry by 87% to 12%. Finally, 90% of the voters who thought the Iraq War was going well for the United States backed Bush, and 82% of those who said the war was going badly for America picked Kerry. For the most part, these are rational choices, sensibly made by the electorate about the dominant issue of the day (whichever side one agrees with).

Political Dimensions

Any observer would be struck by the stability of the presidential vote from 2000 to 2004, as we have shown—from the political maps to the exit poll results. Unavoidably, there were defections in both directions: about one in ten voters switched from Bush to Kerry, or from Gore to Bush. Yet nine in ten Bush voters in 2000 picked Bush again in 2004, and nine in ten Gore voters from 2000 cast a ballot for Kerry in 2004. Again, it just makes basic sense! About 17% of the 2004 voters claimed not to have voted in 2000, and Kerry won these new presidential voters by 54% to 45%. Kerry also won the 3% who voted for other 2000 candidates (mainly Ralph Nader) by 71% to 21%. Interestingly, the exit poll suggests about 5% more 2000 Bush voters than Gore voters showed up at the polls in 2004. Is this true, or another inexplicable artifact of exit poll error? We will never know.

The exit poll also reported that about a quarter of all voters were contacted by the Bush campaign and about a quarter by the

Kerry campaign. No doubt there was some overlap, but one would guess that these quarters were more disjoint sets than intersecting ones. The voters who were contacted by a campaign were very likely to have voted for that candidate, though again, it was probably a matter of the Bush organization getting out the vote of Bush-inclined voters, and the Kerry organization pushing Kerry-leaning voters to the polls.

As our Political Map of America has illustrated, *geography is political destiny*, to a great degree. This axiom is also true when examined from a different demographic perspective. Large cities in both Red and Blue America are heavily Democratic, and Kerry defeated Bush there by 60% to 39%. Smaller cities are less Democratic, but still urban, and when they are added in, the 30% of America in the urban category voted for Kerry by 54% overall. Close to half of the nation's voters can be classified as suburban, and this was fertile GOP territory, with Bush winning by 52% to 47%. The most widespread Republican support, however, is found among the quarter of Americans who reside in rural areas. Ruritania provided Bush's winning margin with a landslide 57% to 42% majority. The Democrats' persistent weakness in rural America is a troubling sign for a party that once drew its fair share of voters in small towns and country outposts.

A concluding, comparative note on the exit polls is in order. As we discussed earlier, the exit polls were less than adequate in 2004, for the third straight national election. The pre-election public opinion polls, at least the final samples before Election Day by most reputable pollsters, fared better as predictors of the final results.[30] And unlike in 2000, when their performance was every bit as bad as the exit pollsters, political scientists came much closer to the final presidential results in their predictive model forecasting that uses advanced statistical techniques. Six of seven recognized models projected Bush to win in a late October publication, though they overshot Bush's final margin. On average, the political scientists conjured up a 53.8% proportion of the two-party vote for the President, compared to Bush's actual 51.2%.[31] (See Appendix, Table 3.)

LESSONS LEARNED IN 2004

Before being changed shortly before publication, this book was entitled *Armageddon*, a word from the Bible with special power and meaning. (As early as 1975, I entitled another monograph, *Aftermath of Armageddon*, about another election where the candidates and their many followers believed the crusade was a battle between good and evil, enlightenment and darkness.)[32] There is little doubt that for most backers of Bush and Kerry, the opposition candidate and party represented the worst of America. In the months following the election, the divisions in America remained firm, with President Bush's approval rating hovering between 49% and 53%—in other words, right where it was on Election Day, with no victory surge or honeymoon sweetener that could be detected.

And yet, the nation survived this pitched battle, and most (though not all) Kerry voters accepted reality and went on about their lives. Thus it has always been, at least since the Civil War. Emotions cool, disappointments are digested, and life goes on. This cannot be said about all societies that inhabit the Earth, and it should not go without remark. In America, there is always a next time, always another election, and the "ins" can become the "outs" in the flash of a few million electronic voting machines.

For now, though, the Republicans are firmly in charge. After the freakishly tight result in 2000, Bush's margin in 2004 appeared to be a relative mandate. Just as important, Bush was able to help his party add seats in both houses of Congress (+3 in the House, +4 in the Senate, net). This was the first time a reelected President had accomplished that feat since Franklin Roosevelt in 1936. Bush's reelection was not a coattail-less event, which makes his 51% potentially more significant legislatively than the "lonely landslides" that Richard Nixon and Ronald Reagan achieved in 1972 and 1984, respectively. Republican members of the Senate and House understood that Bush's strength was theirs, that some of them won due to the turnout generated by Bush's campaign. While controversies galore are inevitable in executive-legislative relations, the underlying political compatibility between the President and his legislative majorities will make the second Bush term more successful than it could otherwise have been.

Of course, exactly how successful Bush will be is, like all of the future, unknowable and highly dependent upon events over which he and others have little or no control. How many analysts in January 2001 believed that popular-vote-loser Bush, installed as President by the Supreme Court, would avoid the fate of all the other popular-vote losers and secure a second term? And how many analysts thought post-September 11, 2001 that a 90%-popular Bush would have to fight for every percentage point to get reelected, come 2004? When it comes to electoral politics, no one is especially prescient in the years, or sometimes just months, prior to our quadrennial presidential spectacle.

After every national election, a multitude of articles and analyses are published purporting to show that the winning party will continue in power as far as the eye can see.[33] After all, it won, and the votes on the map look firm enough. Yet a presidential electoral majority in the modern day is far more like a fragile sand castle built close to the shore than a Mount Rushmore carved into unyielding granite. Modest waves can erode the majority; no tsunami is required, though every generation or two, there is indeed a completely unforeseen tidal wave (the Great Depression, World War II, the JFK assassination, the Iranian hostage crisis, or September 11th, just to name a few in American history).

As Democrats have discussed the disappointing (to them) outcome of the 2004 race for the White House, most have focused on the inadequacies of their nominee. The criticisms are generally categorized in three "L's": liberalism, likeabilty, and leadership. We have already suggested that, by any reasonable legislative measure, John Kerry's entire Senate career was well to the left of the American mainstream, even though it fit Massachusetts well. The Bush campaign had a long list of juicy targets in Kerry's voting record, from national defense to the death penalty to gay rights. Second, to be blunt about it, Kerry was an odd duck—could this be the source of the duck-hunting trip late in the campaign?—and his often emotionless New England manner came across as elitist and chilly to a country that wants to like its President. (Contrast Kerry's dry, humorless persona with that of his hero, John F. Kennedy. Can anyone imagine a best-selling book about Kerry's wit, as there was for JFK in the early 1960s?)[34] Third, Kerry was senatorial to his core, on this side and that side of many issues, and he reminded us why only two senators (JFK and Warren Harding) have ever been elected directly to the Presidency. Senators love nuance, and the debate, and shrewd hedging. If only Kerry's staff had shown him a short excerpt from the first Lincoln-Douglas debate before Kerry cast a Senate vote against the $87 billion supplemental appropriations bill to support American troops in Iraq. During Lincoln's historic 1858 debate with Stephen Douglas while seeking an Illinois U.S. Senate seat, the future President's patriotism was questioned because of his prior opposition to the Mexican-American War while a U.S. House member. But Lincoln cleverly responded that while he had indeed opposed the war, he voted for every appropriation to give the soldiers their salaries and supplies. The issue was defused, and while Lincoln lost the Senate seat, it is easy to see why he became President and Kerry did not.[35]

Even those who mainly blame John Kerry for the Democrats' 2004 defeat agree that the GOP is on top of the political system for now. The presidential results, the congressional gains for the Republicans, favorable trends for the party among women and Latinos, and a solid Southern base argue for its continued dominance. The South alone offers numbers that are particularly daunting for Democrats. Republicans now control 22 of the 26 U.S. Senate seats in the region, an exact reversal of fortunes over the past four decades.[36] Out of 142 U.S. Representatives in the Southern states, the GOP has captured a post-Reconstruction high water mark of 90 seats. In the Congress as a whole, the South generates 40% of all the Republicans holding office. Moreover, George W. Bush was so dominant in the South that he captured almost 85% of the counties in this vast region.[37] And yet, not every trend was positive for the Grand Old Party. A liberal Democrat from Massachusetts whose views were arguably well left of the national mainstream secured 48.3% of the national vote, and was one state (Ohio) away from victory. Democrats made strides with the young, who may well retain their newfound party identification in future elections. In state legislative contests Democrats added 76 seats net across the nation, reversing the slight GOP majority among the 7,382 state legislators; this grassroots strength surprised most observers. Finally, the Democrats raised more money and ginned up more impressive organizational efforts than they have done in modern times. In financing, adding together the Kerry committees and the semi-independent 527s, Democrats actually equaled the $2 billion spent by the Republicans, eliminating a major perceived GOP advantage.[38] Far from being dead, the Democratic party is poised to return to power in the White House *if its candidate is appealing personally and ideologically, and if the issues of the election year tilt in its direction.*

Ah, but that's the rub. An honest evaluation of both parties would suggest that, in a moderate-conservative nation, the right-wing Republicans are probably closer to the voters' ideological mid-point than the left-wing Democrats. The GOP base in the South and Rocky Mountain West is firmer and growing, while the Democratic base in the Northeast and Midwest is shrinking in population,[39] and some of the Midwest pieces of its base are shaky at best. Redistricting (among other factors) has given the GOP a fairly stable, if narrow, governing majority until at least the next post-Census election (2012). Two maps accompany this section, Figures 4 and 5, which depict the party having a majority of House seats in each state from 1992 (the last election of twenty consecutive ones that produced Democratic Houses) and 2004 (the election that gave Republicans their sixth consecutive House majority). The dramatic spread of the sea of Republican red is obvious, but notice also that the House control map has begun to resemble the presidential map.

FIGURE 4
U.S. House Strength After 1992 Election

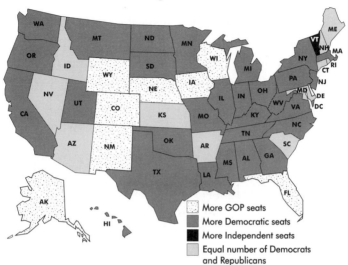

More GOP seats
More Democratic seats
More Independent seats
Equal number of Democrats and Republicans

FIGURE 5
U.S. House Strength After 2004 Election

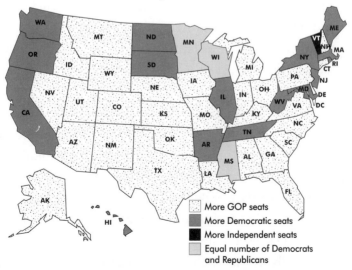

More GOP seats
More Democratic seats
More Independent seats
Equal number of Democrats and Republicans

A similar phenomenon can be observed in the U.S. Senate. Seventy-five of the 100 senators are from the same party as the 2004 presidential candidate who carried their state. This is a substantial increase from recent decades; in the late 1980s and early 1990s, for instance, well less than half the Senate came from the same party as the winning presidential candidate in each state.[40] Not only is this good news for the GOP (at least for now), but it suggests the party polarization of the states is not just a White House phenomenon, but extends down the ballot.

As the governing party, the GOP has all the headaches that come from being in charge. It must produce and achieve, and it is responsible for all the bad things that occur on its watch, from war to recession. But Republicans are in the driver's seat; they can make things happen; they have the initiative; and without a doubt, they have a fairly clear idea of what they stand for and what they would like to do. By contrast, Democrats control nothing at the federal level, and they are merely along for the ride. They can complain and obstruct, but this carries its own risks. A large majority of its national leaders are as far to the left as John Kerry, unable to speak effectively to most of Red or even Purple (mixed Red and Blue) America.

In sum, then, as we look to the political horizon, Republicans face the dangers of any governing party but they appear to be approaching their challenges in sure-footed and methodical fashion. As the out-of-power opposition, Democrats have different choices to make. It is entirely possible that Democrats can simply concentrate on organization and fundraising, and wait out the period of GOP governance, especially at the presidential level. All of American history tells us that a change of party in the White House is almost inevitable within the next several elections. But a refusal by the Democrats to change anything substantively risks delaying the party shift to a moment when the public has become totally fed up and will grab for any alternative. That may be enough to win a single term in the White House but no more. Rather, a better choice for the Democrats would require them to do three things: (1) choose a more moderate presidential nominee, preferably from a Red state, in an attempt to expand their Electoral College base; (2) tone down the party's liberalism on some of the hot-button social and cultural issues, including abortion (support a real partial-birth abortion ban), gay rights (gay marriage is, for now, a bridge much too far), gun control (it isn't going to pass Congress anyway), and the death penalty (in the age of terrorism and school shootings, the public supports it and smart Democrats such as Bill Clinton have, too); and (3) change the party's image from "Blue Elite" to "Down Home." Americans may worship Hollywood idols at the box office, appreciate the intellectuals who teach them college classes, and look to the Washington-New York-Los Angeles trinity for trends in fashion and opinion—but they don't want to be governed by any of them. The first Democratic candidate to be panned by the Blue in-crowd may well be the next Democratic President.

The 2004 presidential election is history, but it will not be quickly forgotten. The intensity level was white-hot, almost frightening at times, and the ripples from its results will be felt for years. Both political parties can learn vital lessons from 2004's big picture down to the precinct returns that created a majority President. If the nation's electoral past is any guide, however, one party will learn its lessons far better than the other, and the identity of that party is yet to be determined.

Larry J. Sabato is a University Professor and the Robert Kent Gooch Professor of Politics at the University of Virginia, and serves as the Director of the University of Virginia Center for Politics.

APPENDIX

TABLES 1–3

TABLE 1
2004 Presidential Vote

	Electoral Vote Rep.	Electoral Vote Dem.	Total Vote	Republican	Democratic	Other	Rep.-Dem. Plurality		Rep.	Dem.	Other
Alabama	9		1,883,415	1,176,394	693,933	13,088	482,461	R	62.5%	36.8%	0.7%
Alaska	3		312,598	190,889	111,025	10,684	79,864	R	61.1%	35.5%	3.4%
Arizona	10		2,012,585	1,104,294	893,524	14,767	210,770	R	54.9%	44.4%	0.7%
Arkansas	6		1,053,694	572,770	468,631	12,293	104,139	R	54.4%	44.5%	1.2%
California		55	12,419,857	5,509,826	6,745,485	164,546	1,235,659	D	44.4%	54.3%	1.3%
Colorado	9		2,129,630	1,101,255	1,001,732	26,643	99,523	R	51.7%	47.0%	1.3%
Connecticut		7	1,578,769	693,826	857,488	27,455	163,662	D	43.9%	54.3%	1.7%
Delaware		3	375,190	171,660	200,152	3,378	28,492	D	45.8%	53.3%	0.9%
Florida	27		7,609,810	3,964,522	3,583,544	61,744	380,978	R	52.1%	47.1%	0.8%
Georgia	15		3,298,790	1,914,254	1,366,149	18,387	548,105	R	58.0%	41.4%	0.6%
Hawaii		4	429,013	194,191	231,708	3,114	37,517	D	45.3%	54.0%	0.7%
Idaho	4		598,376	409,235	181,098	8,043	228,137	R	68.4%	30.3%	1.3%
Illinois		21	5,275,415	2,346,608	2,891,989	36,818	545,381	D	44.5%	54.8%	0.7%
Indiana	11		2,468,002	1,479,438	969,011	19,553	510,427	R	59.9%	39.3%	0.8%
Iowa	7		1,506,908	751,957	741,898	13,053	10,059	R	49.9%	49.2%	0.9%

	Electoral Vote		Total Vote	Republican	Democratic	Other	Rep.–Dem. Plurality		Percentage of Total Vote		
	Rep.	Dem.							Rep.	Dem.	Other
Kansas	6		1,187,756	736,456	434,993	16,307	301,463	R	62.0%	36.6%	1.4%
Kentucky	8		1,795,860	1,069,439	712,733	13,688	356,706	R	59.6%	39.7%	0.8%
Louisiana	9		1,943,106	1,102,169	820,299	20,638	281,870	R	56.7%	42.2%	1.1%
Maine		4	740,752	330,201	396,842	13,709	66,641	D	44.6%	53.6%	1.9%
Maryland		10	2,384,238	1,024,703	1,334,493	25,042	309,790	D	43.0%	56.0%	1.1%
Massachusetts		12	2,912,388	1,071,109	1,803,800	37,479	732,691	D	36.8%	61.9%	1.3%
Michigan		17	4,839,252	2,313,746	2,479,183	46,323	165,437	D	47.8%	51.2%	1.0%
Minnesota*		10	2,828,387	1,346,695	1,445,014	36,678	98,319	D	47.6%	51.1%	1.3%
Mississippi	6		1,139,824	672,660	457,766	9,398	214,894	R	59.0%	40.2%	0.8%
Missouri	11		2,731,364	1,455,713	1,259,171	16,480	196,542	R	53.3%	46.1%	0.6%
Montana	3		450,434	266,063	173,710	10,661	92,353	R	59.1%	38.6%	2.4%
Nebraska	5		778,186	512,814	254,328	11,044	258,486	R	65.9%	32.7%	1.4%
Nevada	5		829,587	418,690	397,190	13,707	21,500	R	50.5%	47.9%	1.7%
New Hampshire		4	677,662	331,237	340,511	5,914	9,274	D	48.9%	50.2%	0.9%
New Jersey		15	3,609,691	1,668,003	1,911,430	30,258	243,427	D	46.2%	53%	0.8%
New Mexico		5	756,304	376,930	370,942	8,432	5,988	R	49.8%	49.0%	1.1%
New York		31	7,391,036	2,962,567	4,314,280	114,189	1,351,713	D	40.1%	58.4%	1.5%
North Carolina	15		3,501,007	1,961,166	1,525,849	13,992	435,317	R	56.0%	43.6%	0.4%

State	R EV	D EV	Total	R Votes	D Votes	Other	Margin	Win	R %	D %	Other %
North Dakota	3		312,833	196,651	111,052	5,130	85,599	R	62.9%	35.5%	1.6%
Ohio	20		5,625,631	2,858,727	2,739,952	26,952	118,775	R	50.8%	48.7%	0.5%
Oklahoma	7		1,463,758	959,792	503,966	0	455,826	R	65.6%	34.4%	
Oregon		7	1,836,782	866,831	943,163	26,788	76,332	D	47.2%	51.3%	1.5%
Pennsylvania		21	5,765,764	2,793,847	2,938,095	33,822	144,248	D	48.5%	51.0%	0.6%
Rhode Island		4	437,134	169,046	259,760	8,328	90,714	D	38.7%	59.4%	1.9%
South Carolina	8		1,617,730	937,974	661,699	18,057	276,275	R	58.0%	40.9%	1.1%
South Dakota	3		388,215	232,584	149,244	6,387	83,340	R	59.9%	38.4%	1.6%
Tennessee	11		2,437,319	1,384,375	1,036,477	16,467	347,898	R	56.8%	42.5%	0.7%
Texas	34		7,410,749	4,526,917	2,832,704	51,128	1,694,213	R	61.1%	38.2%	0.7%
Utah	5		927,844	663,742	241,199	22,903	422,543	R	71.5%	26.0%	2.5%
Vermont		3	312,309	121,180	184,067	7,062	62,887	D	38.8%	58.9%	2.3%
Virginia	13		3,198,367	1,716,959	1,454,742	26,666	262,217	R	53.7%	45.5%	0.8%
Washington		11	2,859,084	1,304,894	1,510,201	43,989	205,307	D	45.6%	52.8%	1.5%
West Virginia	5		755,659	423,550	326,541	5,568	97,009	R	56.1%	43.2%	0.7%
Wisconsin		10	2,997,007	1,478,120	1,489,504	29,383	11,384	D	49.3%	49.7%	1.0%
Wyoming	3		243,428	167,629	70,776	5,023	96,853	R	68.9%	29.1%	2.1%
Dist. of Col.		3	227,586	21,256	202,970	3,360	181,714	D	9.3%	89.2%	1.5%
TOTAL	286	252	122,266,085	62,025,554	59,026,013	1,214,518	2,999,541	R	50.7%	48.3%	1.0%

	Electoral Vote		Total Vote	Republican	Democratic	Other	Rep.–Dem. Plurality		Percentage of Total Vote		
	Rep.	Dem.							Rep.	Dem.	Other
South											
Alabama	9		1,883,415	1,176,394	693,933	13,088	482,461	R	62.5%	36.8%	0.7%
Arkansas	6		1,053,694	572,770	468,631	12,293	104,139	R	54.4%	44.5%	1.2%
Florida	27		7,609,810	3,964,522	3,583,544	61,744	380,978	R	52.1%	47.1%	0.8%
Georgia	15		3,298,790	1,914,254	1,366,149	18,387	548,105	R	58.0%	41.4%	0.6%
Kentucky	8		1,795,860	1,069,439	712,733	13,688	356,706	R	59.6%	39.7%	0.8%
Louisiana	9		1,943,106	1,102,169	820,299	20,638	281,870	R	56.7%	42.2%	1.1%
Mississippi	6		1,139,824	672,660	457,766	9,398	214,894	R	59.0%	40.2%	0.8%
North Carolina	15		3,501,007	1,961,166	1,525,849	13,992	435,317	R	56.0%	43.6%	0.4%
Oklahoma	7		1,463,758	959,792	503,966	0	455,826	R	65.6%	34.4%	
South Carolina	8		1,617,730	937,974	661,699	18,057	276,275	R	58.0%	40.9%	1.1%
Tennessee	11		2,437,319	1,384,375	1,036,477	16,467	347,898	R	56.8%	42.5%	0.7%
Texas	34		7,410,749	4,526,917	2,832,704	51,128	1,694,213	R	61.1%	38.2%	0.7%
Virginia	13		3,198,367	1,716,959	1,454,742	26,666	262,217	R	53.7%	45.5%	0.8%
	168	0	38,353,429	21,959,391	16,118,492	275,546	5,840,899	R	57.3%	42.0%	0.7%
Mountain West											
Alaska	3		312,598	190,889	111,025	10,684	79,864	R	61.1%	35.5%	3.4%
Arizona	10		2,012,585	1,104,294	893,524	14,767	210,770	R	54.9%	44.4%	0.7%

	Electoral Vote Rep.	Electoral Vote Dem.	Total Vote	Republican	Democratic	Other	Rep.–Dem. Plurality		Percentage of Total Vote Rep.	Dem.	Other
Colorado	9		2,129,630	1,101,255	1,001,732	26,643	99,523	R	51.7%	47.0%	1.3%
Idaho	4		598,376	409,235	181,098	8,043	228,137	R	68.4%	30.3%	1.3%
Montana	3		450,434	286,063	173,710	10,661	92,353	R	59.1%	38.6%	2.4%
Nevada	5		829,587	418,690	397,190	13,707	21,500	R	50.5%	47.9%	1.7%
New Mexico	5		756,304	376,930	370,942	8,432	5,988	R	49.8%	49.0%	1.1%
Utah	5		927,844	663,742	241,199	22,903	422,543	R	71.5%	26.0%	2.5%
Wyoming	3		243,428	167,629	70,776	5,023	96,853	R	68.9%	29.1%	2.1%
	47	0	8,260,786	4,698,727	3,441,196	120,863	1,257,531	R	56.9%	41.7%	1.5%
PLAINS STATES											
Kansas	6		1,187,756	736,456	434,993	16,307	301,463	R	62.0%	36.6%	1.4%
Nebraska	5		778,186	512,814	254,328	11,044	258,486	R	65.9%	32.7%	1.4%
North Dakota	3		312,833	196,651	111,052	5,130	85,599	R	62.9%	35.5%	1.6%
South Dakota	3		388,215	232,584	149,244	6,387	83,340	R	59.9%	38.4%	1.6%
	17	0	2,666,990	1,678,505	949,617	38,868	728,888	R	62.9%	35.6%	1.5%
NORTHEAST											
Connecticut		7	1,578,769	693,826	857,488	27,455	163,662	D	43.9%	54.3%	1.7%
Delaware		3	375,190	171,660	200,152	3,378	28,492	D	45.8%	53.3%	0.9%
Maine		4	740,752	330,201	396,842	13,709	66,641	D	44.6%	53.6%	1.9%

	Electoral Vote		Total Vote	Republican	Democratic	Other	Rep.–Dem. Plurality		Percentage of Total Vote		
	Rep.	Dem.							Rep.	Dem.	Other
Maryland		10	2,384,238	1,024,703	1,334,493	25,042	309,790	D	43.0%	56.0%	1.1%
Massachusetts		12	2,912,388	1,071,109	1,803,800	37,479	732,691	D	36.8%	61.9%	1.3%
New Hampshire		4	677,662	331,237	340,511	5,914	9,274	D	48.9%	50.2%	0.9%
New Jersey		15	3,609,691	1,668,003	1,911,430	30,258	243,427	D	46.2%	53.0%	0.8%
New York		31	7,391,036	2,962,567	4,314,280	114,189	1,351,713	D	40.1%	58.4%	1.5%
Pennsylvania		21	5,765,764	2,793,847	2,938,095	33,822	144,248	D	48.5%	51.0%	0.6%
Rhode Island		4	437,134	169,046	259,760	8,328	90,714	D	38.7%	59.4%	1.9%
Vermont		3	312,309	121,180	184,067	7,062	62,887	D	38.8%	58.9%	2.3%
West Virginia	5		755,659	423,550	326,541	5,568	97,009	R	56.1%	43.2%	0.7%
Dist. of Col.		3	227,586	21,256	202,970	3,360	181,714	D	9.3%	89.2%	1.5%
	5	117	27,168,178	11,782,185	15,070,429	315,564	3,288,244	D	43.4%	55.5%	1.2%
INDUSTRIAL MIDWEST											
Illinois		21	5,275,415	2,346,608	2,891,989	36,818	545,381	D	44.5%	54.8%	0.7%
Indiana	11		2,468,002	1,479,438	969,011	19,553	510,427	R	59.9%	39.3%	0.8%
Iowa	7		1,506,908	751,957	741,898	13,053	10,059	R	49.9%	49.2%	0.9%
Michigan		17	4,839,252	2,313,746	2,479,183	46,323	165,437	D	47.8%	51.2%	1.0%
Minnesota*		10	2,828,387	1,346,695	1,445,014	36,678	98,319	D	47.6%	51.1%	1.3%
Missouri	11		2,731,364	1,455,713	1,259,171	16,480	196,542	R	53.3%	46.1%	0.6%

	Electoral Vote		Total Vote	Republican	Democratic	Other	Rep.–Dem. Plurality		Percentage of Total Vote		
	Rep.	Dem.							Rep.	Dem.	Other
Ohio	20		5,625,631	2,858,727	2,739,952	26,952	118,775	R	50.8%	48.7%	0.5%
Wisconsin		10	2,997,007	1,478,120	1,489,504	29,383	11,384	D	49.3%	49.7%	1.0%
	49	58	28,271,966	14,031,004	14,015,722	225,240	15,282	R	49.6%	49.6%	0.8%
Pacific West											
California		55	12,419,857	5,509,826	6,745,485	164,546	1,235,659	D	44.4%	54.3%	1.3%
Hawaii		4	429,013	194,191	231,708	3,114	37,517	D	45.3%	54.0%	0.7%
Oregon		7	1,836,782	866,831	943,163	26,788	76,332	D	47.2%	51.3%	1.5%
Washington		11	2,859,084	1,304,894	1,510,201	43,989	205,307	D	45.6%	52.8%	1.5%
	0	77	17,544,736	7,875,742	9,430,557	238,437	1,554,815	D	44.9%	53.8%	1.4%
NATIONAL	286	252	122,266,085	62,025,554	59,026,013	1,214,518	2,999,541	R	50.7%	48.3%	1.0%

*One Democratic elector from Minnesota cast a presidential ballot for Vice Presidential nominee John Edwards instead of Presidential nominee John Kerry. Because of this "faithless elector," John Kerry received 9 of Minnesota's 10 electoral votes, bringing the actual number of electoral votes he received to 251.

Source: *The Rhodes Cook Letter*, January 2005.

TABLE 2
The 2000 and 2004 Presidential Votes

STATE	2-PARTY VOTE % – 2000				2-PARTY VOTE % – 2004				
	GORE		BUSH		KERRY		BUSH		BUSH GAIN
	VOTES	PERCENT	VOTES	PERCENT	VOTES	PERCENT	VOTES	PERCENT	PERCENT
Alabama	692,611	42.4	9,411,73	57.6	693,933	37.1	1,176,394	62.9	+5.3
Alaska	79,004	32.1	167,398	67.9	111,025	36.8	190,889	63.2	-4.7
Arizona	685,341	46.7	781,652	53.3	893,524	44.7	1,104,294	55.3	+2
Arkansas	422,768	47.2	472,940	52.8	468,631	45	572,770	55	+2.2
California	5,861,203	56.2	4,567,429	43.8	6,745,485	55	5,509,826	45	+1.2
Colorado	738,227	45.5	883,748	54.5	1,001,732	47.6	1,101,255	52.4	-2.1
Connecticut	816,015	59.3	561,094	40.7	857,488	55.3	693,826	44.7	+4
Delaware	180,068	56.7	137,288	43.3	200,152	53.8	171,660	46.2	+2.9
DC	171,923	90.5	18,073	9.5	202,970	90.2	21,256	9.8	+0.3
Florida	2,912,253	50	2,912,790	50	3,583,544	47.5	3,964,522	52.5	+2.5
Georgia	1,116,230	44	1,419,720	56	1,366,149	41.6	1,914,254	58.4	+2.4
Hawaii	205,286	59.8	137,845	40.2	231,708	54.4	194,191	45.6	+5.4
Idaho	138,637	29.2	336,937	70	181,098	30.7	409,235	69.3	-0.7
Illinois	2,589,026	56.2	2,019,421	43.8	2,891,989	55.2	2,346,608	44.8	+1
Indiana	901,980	42	1,245,836	58	969,011	39.6	1,479,438	60.4	+2.4
Iowa	638,517	50.2	634,373	49.8	741,898	49.7	751,957	50.3	+0.5

State									
Kansas	399,276	39.1	622,332	60.9	434,993	37.1	736,456	62.9	+2
Kentucky	638,898	42.3	872,492	57.7	712,733	40	1,069,439	60	+2.3
Louisiana	792,344	46.1	927,871	53.9	820,299	42.7	1,102,169	57.3	+3.4
Maine	319,951	52.7	286,616	47.3	396,842	54.6	330,201	45.4	-1.9
Maryland	1,144,008	58.4	813,827	41.6	1,334,493	56.6	1,024,703	43.4	+1.8
Massachusetts	1,616,487	64.8	878,502	35.2	1,803,800	62.7	1,071,109	37.3	+2.1
Michigan	217,0418	52.6	1,953,139	47.4	2,479,183	51.7	2,313,746	48.3	+0.9
Minnesota	1,168,266	51.3	1,109,659	48.7	1,445,014	51.8	1,346,695	48.2	-0.5
Mississippi	404,614	41.4	572,844	58.6	457,766	40.5	672,660	59.5	+0.9
Missouri	1,111,138	48.3	1,189,924	51.7	1,259,171	46.4	1,455,713	53.6	+1.9
Montana	137,126	36.4	240,178	63.6	173,710	39.5	266,063	60.5	-3.1
Nebraska	231,780	34.8	433,862	65.2	254,328	33.2	512,814	66.8	+1.6
Nevada	279,978	48.1	301,575	51.9	397,190	48.7	418,690	51.3	-0.6
New Hampshire	266,348	49.3	273,559	50.7	340,511	50.7	331,237	49.3	-1.4
New Jersey	1,788,850	58.2	1,284,173	41.8	1,911,430	53.4	1,668,003	46.6	+4.8
New Mexico	286,783	50	286,417	50	370,942	49.6	376,930	50.4	+0.4
New York	4,107,697	63.1	2,403,374	36.9	4,314,280	59.3	2,962,567	40.7	+3.8
North Carolina	1,257,692	43.5	1,631,163	56.5	1,525,849	43.8	1,961,166	56.2	-0.3
North Dakota	95,284	35.3	174,852	64.7	111,052	36.1	196,651	63.9	-0.8
Ohio	2,183,628	48.2	2,350,363	51.8	2,739,952	48.9	2,858,727	51.1	-0.7
Oklahoma	474,276	38.9	744,337	61.1	503,986	34.4	959,792	65.6	+4.5
Oregon	720,342	50.2	713,577	49.8	943,163	52.1	866,831	47.9	-1.9

2-PARTY VOTE % – 2000

STATE	GORE VOTES	GORE PERCENT	BUSH VOTES	BUSH PERCENT
Pennsylvania	2,485,967	52.1	2,281,127	47.9
Rhode Island	249,508	65.6	130,555	34.4
South Carolina	566,039	41.8	786,892	58.2
South Dakota	118,804	38.4	190,700	61.6
Tennessee	981,720	48	1,061,949	52
Texas	2,433,746	39	3,799,639	61
Utah	203,053	28.3	515,096	71.7
Vermont	149,022	55.4	119,775	44.6
Virginia	1,217,290	45.9	1,437,490	54.1
Washington	1,247,652	52.9	1,108,864	47.1
West Virginia	295,497	46.8	336,475	53.2
Wisconsin	1,242,987	50.1	1,237,279	49.9
Wyoming	60,481	29	147,947	71
Total	50,996,039	50.3	50,456,141	49.7

2-PARTY VOTE % – 2004

STATE	KERRY VOTES	KERRY PERCENT	BUSH VOTES	BUSH PERCENT	BUSH GAIN PERCENT
Pennsylvania	2,938,095	51.3	2,793,847	48.7	+0.8
Rhode Island	259,760	60.6	169,046	39.4	+5
South Carolina	661,699	41.4	937,974	58.6	+0.4
South Dakota	149,244	39.1	232,584	60.9	-0.7
Tennessee	1,036,477	42.8	1,384,375	57.2	+5.2
Texas	2,832,704	38.5	4,526,917	61.5	+0.5
Utah	241,199	26.7	663,742	73.3	+1.6
Vermont	184,067	60.3	121,180	39.7	-4.9
Virginia	1,454,742	45.9	1,716,959	54.1	+0
Washington	1,510,201	53.6	1,304,894	46.4	-0.7
West Virginia	326,541	43.5	423,550	56.5	+3.3
Wisconsin	1,489,504	50.2	1,478,120	49.8	-0.1
Wyoming	70,776	29.7	167,629	70.3	-0.7
Total	59,026,013	48.8	6,202,5554	51.2	+1.5

Sources: 2000 figures adapted from http://www.thegreenpapers.com/G00/PresidentLong.html.
2004 figures adapted from *The Rhodes Cook Letter*, January 2005.

TABLE 3
U.S. President Election Results—National Exit Poll

Vote by Gender

	Bush		Kerry	Nader
	2004	Change from 2000	2004	2004
Total				
Male (46%)	55%	+2%	44%	0%
Female (54%)	48%	+5%	51%	0%

Vote by Race and Gender

	Bush		Kerry	Nader
	2004	Change from 2000	2004	2004
Total				
White Men (36%)	62%	n/a	37%	0%
White Women (41%)	55%	n/a	44%	0%
Non-White Men (10%)	30%	n/a	67%	1%
Non-White Women (12%)	24%	n/a	75%	1%

Vote by Race

	Bush		Kerry	Nader
	2004	Change from 2000	2004	2004
Total				
White (77%)	58%	+4%	41%	0%
African-American (11%)	11%	+2%	88%	0%
Latino (8%)	44%	+9%	53%	2%
Asian (2%)	44%	+3%	56%	*
Other (2%)	40%	+1%	54%	2%

Vote by Age

Total	Bush		Kerry	Nader
	2004	Change from 2000	2004	2004
18−29 (17%)	45%	n/a	54%	0%
30−44 (29%)	53%	+4%	46%	1%
45−59 (30%)	51%	+2%	48%	0%
60 and Older (24%)	54%	+7%	46%	0%

Vote by Income

Total	Bush		Kerry	Nader
	2004	Change from 2000	2004	2004
Under $15,000 (8%)	36%	n/a	63%	0%
$15−30,000 (15%)	42%	n/a	57%	0%
$30−50,000 (22%)	49%	n/a	50%	0%
$50−75,000 (23%)	56%	n/a	43%	0%
$75−100,000 (14%)	55%	n/a	45%	0%
$100−150,000 (11%)	57%	n/a	42%	1%
$150−200,000 (4%)	58%	n/a	42%	*
$200,000 or More (3%)	63%	n/a	35%	1%

Vote by Income

Total	Bush		Kerry	Nader
		Change from		
	2004	2000	2004	2004
Less Than $50,000 (45%)	44%	n/a	55%	0%
$50,000 or More (55%)	56%	n/a	43%	0%

Vote by Income

Total	Bush		Kerry	Nader
		Change from		
	2004	2000	2004	2004
Less Than $100,000 (82%)	49%	n/a	50%	0%
$100,000 or More (18%)	58%	n/a	41%	1%

Anyone in household in a union?

Total	Bush		Kerry	Nader
		Change from		
	2004	2000	2004	2004
Yes (24%)	40%	n/a	59%	1%
No (76%)	55%	n/a	44%	0%

Do you work full-time?

Total	Bush		Kerry	Nader
		Change from		
	2004	2000	2004	2004
Yes (60%)	53%	+5%	45%	1%
No (40%)	51%	+3%	49%	0%

Vote by Education

Total	Bush		Kerry	Nader
		Change from		
	2004	2000	2004	2004
No High School (4%)	49%	+10%	50%	0%
H.S. Graduate (22%)	52%	+3%	47%	0%
Some College (32%)	54%	+3%	46%	0%
College Graduate (26%)	52%	+1%	46%	1%
Postgrad Study (16%)	44%	0	55%	1%

Vote by Party ID

Total	Bush		Kerry	Nader
		Change from		
	2004	2000	2004	2004
Democrat (37%)	11%	0%	89%	0%
Republican (37%)	93%	+2%	6%	0%
Independent (26%)	48%	+1%	49%	1%

Vote by Ideology

Total	Bush		Kerry	Nader
		Change from		
	2004	2000	2004	2004
Liberal (21%)	13%	0%	85%	1%
Moderate (45%)	45%	+1%	54%	0%
Conservative (34%)	84%	+3%	15%	0%

Have you ever voted before?

Total	Bush		Kerry	Nader
		Change from		
	2004	2000	2004	2004
No (11%)	46%	+3%	53%	0%
Yes (89%)	51%	+3%	48%	0%

Vote by Religion

Total	Bush		Kerry	Nader
		Change from		
	2004	2000	2004	2004
Protestant (54%)	59%	+3%	40%	0%
Catholic (27%)	52%	+5%	47%	0%
Jewish (3%)	25%	+6%	74%	*
Other (7%)	23%	−5%	74%	1%
None (10%)	31%	+1%	67%	1%

White Evangelical/Born-Again

Total	Bush		Kerry	Nader
		Change from		
	2004	2000	2004	2004
Yes (23%)	78%	n/a	21%	0%
No (77%)	43%	n/a	56%	0%

Vote by Church Attendance

	Bush		Kerry	Nader
		Change from		
Total	2004	2000	2004	2004
More Than Weekly (16%)	64%	+1%	35%	1%
Weekly (26%)	58%	+1%	41%	0%
Monthly (14%)	50%	+4%	49%	*
A Few Times a Year (28%)	45%	+3%	54%	0%
Never (15%)	36%	+4%	62%	1%

Have you ever served in the military?

	Bush		Kerry	Nader
		Change from		
Total	2004	2000	2004	2004
Yes (18%)	57%	n/a	41%	0%
No (82%)	49%	n/a	50%	0%

Are you married?

	Bush		Kerry	Nader
		Change from		
Total	2004	2000	2004	2004
Yes (63%)	57%	+4%	42%	0%
No (37%)	40%	+2%	58%	0%

Are you gay, lesbian, or bisexual?

	Bush		Kerry	Nader
		Change from		
Total	2004	2000	2004	2004
Yes (4%)	23%	−2%	77%	0%
No (96%)	53%	+3%	46%	0%

Gun owner in household?

	Bush		Kerry	Nader
		Change from		
Total	2004	2000	2004	2004
Yes (41%)	63%	+2%	36%	1%
No (59%)	43%	+4%	57%	0%

When did you decide who to vote for?

	Bush		Kerry	Nader
		Change from		
Total	2004	2000	2004	2004
Within the Last Week (11%)	46%	n/a	52%	1%
Earlier Than That (89%)	52%	n/a	47%	0%

Most Important Issue

Total	Bush		Kerry	Nader
		Change from		
	2004	2000	2004	2004
Taxes (5%)	57%	n/a	43%	0%
Education (4%)	26%	n/a	73%	*
Iraq (15%)	26%	n/a	73%	0%
Terrorism (19%)	86%	n/a	14%	0%
Economy/Jobs (20%)	18%	n/a	80%	0%
Moral Values (22%)	80%	n/a	18%	1%
Health Care (8%)	23%	n/a	77%	*

How Bush Is Handling His Job

Total	Bush		Kerry	Nader
		Change from		
	2004	2000	2004	2004
Approve (53%)	90%	n/a	9%	0%
Disapprove (46%)	6%	n/a	93%	0%

Most Important Quality

Total	Bush		Kerry	Nader
		Change from		
	2004	2000	2004	2004
Cares About People (9%)	24%	n/a	75%	1%
Religious Faith (8%)	91%	n/a	8%	*
Honest/Trustworthy (11%)	70%	n/a	29%	1%
Strong Leader (17%)	87%	n/a	12%	0%
Intelligent (7%)	9%	n/a	91%	0%
Will Bring Change (24%)	5%	n/a	95%	0%
Clear Stand on Issues (17%)	79%	n/a	20%	0%

Compared to four years ago, U.S. is...

Total	Bush		Kerry	Nader
		Change from		
	2004	2000	2004	2004
Safer from terrorism (54%)	79%	n/a	20%	0%
Less safe (41%)	14%	n/a	85%	0%

Decision to Go to War in Iraq

Total	Bush		Kerry	Nader
		Change from		
	2004	2000	2004	2004
Approve (51%)	85%	n/a	14%	0%
Disapprove (45%)	12%	n/a	87%	0%

How are things going for U.S. in Iraq?

Total	Bush		Kerry	Nader
		Change from		
	2004	2000	2004	2004
Well (44%)	90%	n/a	9%	1%
Badly (52%)	17%	n/a	82%	0%

Family's Financial Situation

Total	Bush		Kerry	Nader
		Change from		
	2004	2000	2004	2004
Better (32%)	80%	+44%	19%	0%
Worse (28%)	20%	–43%	79%	0%
Same (39%)	49%	–11%	50%	1%

Your vote for President was mostly...

Total	Bush		Kerry	Nader
		Change from		
	2004	2000	2004	2004
For your candidate (69%)	59%	n/a	40%	0%
Against his opponent (25%)	30%	n/a	70%	0%

Were you contacted by Kerry campaign?

	Bush		Kerry	Nader
		Change from		
Total	2004	2000	2004	2004
Yes (26%)	33%	n/a	66%	1%
No (74%)	57%	n/a	42%	0%

Were you contacted by Bush campaign?

	Bush		Kerry	Nader
		Change from		
Total	2004	2000	2004	2004
Yes (24%)	62%	n/a	38%	0%
No (76%)	47%	n/a	52%	1%

Abortion should be...

	Bush		Kerry	Nader
		Change from		
Total	2004	2000	2004	2004
Always Legal (21%)	25%	0%	73%	1%
Mostly Legal (34%)	38%	0%	61%	0%
Mostly Illegal (26%)	73%	+4%	26%	0%
Always Illegal (16%)	77%	+3%	22%	0%

Policy Toward Same-Sex Couples

	Bush		Kerry	Nader
		Change from		
Total	2004	2000	2004	2004
Legally Marry (25%)	22%	n/a	77%	1%
Civil Unions (35%)	52%	n/a	47%	0%
No Legal Recognition (37%)	70%	n/a	29%	0%

Presidential Vote in 2000

	Bush		Kerry	Nader
		Change from		
Total	2004	2000	2004	2004
Did not vote (17%)	45%	n/a	54%	1%
Gore (37%)	10%	n/a	90%	0%
Bush (43%)	91%	n/a	9%	0%
Other (3%)	21%	n/a	71%	3%

Is U.S. going in right direction?

	Bush		Kerry	Nader
		Change from		
Total	2004	2000	2004	2004
Yes (49%)	89%	+53%	10%	0%
No (46%)	12%	−62%	86%	0%

Vote by Size of Community

	Bush		Kerry	Nader
		Change from		
Total	2004	2000	2004	2004
Urban (30%)	45%	+10%	54%	0%
Suburban (46%)	52%	+3%	47%	0%
Rural (25%)	57%	−2%	42%	0%

Source: CNN
http://www.cnn.com/ELECTION/2004/pages/results/states/US/P/00/epolls.0.html.

NOTES

1. It was unclear whether this was intentional, or simply a mix-up by a confused elector. No one owned up to the action, though it was reminiscent of the decision by a Democratic elector in West Virginia in 1988 to cast a presidential vote for the party's vice presidential candidate Lloyd Bentsen, relegating presidential nominee Michael Dukakis to the Veep spot.

2. On a somewhat sillier note, Bush broke another presidential curse. Until him, all Presidents with four letters in their surname had served but a single term: Polk, Taft, Ford, Bush Sr.

3. Larry J. Sabato, *Overtime: The Election 2000 Thriller*. New York: Longman Publishers, 2002.

4. Nader secured 456,471 votes nationwide, Badnarik 396,895 votes, the Green party nominee David Cobb 119,536, the Constitution party nominee Michael Peroutka 142,843; and a smattering of other candidates garnered 51,382.

5. This was not strictly a reelection, since Truman succeeded the deceased FDR in April 1945, but he had served virtually the entire term to which Roosevelt had been elected.

6. This number grows substantially when one considers the many incumbent Presidents who publicly or privately wanted to be re-nominated but were spurned by their own party, especially in the nineteenth century but also including Teddy Roosevelt in 1912 and Woodrow Wilson in 1920.

7. A good estimate of the total number of *registered* voters on November 2, 2004 is 156 million, which means that 78% of the registered voters cast a ballot—an impressive figure.

8. Some researchers have long noted that, once the disqualified ex-felons, non-citizen residents, and the imprisoned and institutionalized populations are excluded, voter turnout in the United States is considerably higher than the numbers cited here suggest. See, for instance, Michael McDonald and Samuel Popkin, "The Myth of the Vanishing Voter," *American Political Science Review* 90 (December 2001): 963–974; and Michael McDonald, "The Turnout Rate Among Eligible Voters in the States, 1980–2000," *State Politics and Policy Quarterly* 2 (Summer 2002): 199–212.

9. Michael McDonald, "Up, Up and Away! Voter Participation in the 2004 Presidential Election," *The Forum* 2:4 (2004): article four. http://www.bepress.com/forum/vol2/iss4/art4.

10. Barry C. Burden, "An Alternative Account of the 2004 Presidential Election," *The Forum* 2:4 (2004): article two. http://www.bepress.com/forum/vol2/iss4/art2.

11. States that gained electors as of 2001 were: Arizona (2), California (1), Colorado (1), Florida (2), Georgia (2), Nevada (1), North Carolina (1), and Texas (2). All but California were Bush states in 2000 and 2004. The states that lost electors were: Connecticut (1), Illinois (1), Indiana (1), Michigan (1), Mississippi (1), New York (2), Ohio (1), Oklahoma (1), Pennsylvania (2), and Wisconsin (1). The Democrats carried all but Indiana, Mississippi, Ohio, and Oklahoma in both elections. Thus, the net gain for Bush among this set of electoral winner and loser states was +6.

12. Matt Bai, "Who Lost Ohio?," *The New York Times Magazine*, November 21, 2004.

13. These figures were compiled by journalist Lynn Hulsey of Cox News Service, and shared with me in an e-mail dated November 12, 2004. Hulsey also shows that the Kerry "Blue" counties in Ohio had a total of 4,093,761 registered voters, while the Bush "Red" counties contained just 3,885,878 voters. But on Election Day, the under-populated Bush counties actually out-voted the Kerry counties, 2,788,806 to 2,785,670. These numbers were no doubt marginally changed in Kerry's favor during the Ohio recount, which shaved Bush's overall Ohio margin by about 18,000 votes. But the Bush counties would still have maintained a considerable turnout edge over the Kerry counties.

14. New York: Longman Publishers, 2002. pp. 103–105.

15. Larry J. Sabato, *Overtime: The Election 2000 Thriller*. New York: Longman Publishers, 2002. pp. 105–110. Larry J. Sabato, *Midterm Madness: The Elections of 2002*. Lanham, Md.: Rowman & Littlefield Publishers, Inc. pp. 10–14.

16. See Kausfiles, "Kf Cops a Blog," http://slate.msn.com/id/2109381, accessed January 2005. Also see Nick Anderson and Faye Fiore, "Early Data for Kerry Proved Misleading," *Los Angeles Times,* November 4, 2004, p. A-17. The *Post* editor quoted here was Steve Coll, the *Washington Post*'s managing editor. See also David Hill, "More Mitofsky Mischief," *The Hill,* November 17, 2004, p. 21; and Richard Morin, "Surveying the Damage: Exit Polls Can't Predict Winners, So Don't Expect Them To," *Washington Post,* November 21, 2004, pp. B1, 4.

17. Mike McCurry speaking at the seventh annual American Democracy Conference hosted by the University of Virginia Center for Politics and *The Hotline* on December 3, 2004: "I don't know whether this was unreported or not, but it is absolutely true. On election night for four hours, John Kerry sat in a Boston hotel room doing satellite feeds to all the key battleground states urging people to go out to vote while his loyal staff—me, John Sasso, and Bob Shrum—sat up looking at all these exit poll numbers that were coming across our Blackberries, talking to our state directors in all the key battleground states who reported in fact they were achieving a hundred percent of their targeted performance numbers county by county, and we said we've won. And the end of four hours of making John Kerry work there, because, of course, we did not tell him that it looked like he'd won, because he never would've sat there continuing to do the interviews, but when he got up out of the chair and went to go out, Shrum, I think, said to him, well, let me be the first to call you Mr. President, so you can imagine what kind of rollercoaster we were on that night…" Aired on C-SPAN throughout December, 2004.

18. See Kausfiles, "Kf Cops a Blog," http://slate.msn.com/id/2109381, accessed January 2005. Also see Nick Anderson and Faye Fiore, "Early Data for Kerry Proved Misleading," *Los Angeles Times,* November 4, 2004, p. A-17.

19. Changes include waiting until 6:00 p.m. on Election Day to release any data collected by the NEP and sharing possible inaccuracies with both NEP members and subscribers on Election Day instead of members only. See Evaluation of Edison/Mitofsky Election System 2004 for further recommended changes: http://www.exit-poll.net/election-night/EvaluationJan192005.pdf.

20. See Gregg Sangillo, "The GOP and Blacks: An Inch at a Time," *National Journal* 37 (January 1 & 8, 2005): 57–58.

21. See the William C. Velasquez Institute's exit polls conducted November 2, 2004, http://www.wcvi.org/latino_voter_research/polls/national/2004/exit_poll_results_110204.html, accessed January 17, 2005. See "Fallout: Whoops," *The Hotline,* December 3, 2004, p. 14.

22. See Darryl Fears, "Pollsters Debate Hispanics' Presidential Voting," *Washington Post,* November 26, 2004, p. A4.

23. The Annenberg survey was conducted by the Schulman, Ronca, Bucavalas polling firm, with about 5,000 Hispanic registered voters surveyed from 2000 to mid-November 2004. Republicans fare best with Cuban-Americans and Spanish-Americans, while Democrats have their greatest strength with Puerto Ricans and Central American U.S. citizens.

24. Pontell and Coker produced a white paper entitled, "Generation Jones: The 'Invisible Generation' Elects a President," November 2004, provided to the author by Mr. Coker, the managing director of Mason-Dixon Polling & Research, Inc., of Jacksonville, Florida.

25. Matt Bai, "Who Lost Ohio?," *The New York Times Magazine,* November 21, 2004.

26. While there are no hard data known to this author to prove it, some major Jewish groups privately have insisted to me that Bush fared considerably better than the NEP exit poll reported, mainly because of his rock-solid support for Israel in his first term. The proportions most mentioned are 30–35%, but again, this is conjecture. The exit poll does indeed show progress for Bush among American Jews, in any event.

27. See Neil Munro and Corine Hegland, "The Faithful Evangelical, Not Fundamentalist," *National Journal* 36 (December 5, 2004): 3451–3457.

28. Few post-election subjects generated more reaction than the misleading 'moral values' component of the 2004 exit poll. Four of the best commentaries were: Louis Menand, "Permanent Fatal Errors," *The New Yorker*, December 6, 2004, pp. 54–60; Gregory L. Giroux, "Effect of 'Moral Values' Voters Exaggerated, Say Analysts," *Congressional Quarterly Weekly* 62 (November 13, 2004): 2688; Christopher Muste, "Hidden in Plain Sight: Polling Data Shows Moral Values Aren't a New Factor," *The Washington Post*, December 12, 2004, p. B4; and Brian Friel, "Polling's Moral Dilemma," *National Journal* 36 (November 20, 2004): 3552–3553.

29. See, for instance, Sue Kirchhoff, "Economic predictors don't track vote results," *USA Today*, November 15, 2004, p. 4B.

30. See Summary of Election 2004 polls at Real Clear Politics http://www.realclearpolitics.com/polls.html.

31. Remember, the "two-party vote" means that all votes for third-party candidates and independents are excluded before the proportions are determined. See James E. Campbell, Alan I. Abramowitz, et al., "Forecasting the 2004 Presidential Election," *PS: Political Science and Politics* 37 (October 2004): 733–767. The models are quite different, and use various economic and public opinion data as a basis to project the likely results of the presidential contest.

32. Larry J. Sabato, *Aftermath of Armageddon* (Charlottesville, Va.: University of Virginia Institute of Government, 1975). This was the story of the epic 1973 gubernatorial battle in the Old Dominion between populist liberal Henry Howell and conservative Democrat-turned-Republican Mills Godwin. Godwin very narrowly defeated Howell to secure a second, non-consecutive term as Governor.

33. See, for example, John F. Harris, "'04 Voting: Realignment—Or a Tilt?," *Washington Post*, November 28, 2004, pp. A1, 8.

34. Bill Adler, *The Kennedy Wit*. New York: Bantam, 1964.

35. I am grateful to my colleague, Professor James Savage, for pointing out this instructive excerpt, for which Lincoln received loud applause. See Andrew Delbanco, *The Portable Abraham Lincoln* (New York: Penguin Books, 1992), p. 116. The first Lincoln-Douglas debate was held in Ottawa, Illinois on August 21, 1858.

36. Democrats controlled 22 of 26 Southern Senate seats in 1965.

37. Ron Brownstein, "GOP Has Lock on South, and Democrats Can't Find Key; A *Times* analysis shows that Bush's sweep of the region went even deeper than first appeared.," *Los Angeles Times*, December 15, 2004, p. A1. Out of about 11,100 counties in the eleven states of the Confederacy, plus Oklahoma and Kentucky, John Kerry won just 90 majority-white counties. By contrast, Bill Clinton had carried 510 majority-white Southern counties in 1996.

38. Thomas B. Edsall and James V. Grimaldi, "On Nov. 2, GOP Got More Bang For Its Billion, Analysis Shows," *Washington Post*, December 30, 2004, pp. A1, 7.

39. Very early Census Bureau projections suggest that Republicans are likely to gain again from the 2010 Census. If current trends continue, Texas will gain three electoral votes and Florida two, with Arizona, California, Georgia, Nevada, and Utah all adding one vote. New York and Ohio may lose two electoral votes each, with Illinois, Iowa, Louisiana, Massachusetts, Missouri, and Pennsylvania each losing one vote. This adds up, using the Bush-Kerry results, to a GOP gain of *eight* more electoral votes in the next decade.

40. Brian Faler, "Redder Reds, Bluer Blues Tilting the Senate," *Washington Post*, January 9, 2005, p. A4.

CHAPTER FIVE

A Bush Mandate?
It's in the Eye of the Beholder

Rhodes Cook
THE RHODES COOK LETTER

From the beginning, everyone knew the election of 2004 was for high stakes. It was the first presidential contest to be held after the terrorist attacks of 9/11; the first after the start of the bloody war in Iraq; the first after a state court in Massachusetts approved gay marriage; and the first since George W. Bush initially won the White House in 2000 on a split decision—winning the electoral vote but losing the popular vote.

To his critics, virtually everything about Bush was controversial—from the furor over his initial election to the president's embrace of an ideologically conservative agenda driven by an assertive leadership style. And the campaign of 2004 was waged against the backdrop of an uncertain economy, with both parties evenly matched—unified and well-financed for their rendezvous with the electorate.

Taken together, it created a volatile political cocktail, which for the first time in decades produced an election in which nearly everyone agreed that it made a difference who won.

In the end, there was little doubt that the election of 2004 was a victory for Bush and his Republican Party. But how great a victory is in the eye of the beholder.

Viewed from one angle, Republicans scored a decisive triumph that gives President Bush the mandate he so quickly claimed after the Nov. 2 balloting. Yet from another perspective, it is a different story. The president's victory over Democrat John Kerry appears tepid at best.

CASE FOR A MANDATE

Looking at the results from the GOP vantage point, the election of 2004 was a remarkable success. Republicans fashioned a clear message that combined support for traditional family values and the president's decisive leadership both home and abroad, while sharply questioning the suitability of Kerry to lead in troubled times. And the GOP buttressed its effort with a focused advertising campaign and a quietly effective voter-targeting operation that in the end the Democrats could not match.

The result: Republicans strengthened their grip on both ends of Pennsylvania Avenue, and maintained a clear majority of the nation's governorships, in a history-making election that produced the nation's highest voter turnout ever.

For the first time since 1988, a presidential candidate of either party captured a majority of the popular vote; Bush took 51%.

For the first time since 1924, the GOP both reelected a president and won control of both the Senate and the House of Representatives.

For the first time ever, a presidential candidate won more than 60 million votes, as Bush easily surpassed the previous record of nearly 54.5 million set by Ronald Reagan in 1984.

And the incumbent prevailed in the face of a record high turnout of 122 million voters, almost 17 million more than turned out four years earlier. On the eve of the election, there was a widespread belief that a huge turnout would benefit the challenger. But rather than fueling a vote for change, it was Bush who benefited most from the additional ballots.

While Kerry won 59 million votes, fully 8 million more than Democratic nominee Al Gore received in 2000, Bush hiked his own total by 11.5 million votes from four years earlier—the largest jump in a president's tally since Richard Nixon increased his total by more than 15 million votes from 1968 to 1972.

In every state, Bush received more votes this time than in 2000, as Kerry received more votes than Gore in every state except Alabama. Yet in the vast majority of states, 38, to be precise, there were more additional ballots for Bush than Kerry.

The power of the moral values issue no doubt played a hand in the Bush upsurge. In the 11 states where a ban on gay marriage was also on the November ballot—which were primarily smaller states in the Republican heartland—Bush gained more than two and a quarter million votes from 2000.

But the trauma of 9/11 was also a driving force, very evident in the three states within a close radius of ground zero—New York, New Jersey, and Connecticut. In those three states alone, Bush gained more than one million votes from four year earlier. The increase was not enough for the president to come close to carrying any of the three. But the huge gain in his vote total spoke to the power of terrorism, and the president's handling of it, in the 2004 election.

The increase in Bush's vote from four years earlier was not a regional phenomenon. It was broad based, as his share of the vote went up from 2000 in all but three states—North Carolina, South Dakota, and Vermont. In a majority of states—29—Bush captured at least 50% of the vote.

And nationwide exit polls showed the president running better than 2000 among Hispanics, Jews, Catholics, women, and suburbanites—all groups that some observers had figured would be pillars of an emerging Democratic majority.

It may be too soon to talk of a Republican realignment. But there is little doubt that the election of 2004 provided new evidence that the pendulum of American politics continues to swing steadily in the Republicans' direction since "the perfect tie" of 2000.

ON THE OTHER HAND…

Yet this was an election where the outcome could be argued round or argued flat. In short, there is also a compelling set of data that points to a more hopeful scenario for the Democrats.

Bush's margin of victory in the popular vote—3 million—was the smallest for any reelected president since Harry Truman scored his fabled come-from-behind victory in 1948. And then, less than half as many votes were cast as this time.

Bush's margin of victory in the electoral vote—35—was the smallest for any reelected president since Woodrow Wilson won by 23 in 1916. And other than Wilson's, there has been no other successful presidential reelection in the Electoral College as narrow as Bush's since the founding of the Republic.

To boot, Bush's margin of victory percentage-wise in the popular vote—2.4 points—was the smallest for a reelected president in the nation's history, bar none.

The scope of Bush's victory this year looks impressive when compared to his father's 1992 reelection defeat or "W's" own win on a split decision in 2000, when he won the electoral vote by five, but lost the popular vote by more than a half million.

But it looks a lot less gaudy when compared to recent incumbents such as Lyndon Johnson, Richard Nixon and Ronald Reagan, who parlayed their popularity (and their opponents' weakness) into reelection landslides that exceeded 15 million votes, or for that matter, Bush's predecessor, Bill Clinton, who won a second term in 1996 by a margin of more than 8 million votes.

Neither Bush nor Kerry came close to running a 50-state campaign in 2004, operating instead off the closely divided electoral map from 2000 with its sharply defined red and blue shadings. Both candidates conceded huge chunks of the country to the other, to the extent that it could be argued that Bush's triumph in 2004 was less a rousing nationwide vote of approval than a more limited triumph based largely in one region, the South.

The president swept the 13 states of the South (the 11 of the old Confederacy plus Kentucky and Oklahoma) by nearly 6 million votes, but was beaten by Kerry in the rest of the country by 3 million. In electoral votes, it was 168-to-0 for Bush inside the South, 251-to-118 for Kerry outside the South. If Democrats have problems in rural America, Republicans have concerns almost as troublesome in the large metropolitan areas of the Northeast, Midwest, and the West.

Clearly, the Democrats are not the woebegone force they were at the presidential level in the 1970s and 1980s. In those two decades they not only lost four of five presidential elections, but in three of them fell below 50 electoral votes and barely reached 100 in another.

By contrast, the Democrats have won at least 250 electoral votes of the 270 needed to take the White House in each of the last four elections. In the process, they have won with regularity big electoral vote prizes such as California, New York, New Jersey, Pennsylvania, Illinois, and Michigan. And in many of these mega-states, the vote has not even been close.

In every presidential election since 1992, the Democrats have carried California by at least 1.2 million votes, New York by at least 1 million, and Illinois by at least 500,000 votes. A part of the vast Republican presidential terrain in the eras of Nixon and Reagan, these vote-rich states have become cornerstones of the Democratic presidential coalition.

VICTORY FOR "TEAM REPUBLICAN"

There are many who believe that the reelection of a controversial president in highly polarized times was a feat in itself. Yet throughout the campaign, Bush enjoyed some significant advantages.

He benefited from money and the map. The map in terms of a post-2000 shuffling of electoral votes that transformed his tenuous total of 271 in 2000 into a more comfortable starting point of 278. Money in the form of a virtually bottomless campaign chest that did not require the spending of a single dollar to dispense to an intra-party rival; there was none.

Unopposed for renomination (always a favorable sign for a president's reelection), Bush was free to launch a relentless advertising attack on Kerry from March on, that effectively pilloried the Democratic challenger as a liberal legislator from Massachusetts and a "flip-flopper," particularly in his approach to the war in Iraq.

The incumbent also enjoyed the bully pulpit of the White House with surrogates galore, and was able to portray himself as a wartime president tenaciously fighting a new kind of terrorist enemy. "9/11 changed everything," was the campaign's answer to practically any criticism.

Yet by shedding the mantle of the "compassionate conservative" that he wore in 2000 for that of the highly partisan warrior president, Bush virtually ensured that the votes of Democrats and many independents would be tough to come by and a narrow reelection victory was likely the best he could hope for.

As a consequence, the Republican showing in the election of 2004 was truly impressive only when one moves beyond the presidential race to consider the totality of the GOP victory. In short, it was a notable victory for "Team Republican" as a whole.

Republicans in 2004 continued to strengthen their majorities on Capitol Hill. Since the election of 2000, GOP numbers in the Senate have swelled to 55 seats from 50, and in the House to 232 seats from 221. The Republican Senate total after this election ties the party's highest number since the eve of the New Deal; the number of Republican House members is the highest post-election total for the party since 1946.

In the process, Republicans have gone from razor-thin majorities in both houses of Congress to a more clear-cut advantage, which could enable Bush to pursue a more activist second term agenda than many presidents in his position have been able to pursue.

The 2004 election produced an unusual congruency in the nationwide voting for president and the House of Representatives—with the size of the GOP majorities almost identical. This congruency was literally a generation in the making. Through much of the latter half of the 20th century, Republicans dominated the balloting for president, Democrats for Congress. In 2000, the popular vote for president leaned slightly Democratic, the aggregate House vote leaned slightly Republican—each by roughly a half million votes.

But in 2004, Republicans enjoyed a similar advantage in both the presidential and congressional balloting. Bush defeated Kerry in the presidential vote by 2.4 percentage points—50.7% to 48.3%—and took 53% of the electoral vote. Republicans outpolled the Democrats in the nationwide House vote by 2.7 points—50.1% to 47.5%—and took 53% of all House seats.

Yet this election was arguably as much about incumbency as anything else. Only one Senate incumbent was defeated in the November balloting, Democratic Senate Minority Leader Tom Daschle of South Dakota. He was ousted by the margin of one percentage point.

Only seven incumbents lost in the House of Representatives, with most of the carnage concentrated in the president's home state of Texas. There, a controversial GOP-orchestrated remap in 2003 led to the defeat of four veteran Democratic House members last fall.

Two of the passel of governors up this year lost their bids for another term, but only one, Craig Benson of New Hampshire, had been elected to the post. The other, Joe Kernan of Indiana, ascended to the governorship in 2003 upon the death of his predecessor, Frank O'Bannon.

And in the presidential race, Bush effectively underscored the value of incumbency in 2004 as he made an updated version of "don't change horses in the middle of the stream" a major theme that played particularly well in a campaign where fear of terrorism was a driving concern.

Republicans can act cocky at their peril. The GOP came out of the election with a 22-to-4 edge in Southern Senate seats, and 91-to-51 advantage in Southern House seats. Yet without the South, Kerry would be in the White House and Democrats in control of both chambers of Congress.

In California, New York, and Illinois—each a keystone of the electoral map in their region—Republicans currently have problems not only at the presidential level, but the congressional level as well. Democrats hold 25 more House seats than the Republicans in these three states, plus all six Senate seats.

In last year's Senate races, the GOP barely managed a blip on the radar screen in any of these three states. Democrats Barbara Boxer in California, Barack Obama in Illinois, and Charles Schumer in New York all won by more than two million votes—in each case, rolling up a record margin of victory for a contested Senate race in their state.

After all the effort, all the money spent—neither the presidential nor the congressional map really changed that much in 2004. Republican Senate gains were concentrated in the GOP's strongest region, the South, where they picked up five open Democratic seats. Republican House gains were mainly in Texas, where the party picked up four seats. And in the presidential election, only three states switched from one party to another: New Hampshire to Kerry, Iowa and New Mexico to Bush. All were states decided by less than 10,000 votes in 2000 and all were close again this time.

Undeniably, the election of 2004 was a Republican victory. But by historical standards, it was a tenuous one, in which the lines between the Democratic and Republican parts of the country so evident in 2000 continued to be etched deeply.

Rhodes Cook is author of *The Rhodes Cook Letter.*

CHAPTER SIX

Kerry in the Red States: Fighting an Uphill Battle from the Start

Susan A. MacManus

(with the assistance of Matthew Cillian, Andrew Quecan,
Thomas A. Watson, & Brittany L. Penberthy)

UNIVERSITY OF SOUTH FLORIDA, TAMPA

In the red states, Democratic presidential candidate John Kerry used two principal strategies: (1) target the states that might be won, and (2) focus on the twin issues of the President's bungling the war in Iraq and his ineptness in reversing a sluggish economy. Many in his camp believed these strategies would unseat a President who they believed really didn't win the first time around. But in the end, the strategies missed the mark. Bush won both the popular and the Electoral College votes... and many of the red states turned even redder.

Of the 29 states carried by Republican George Bush in 2000, Kerry won back only one—tiny New Hampshire. Despite early boasts of being competitive in these red states, he ended up losing ground in all but a handful.[1] (See Figure 1.) His choice of issues rallied many voters, but more aligned with Bush's appeals to traditional moral values and the need for security in a world afire with terrorism.

With nearly half the red states—14 of 29—in the South,[2] Kerry faced a tough climb from the start. The South had long been viewed as a must-have region for a Democrat to capture the White House. And the region had gained political clout following reapportionment after the 2000 Census.[3] (So, too, had several red states in the West.[4])

From the outset, many Democratic strategists felt that most of the southern red states would be tough to win. In January 2004, heading into the presidential primaries, one Seattle journalist painted this picture of the challenge Democrats faced:

> *Over the past four presidential elections, GOP candidates have tapped into the region's inherent conservatism, its increasing wealth, and most of all, its growing antipathy toward liberal Democrats, to dominate one of the nation's most populous regions...*Democrats privately acknowledge the steep hill in the South, *but they believe some states show promise for Democrats. The strategy, they say, is rather than running across the South as a whole, to target states where they have [a] chance of winning...Despite recent history, Democrats believe there is a chance. The worsening economy and questions about the war in Iraq could convince voters who went Republican in the past to switch back, they say.*[5] (emphasis added)

The uphill nature of the race for red states proved prophetic. "By the campaign's final days," noted one *Los Angeles Times* reporter, "Kerry was seriously bidding for only three states that Bush carried last time—Florida, Ohio, and New Hampshire."[6]

Overall, compared to his predecessor Al Gore, Kerry lost ground in a majority (53%) of the red states—16 of the 30, the biggest losses occurring in the South. (See Figure 1.) He moved ahead of Gore in just 11 (37%). Six were in the West (Alaska, Colorado, Idaho, Montana, Nevada, Wyoming), two in the Midwest (North Dakota and Ohio), two in the South (North Carolina and Virginia), and one, New Hampshire, in the Northeast.[7]

Steve Elmendorf, Kerry's deputy campaign manager, acknowledged that Bush's strong position in the red states enabled the President to force Kerry to scramble for some of the blue states that should have been sure wins:

> *We were working from a pretty small map here. He [Bush] was pressuring us much more in places where Gore had won than we were pressuring him where he had won, like New Hampshire and Nevada: those were only four electoral votes. He [Bush] had us in New Mexico, Iowa, Wisconsin and Minnesota, and in Pennsylvania and Michigan we could never take our eye off the ball. It wasn't a resource question as much as we weren't competitive in places like Missouri and Arkansas that Bush had won, so he was able to take enormous resources and really pour them into those states.[8]*

At the final bell, Kerry fell short of Bush in three of the Democrats' top priority states: Florida by 5%, Ohio by 2%, and Nevada by 2%. Kerry won back New Hampshire by a slim 1%. (See Figure 2 for Kerry vote percentages in the red states.)

TARGETING: KERRY'S BLOOPER

On March 22, 2003, Senator Kerry gave his fellow U.S. Senators a copy of a speech he had made at a fund-raiser in California nearly a year ahead of the official opening of the presidential nominating

FIGURE 1
Kerry Vote Percentage Gains Over Gore 2000

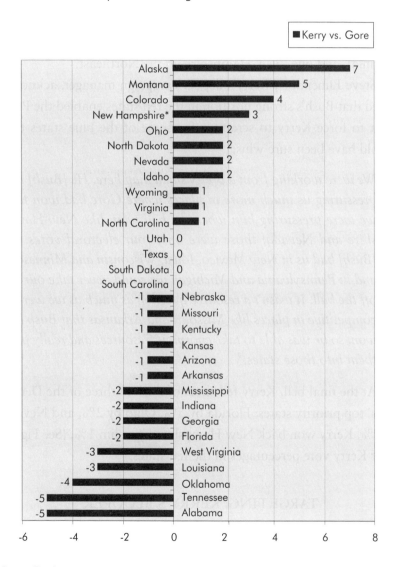

Source: Election returns.

FIGURE 2
Kerry in the Red States 2004

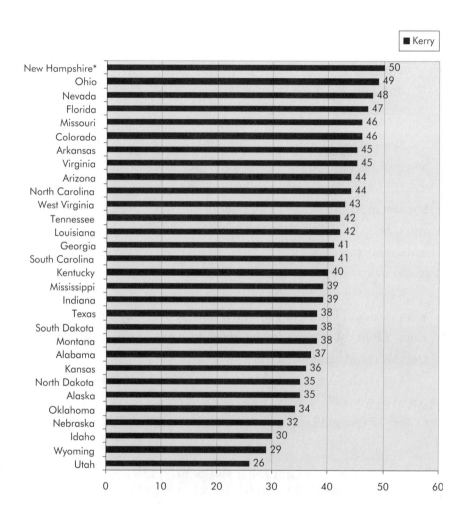

Source: Election returns.

season. Kerry's remarks, which the press widely publicized, plagued him throughout the campaign:

> *Al Gore proved that you can get elected president of the United States without winning one Southern state—if he had simply won New Hampshire or West Virginia or Ohio or Colorado or a number of other states. We are the leaders. Democrats have to stop looking at the small solution that the country is compartmentalized in that way.*[9]

Not having to win a single southern state? Heresy. Kerry spent much of his time on the stump backtracking that part of his statement: "[W]e can win a number of states [in the South], Florida, Louisiana, Arkansas, and a number of others."[10] He chose a Southerner, Sen. John Edwards (NC), as his vice presidential running mate, and the two, either singly or together, campaigned in key southern states that were seen as target or swing states.

Kerry also had to produce on the other half of his statement—winning possible red pick-up states like New Hampshire, West Virginia, Ohio, or Colorado. He tried to carry it off by mounting credible campaign efforts there.

The truth is, however, that many of the red states were not perceived as winnable to begin with. The best proof? Kerry's decision not to visit 17 of the 29 states in the final two months of the campaign.

TARGETING: IDENTIFYING
BATTLEGROUND RED STATES

Presidential campaigns are grueling affairs—draining the time, resources, and energy of the candidates—thereby forcing them to pick and choose where to concentrate their efforts. They usually begin in the states perceived to be winnable based on the results of the most recent election. (See Figure 3.)

FIGURE 3
Gore in the Red States 2000

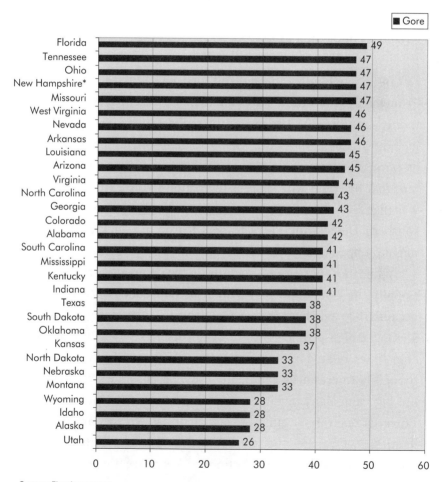

Source: Election returns.

Early handicapping of the race in March 2004, largely stemming from Al Gore's performance in 2000, identified more blue
than red states as competitive battlegrounds for Kerry. Political analysts projected the nine competitive blue states to be Michigan,
Washington state, Maine, Minnesota, Pennsylvania, Iowa, Oregon,
Wisconsin, and New Mexico. The seven competitive red states were
expected to be Nevada, New Hampshire, West Virginia, Missouri,
Arizona, Ohio, and Florida.[11]

Five other red states were cast as longer shots: Tennessee,
Arkansas, Louisiana, Arizona, and Virginia. (With the exception of
Tennessee, each of these states did manage to get Kerry's attention,
if only sporadically.) The rest of the red states looked out of reach,
including many in the South. And yet, media attention on the South
as a must-have region never dissipated. One reason was Kerry's
hint that he could win without the region's votes. Another reason
was that several states had competitive, open U.S. Senate seats, and
southern Democratic Party leaders feared any lack of attention
might dampen their supporters' turnout.

While most of a ticket's focus is on the competitive states, occasionally the candidates may visit relatively noncompetitive states
because they live there or they want to help other party candidates
seeking a high profile office (e.g., an open U.S. Senate seat). But
sometimes relatively noncompetitive states may merit attention,
though not necessarily candidate visits, because the state's citizens
are big campaign contributors. Such was the case for the Kerry-
Edwards team in Virginia, Texas, Georgia, North Carolina, and
Tennessee. Of these, the team visited only one, North Carolina.
(For a list of red-state contributions to Kerry, see Table 1.)

TABLE 1

Ranking the Red States: Campaign Contributions to Sen. John Kerry (D)

STATE	TOTAL TO PRESIDENTIAL CANDIDATE JOHN KERRY
Florida	$6,174,844
Virginia	$5,635,323
Texas	$4,665,975
Ohio	$3,170,253
Colorado	$2,644,586
Georgia	$2,152,002
North Carolina	$1,708,902
Missouri	$1,417,459
Arizona	$1,414,710
Tennessee	$1,140,257
Louisiana	$955,059
Kentucky	$907,923
New Hampshire*	$736,370
Indiana	$594,223
Nevada	$577,204
Alabama	$483,589
West Virginia	$446,010
South Carolina	$443,516
Arkansas	$413,494
Mississippi	$393,665
Kansas	$387,234
Idaho	$329,211
Oklahoma	$324,038
Utah	$251,081
Wyoming	$240,375
Alaska	$170,483

TABLE 1 continued

STATE	TOTAL TO PRESIDENTIAL CANDIDATE JOHN KERRY
Nebraska	$157,880
Montana	$142,179
South Dakota	$75,553
North Dakota	$36,600

Source: Federal Election Commission, data released December 13, 2004.

TARGETING: WHERE DEMOCRATS VISITED—OR NOT

Campaigning is a team effort—a family affair. In the last two months of the campaign, the candidates and their spouses made 224 visits to red states. The number of Kerry-Edwards visits actually exceeded that of the Bush-Cheney ticket (122 vs. 102 respectively). The presidential contenders visited red states in almost equal numbers (45 Kerry, 42 Bush). But Democratic vice presidential nominee Edwards visited considerably more than Cheney (44 vs. 33). Edwards was doing his job of helping the ticket in the South … or trying to.[12] (See Table 2.)

Predictably, the number of the Kerry-Edwards visits closely corresponded with the perceived competitiveness of a state:

Highly competitive/frequent-visit states: Ohio (68), Florida (53).

Highly competitive/occasional[13]-visit states: New Hampshire (9), West Virginia (8), North Carolina (8), Nevada (6), Colorado (5), Missouri (5).

Somewhat competitive/minimal-visit states: Arizona (3), Arkansas (1), Kentucky(1), Louisiana (1), South Carolina (1).

Noncompetitive/no-visit states: Texas, North Dakota, South Dakota, Alaska, Georgia, Idaho, Kansas, Mississippi, Montana, Nebraska, Utah, Indiana, Oklahoma, Tennessee, Alabama, Virginia, Wyoming.

TABLE 2
One-Third of Red States Get the Bulk of the Visits from Candidates and Spouses in Last Two Months of Campaign

STATE	PRESIDENTIAL		VICE PRESIDENTIAL		PRES. SPOUSES		VP SPOUSES		STATE TOTALS
	BUSH	KERRY	CHENEY	EDWARDS	LAURA	TERESA	LYNNE	ELIZABETH	
Alabama	1	0	0	0	0	0	0	0	1
Alaska	0	0	0	0	0	0	0	0	0
Arizona	2	1	1	1	0	1	0	0	6
Arkansas	0	0	0	0	0	0	0	1	1
Colorado	4	2	3	1	0	1	0	1	12
Florida	9	13	6	13	3	4	2	3	53
Georgia	0	0	0	0	0	0	0	0	0
Idaho	0	0	0	0	0	0	0	0	0
Indiana	0	0	0	0	1	0	0	0	1
Kansas	0	0	0	0	0	0	0	0	0
Kentucky	0	0	0	1	0	0	0	0	1
Louisiana	0	1	1	0	1	0	0	0	3
Mississippi	0	0	0	0	0	0	0	0	0
Missouri	4	2	2	1	0	1	0	1	11
Montana	0	0	0	0	0	0	0	0	0
Nebraska	0	0	0	0	0	0	0	0	0
Nevada	2	4	3	1	3	1	0	0	14
New Hampshire	3	3	1	3	2	0	0	3	15

TABLE 2 continued

STATE	PRESIDENTIAL		VICE PRESIDENTIAL		PRES. SPOUSES		VP SPOUSES		STATE TOTALS
	BUSH	KERRY	CHENEY	EDWARDS	LAURA	TERESA	LYNNE	ELIZABETH	
N. Carolina	1	1	0	4	0	0	0	4	10
N. Dakota	0	0	0	0	0	0	0	0	0
Ohio	11	17	10	14	4	3	3	6	68
Oklahoma	0	0	1	0	0	0	0	0	1
S. Carolina	0	0	0	1	1	0	0	0	2
S. Dakota	0	0	0	0	0	0	0	0	0
Tennessee	0	0	0	0	0	0	0	0	0
Texas	2	0	0	0	2	0	0	0	4
Utah	0	0	0	0	0	0	0	0	0
Virginia	0	0	0	0	0	0	1	0	1
W. Virginia	2	1	3	4	1	0	2	3	16
Wyoming	0	0	2	0	0	0	1	0	3
Total	41	45	33	44	18	11	9	22	223

Note: Figures reflect state visits from September 2–November 2, 2004.
Source: Compiled by Andrew Quecan from ABC News's *The Note*, candidate web sites, and various news sources.

Travel by the candidates' wives was driven by their popularity within the more traditional red-state America. Democrats relied more heavily on Elizabeth Edwards, a native-born Floridian, than on Teresa Heinz Kerry to campaign on the ticket's behalf (22 vs. 11 visits respectively). Clearly, the less traditional Ms. Kerry was not as helpful to her husband's campaign in the red states as was Ms. Bush to the President.[14] The First Lady took nearly twice the number of trips to the red states as Ms. Kerry (18 vs. 11). An Ohio voter sums up Laura Bush's popularity in America's heartland: "She is a good mother, a good wife, a good American citizen and a lovely, lovely lady. She's a big, big help to her husband."[15]

In the closing days of the long and contentious campaign, the Kerry campaign put most of its red-state efforts (as measured by visits) into five states: Ohio, Florida, Colorado, New Hampshire, and Nevada. (See Figure 4.)

Several post-election pundits blamed Kerry for not trying just a little harder in some of the red states he abandoned. Chuck Todd of the *National Journal* had this post-mortem analysis:

> *The party should have spent more time cultivating places like Arkansas, Colorado, Virginia and Arizona this cycle. None of these are old-time labor states, but all have growing, diverse electorates with fast-growing suburbs that could have been edged into battleground status—if they'd gotten the sort of resources that Ohio, Pennsylvania, New Mexico, Nevada, Wisconsin and Iowa received. There were flirtations with all those states, of course, but no real commitments beyond money for TV. Colorado is probably the biggest flub by Democrats. In this election that saw Republicans do well across the country, Democrats won control of Colorado's entire state Legislature for the first time in nearly 50 years, and the party won a U.S. Senate seat in the state for the first time in over a decade...*[16]

In the end, the Kerry-Edwards efforts to court the red states fell flat. Kerry simply couldn't get a majority of red-state voters to rank his issues ahead of the President's. Nor could Kerry convince red-state voters that he had the right leadership skills in a time of war. And the Kerry campaign's over-reliance on labor unions and 527 groups to turn out the vote fell short of the Bush team's same efforts in the competitive red states.

FIGURE 4
Presidential and Vice Presidential Visits to Red States:
September 2–November 2, 2004

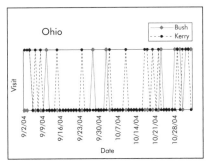

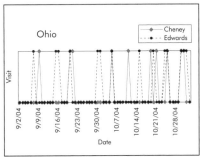

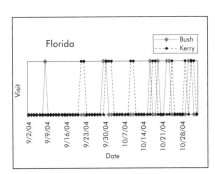

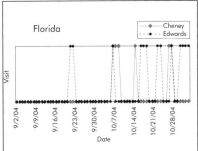

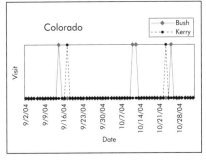

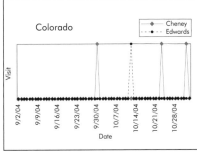

FIGURE 4 CONTINUED

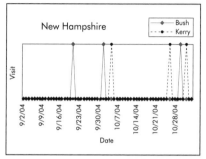

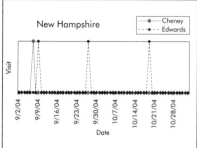

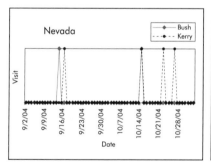

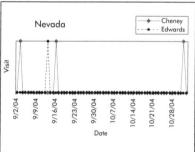

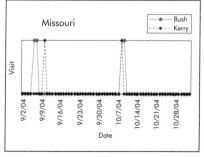

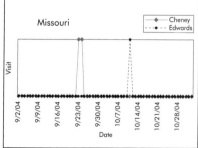

FIGURE 4 CONTINUED

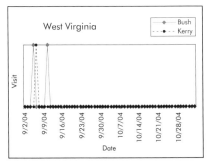

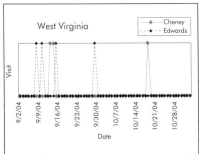

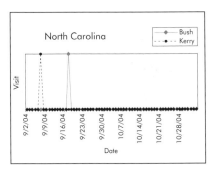

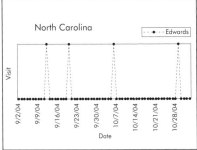

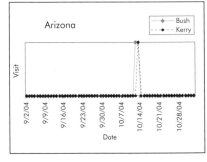

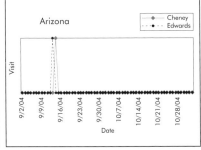

FIGURE 4 CONTINUED

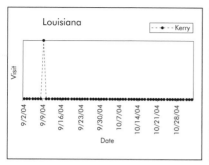
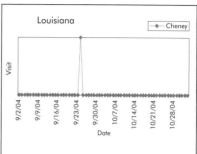

Sources: Compiled by Andrew Quecan from ABC News's The Note, candidate web sites, and various news accounts.

TARGETING: DEMOCRATS COULDN'T BEAT GOP AT TURNOUT GAME

In spite of the fact that Democratic registrants outnumbered Republicans in many red states, including the must-have Florida,[17] the Kerry-Edwards team couldn't drag enough of them to the polls.[18] One reason was the Democrats' get-out-the-vote efforts relied more heavily on paid workers, often out-of-staters recruited by 527 groups like MoveOn.org and America Coming Together. By contrast, the Republicans assembled friends and neighbors as volunteers. As one independent pollster put it: "One volunteer is worth 100 paid workers in a get-out-the-vote campaign. They don't have the same enthusiasm as the guy who believes in the candidate and makes sure his neighbors and friends of neighbors are going to show up at the polls."[19] In short, "'Volunteers' who are bought and paid for cannot beat volunteers who come from the neighborhood, church, workplace and reading group."[20]

Another reason was that the Democrats lagged behind the GOP in using sophisticated methods of refining and testing databases of potential supporters. Research firms hired by the Republican National Committee meshed information from commercial databases with that from political polls to identify people who were inclined to vote for Bush but either had not registered or didn't feel motivated to vote, so-called soft Republicans. The result: a four-fold increase in the number of Republican voters who could be targeted.[21]

"Very few people understand how much work it takes to get this technology to actually produce political results," said one Democrat who helped coordinate the GOTV effort. "We are one election cycle behind them [the GOP] in this area."[22]

Early GOP research identified trigger issues such as abortion and trial lawyer fees that were used in tailoring messages to specific groups via direct mail, phone calls, and personal visits. "They [the Bush campaign] were smart," said Democratic National Committee Chairman Terence R. McAuliffe. "They came into our neighborhoods. They came into Democratic areas with very specific targeted messages to take Democratic voters away from us."[23]

Democratic voters turned out in greater numbers, as revealed in exit poll data, in only four red states: Arkansas, Kentucky, Louisiana, and Mississippi. (See Table 3.) Ironically, however, many Democrats in these Deep South states are conservatives who historically support Republican presidential candidates. When a Massachusetts liberal was the Democratic nominee, Republicans could roust conservative southern voters by pointing out that Kerry was even more liberal than Sen. Edward Kennedy.[24]

In every red state, conservative voters significantly outnumbered liberals. (See Table 3.) Only in New Hampshire, Mississippi, and

North Dakota did the proportion of conservative voters dip below the national average of 34%. Conversely, in only one state, Colorado, did the proportion of liberal voters exceed the national average, and by only 1%.

The electorate's larger-than-average Republican and conservative profiles clearly show why Kerry had trouble breaking the GOP's hold on the red states. In all but two states—Ohio and New Hampshire—voters identified moral values or terrorism as the most important issue in their decision-making. On these issues, Bush came out better than Kerry. The sluggish economy and the dismal news from Iraq were leading issues in Ohio and New Hampshire— and that's where Kerry did best.

TABLE 3
The Red State (2000) Voters in 2004: Party, Ideology, and Major Issue

STATE	PARTISAN COMPOSITION OF ELECTORATE		IDEOLOGICAL COMPOSITION OF ELECTORATE		MAIN ISSUE AMONG ELECTORATE	
	% REPUBLICAN	% DEMOCRAT	% CONSERVATIVE	% LIBERAL	ISSUE	PERCENT
Alabama	48	34	44	15	N/A	n/a
Alaska	37	22	34	20	Moral values	27
Arizona	44	30	38	19	Moral values Terrorism*	22
Arkansas	31	41	42	13	Moral values	33
Colorado	38	29	35	22	Moral values	24
Florida	41	37	34	20	Terrorism	24
Georgia	42	34	41	14	Moral values	24
Idaho	50	22	39	17	N/A	n/a
Indiana	46	32	42	14	Moral values	24
Kansas	50	27	38	14	N/A	n/a

TABLE 3 continued

STATE	PARTISAN COMPOSITION OF ELECTORATE		IDEOLOGICAL COMPOSITION OF ELECTORATE		MAIN ISSUE AMONG ELECTORATE	
	% REPUB-LICAN	% DEMO-CRAT	% CONSER-VATIVE	% LIBERAL	ISSUE	PERCENT
Kentucky	40	44	39	15	Moral values	26
Louisiana	40	42	40	17	Terrorism	22
Mississippi	32	41	31	21	N/A	n/a
Missouri	36	35	36	19	Moral values	24
Montana	39	32	35	19	N/A	n/a
Nebraska	53	24	41	13	N/A	n/a
Nevada	39	35	34	18	Terrorism	25
New Hampshire	32	25	30	21	Iraq	26
North Carolina	40	39	40	17	Moral values	24
North Dakota	41	27	33	13	N/A	n/a
Ohio	40	35	34	19	Economy/jobs	24
Oklahoma	43	40	43	13	Moral values	29
South Carolina	44	33	39	15	Moral values Terrorism*	23
South Dakota	47	32	39	16	Moral values	25
Tennessee	41	31	47	15	Moral values	29
Texas	42	33	44	15	N/A	n/a
Utah	58	19	45	11	N/A	n/a
Virginia	39	35	38	17	Moral values Terrorism*	22
West Virginia	32	50	33	17	Moral values	25
Wyoming	52	26	38	14	N/A	n/a
U.S At-Large	37	37	34	21	Moral values	22

*Statistical tie between moral values and terrorism.

Source: Compiled by Matthew Cillian. All data come from the exit poll surveys conducted by Edison Media Research/Mitofsky International for the AP and television networks; the polls were then pulled from the *Washington Post* web site, http:// www.washingtonpost.com/wp-srv/politics/elections/2004/graphics/exitPolls_(state).html.

THE RED-STATE ISSUES:
WHY MORAL VALUES?

It is not coincidental that moral values ranked highest as a voting cue issue[25] in many red states—namely, Alabama, Arkansas, Georgia, Indiana, Kentucky, Idaho, Nebraska, North Carolina, Oklahoma, Tennessee, Texas, and Utah. These 12 states had significantly more conservatives than liberals and higher-than-average proportions of voters who attend church weekly or more often.

The importance of moral values as an issue began to appear in early 2004 in a number of warning signs: the public outrage over Janet Jackson's "revealing" halftime show episode at the Super Bowl; the long box office lines for *The Passion of the Christ*; and the nation's week-long grieving over the death of President Ronald Reagan and reminders of his life's moral attributes. Not the least of these signs—and a political red flag—was the rejection of gay marriage in a moderate red swing state (Missouri), where turnout reached record levels for a primary election. (Nine red states had anti-gay marriage amendments on their November 2004 ballots; all passed by overwhelming margins.[26])

In looking at the candidates, red-state voters could hardly miss the Kerry campaign's endorsements from Hollywood celebrities, rock and rap musicians, and other avant garde personalities. "When he stood on stage basking in a raunchy, raucous show by Hollywood celebrities helping his campaign—and said they 'conveyed the heart and soul of our country'[27]—Kerry enhanced his image as someone out of touch with Main Street."[28]

If he was out of touch with red-state voters on the culture front, Kerry was well aware of attitudes toward religion. Indeed, polls showed that 68% of Americans think it's important for a president to have strong religious beliefs.[29] Kerry tried hard to reach the large evangelical and Catholic religious communities in the red states without alienating his own separation-of-church-and-state supporters. One writer in the *Wall Street Journal* observed:

> *Aware of the church-attendance gap*[30]*—at-least-weekly church-goers tend to vote Republican, less-than-weekly churchgoers (and never-goers) tend to vote Democratic—Mr. Kerry sought to discuss his own faith and thereby convey his deepest values. Yet here the Catholic Kerry encountered problems. He said that he believes life to begin at conception but that he could not "legislate" a pro-life bill (given the First Amendment ban on establishing religion) because his belief was a Catholic teaching. Then he cited other aspects of his faith—touching on the environment, equality and justice—that he said would shape his policies. Mr. Kerry was trying to shift the values debate to his terrain—to a discussion of how to pursue "a society of the common good."* Yet his position on abortion only served to remind pro-life Catholics (and non-Catholics) where he stood on the issue. *Meanwhile, his effort to call forth voters inspired by a social gospel didn't work.*[31] *(emphasis added)*

Kerry's attempts to appeal to religious conservatives were not enough to erase the image of his "immoral" supporters ("trashy" Hollywood and pro-choice supporters). The moral values issue resonated with women voters in the red states, most notably those married with children. Why? "The culture wars," according to a *Washington Times* columnist, "are about how we raise our children, what the schools teach them, how we teach them what's right and what's wrong."[32] On these questions, women leaned toward

Bush. Among women in the red states, Kerry fared worse in 2004 than Gore had in 2000.[33] Kerry also lost ground among Hispanic and African American voters in the red states over moral issues like abortion and gay marriage.[34]

THE RED-STATE ISSUES:
WHY TERRORISM?

In the red states, as in the rest of the nation, terrorism proved to be a major issue. As David Broder noted: "Terrorism was Bush's trump card in this political game, a high card he had picked up by his stalwart performance following the 9-11 attacks and the emotional bond he formed with millions of Americans at that time."[35]

Terrorism ranked as *the* most important issue in three red states: Nevada, Louisiana, and Florida and tied with moral values in Arizona, South Carolina, and Virginia. These states have large numbers of veterans and active-duty military and thus were more receptive to the Bush preemption policy on invading Iraq. Voters in these states were also more likely to believe the ad of the Swift Boat Veterans for Truth challenging Kerry's fitness to serve as commander-in-chief in a time of war.[36] The ad did not air in all these states, but it generated enormous news and talk radio coverage. The executive director of the Center for Public Integrity labeled the ad the most effective of any television ads run by an advocacy group in the 2004 campaign.[37] So, too, did Mary Beth Cahill, Kerry's campaign manager: "This is the best $40,000 investment made by any political group but it was only because of the news coverage that it got where it did."[38] For Kerry, the ad and its fallout were devastating.

Interestingly, the red states where terrorism ranked as the most

important voting cue are also among the most vulnerable to terrorist attack, a fact that became more apparent after 9-11. Particularly vulnerable are deep-water ports in Louisiana and Florida, the
tourism-dependent economies of Florida, Nevada, and Virginia,
and the porous borders of Arizona and Florida. Another factor fan-
ning the terrorism flame was the competitive, open U.S. Senate seats
in South Carolina, Louisiana, and Florida. (The Republicans ended
up winning all three.[39])

In the states where terrorism was the leading issue, higher-than-
average proportions of voters identified "strong leader" as the most
important personal quality they looked for in a president.[40] Kerry
had trouble portraying himself as a strong leader, especially in the
highly competitive states of Florida and Nevada. How did this happen? One *USA Today* observer suggested that "…Kerry's long, con-
fusing series of votes and statements on Iraq gave Bush an opening
to paint him as a waffling political opportunist who'd say anything
he thought people wanted to hear."[41] For those most concerned
about terrorism, the flip-flop image was less than comforting.

THE RED-STATE ISSUES: WHY NOT THE ECONOMY OR JOBS?

According to U.S. Bureau of Labor Statistics, the nation lost almost
1.9 million jobs during the first three years of the Bush administration. Labor data also showed the unemployment rate rose from a
low of 4.2 percent in January 2001 and hovered around 5.8 percent
through much of 2002.[42] To Kerry, jobs and the economy seemed
an indisputable issue.

But in the red states, economic conditions were generally better than those in the blue states, particularly the blue Rust Belt states of the Midwest. The only state where the issue hit home for Kerry was Ohio. Even when he tried to use it in mining states like West Virginia, Nevada, and Indiana, the Americans for Coal Jobs (originally the Coal Miners for Truth, a 527 group[43]) ran an ad suggesting that if Kerry were elected, his environmental policies would threaten mining jobs.

The issue also lost some teeth when national economic reports published in the two periods prior to the election started showing job growth, even in the manufacturing sector. An ABC News/Money poll ending October 31, just prior to the election, showed that consumer confidence had jumped to its highest level in nine months. A majority (57%) rated their personal finances positively.[44]

Proof of the issue's weakness for Kerry came in the results of the nationwide exit poll taken Election Day. That survey showed that a majority of the voters thought the job situation was at least as good as it was when Bush took office in 2001. A majority said they personally had not lost work over the past four years.[45] And a higher-than-average proportion in all but three red states said their family's financial situation was the same as or better than it was when Bush first took office. (See Table 4.)

TABLE 4

STATE	PERCENT OF ELECTORATE WHOSE FINANCIAL SITUATION IMPROVED OR REMAINED THE SAME DURING BUSH'S FIRST TERM
Wyoming	83
Alaska	79
South Dakota	79
Idaho	78
Idaho	78

TABLE 4 continued

STATE	PERCENT OF ELECTORATE WHOSE FINANCIAL SITUATION IMPROVED OR REMAINED THE SAME DURING BUSH'S FIRST TERM
Idaho	78
North Dakota	77
Utah	77
Virginia	77
Arizona	76
Nevada	76
Alabama	75
Nebraska	75
Georgia	74
South Carolina	74
Louisiana	73
Montana	73
Oklahoma	73
Florida	72
New Hampshire	72
Colorado	71
Indiana	71
Kansas	71
Kentucky	71
Mississippi	71
North Carolina	71
Tennessee	71
Texas	71
West Virginia	71
Missouri	70
Arkansas	68
Ohio	66
U.S. At-Large	71

Source: Compiled by Matthew Cillian. All data come from the exit poll surveys conducted by Edison Media Research/Mitofsky International for the AP and television networks; the polls were then pulled from the *Washington Post* web site, http://www.washingtonpost.com/ wp-srv/politics/elections/2004/graphics/exitPolls_(state).html.

THE RED-STATE ISSUES:
WHY NOT THE WAR IN IRAQ?

The only red state where the war in Iraq was the most cited issue was New Hampshire, the next-door neighbor to Kerry's home state of Massachusetts. New Hampshire's residents much more closely resemble the residents of Massachusetts than those of the other red states. New Hampshire's voters are notoriously independent; 43% described themselves in the exit poll as neither a Democrat nor a Republican. The gap between conservative and liberal voters (30% vs. 21%) is narrower there than elsewhere. Historically, the state has voted Republican when tax issues dominate (Bush in 2000) but Democratic when foreign policy prevails. When Kerry rebuked the Bush administration for its handling of the war in Iraq, many New Hampshire voters, like those in nearby blue states, lined up behind Kerry. Exit poll data show that New Hampshire was the only red state with a higher-than-average proportion of its electorate opposed to going to war in Iraq. (See Table 5.)

TABLE 5

STATE	PERCENT OF ELECTORATE WHO DISAPPROVED SOMEWHAT OR STRONGLY TO GOING TO WAR IN IRAQ
New Hampshire	48
Colorado	45
Florida	45
Nevada	45
Virginia	45
Missouri	44
Montana	44

TABLE 5 continued

STATE	PERCENT OF ELECTORATE WHO DISAPPROVED SOMEWHAT OR STRONGLY TO GOING TO WAR IN IRAQ
Alaska	43
Arizona	43
Arkansas	43
North Carolina	43
Ohio	42
Tennessee	41
Georgia	40
Kentucky	40
Louisiana	40
South Carolina	40
Indiana	39
South Dakota	39
Mississippi	38
North Dakota	38
Alabama	37
Texas	36
West Virginia	36
Kansas	35
Nebraska	34
Oklahoma	33
Idaho	32
Wyoming	31
Utah	29
U.S. At-Large	46

Source: Compiled by Matthew Cillian. All data come from the exit poll surveys conducted by Edison Media Research/Mitofsky International for the AP and television networks; the polls were then pulled from the *Washington Post* web site, http://www.washingtonpost.com/wp-srv/politics/elections/2004/graphics/exitPolls_(state).html.

THE FINAL ANALYSIS: KERRY OUT-OF-SYNC FROM THE START

A national post-election survey by Gallup[46] underscored what exit polls taken in the red states on Election Day 2004 vividly portrayed:

> Kerry voters *"were most likely to cite Iraq, economic issues, dissatisfaction with Bush's job performance, overall dislike of Bush, and favoring Kerry's agendas as the reasons for their choices."*

> Bush voters *"were most likely to cite moral values, terrorism, satisfaction with Bush's job performance, leadership qualities, Iraq, dislike of Kerry and honesty and ethics as reasons for their vote."*

The election returns confirmed what many Democratic strategists had predicted from the beginning: converting red states to blue was going to be tough. It turned out to be an even tougher challenge than they had anticipated. It was particularly difficult in the South where Kerry and all five Democratic candidates for the five open U.S. Senate seats lost handily. As Doug Schoen, Bill Clinton's pollster said, "The entire South is gone ... an across the board rejection of the Democratic Party." [47]

Of the seven red states seen as the most likely Kerry converts way back in March 2004, only one came through on November 2—New Hampshire. While Kerry did slightly better than Gore in Nevada (+2%) and Ohio (+2%), he actually lost ground in the other four "likely competitive" red states (Missouri −1%, Arizona −1%, Florida −2%, and West Virginia −3%). Overall, he lost ground in 15 of the 29 red states and made no gains in another four.

The *Boston Globe*'s Peter Canellos captured the dynamics: "Through all the darkest moments of his presidency ... Bush's supporters in Southern and Western states remained loyal, restricting the competitive landscape for the 2004 election to a handful of swing states ... Election Day was another show of loyalty of 'red-state America' to the president it admires."[48]

Simply put, Kerry could not carry red-state America. He was out-of-sync with its voters, both on the issues they deemed most important and in the personal qualities they sought in their president.

There is no bigger challenge to the Democratic Party than to figure out a way to capture the hearts and minds of at least a portion of red-state America. The urgency is palpable. A Census list, released in December 2004, showed the 10 fastest growing states were mostly in the West and the South.[49] A hypothetical reapportionment based on those numbers "would result in a continuing flow of congressional [and Electoral College] power to the Sun Belt. All four states that would gain House seats are in the South or West [all red states], while all four that would lose are in the East or Midwest."[50]

Democratic leaders have begun rethinking strategy and tactics. Donna Brazile, Gore's campaign manager in 2000, urged the party to "evaluate our get-out-the-vote efforts, not only in the so-called battleground states but in key House and Senate races outside those swing states. ... We can no longer rely on union members and black churches to get voters to the polls."[51]

Political observers recommend recasting the issues for greater appeal to middle America. On the cultural front, "... Democratic leaders don't need to carry guns to church services and shoot grizzlies on the way" said one *New York Times* op-ed columnist. "But a starting point would be to shed their inhibitions about talking about faith, and to work more with religious groups. Otherwise, the Democratic Party's efforts to improve the lives of working-class Americans in the long run will be blocked by the very people the Democrats aim to help."[52]

On terrorism, some Democratic leaders urge rejection of the party's anti-war wing: "We must leave no doubt that Michael Moore [*Fahrenheit 9-11* director] neither represents, nor defines our party."[53] Others argue that terrorism can be contained and reduced without resorting to preemptive war. The Republican approach, said former U.S. Rep. Martin Frost of Texas, "is not only irresponsible, it is dangerous."[54] (But then again, Frost lost in a red state!)

Given Kerry's poor showing, some Democratic Party leaders have begun looking around for the next candidate. But this could be a mistake, said David Gergen, director of the Center for Public Leadership in the Kennedy School of Government at Harvard. He believes it far more important to focus first on the party's ideas and principles and then find someone to carry their banner: "The Democrats have got some soul-searching to do about what they believe in."[55]

He points to the facts: the Democrats "haven't won a majority of the white vote since 1964. They haven't won 50% of the national vote since 1976. And in the last six congressional elections—starting with 1994—they haven't cracked 48.5 percent of the national vote. This is a party that needs to have some deep rethinking—not simply go out and turn a few dials."[56]

If Gergen's right, Democrats must grapple with more than which red states to target and whether to move toward the middle or the right on the issues. Otherwise, they may find the 2008 election an even steeper hill to climb.

Susan MacManus is a professor of politics at the University of South Florida, Tampa.

NOTES

1. And in some of those, the size of his gains was primarily due to the poor race run by Nader in 2004 compared to 2000.

2. Of the remainder, eight are in the West, seven in the Midwest, and one in the Northeast.

3. Florida (2), Texas (2), Georgia (2), North Carolina (1), Louisiana (1) each gained Electoral College votes. Only Mississippi and Oklahoma lost votes—1 each. Overall, the red states gained 7 Electoral College votes as a consequence of reapportionment before the election even began.

4. Western red states that gained Electoral College votes were: Arizona (2), Colorado (1), and Nevada (1).

5. Charles Pope, "Democrats Face a Steep Hill in the New South," *Seattle Post-Intelligencer*, January 31, 2004; http://seattlepi.nwsource.com/printer2/index.asp?ploc=t&refer=http://seattlepi.newsource.com/ national, accessed December 21, 2004.

6. Ronald Brownstein, "Democrats' Losses Go Far Beyond One Defeat," *Los Angeles Times*, November 4, 2004.

7. To make matters worse, Bush reduced the Democratic margin in 13 of the 20 blue states Gore won in 2000. And Bush *won* two of those blue states in 2004—New Mexico and Iowa. Only in Vermont did Kerry actually win bigger than did Gore in 2000. See Louis Jacobson, "Is the Red-Blue Divide Growing or Narrowing?" *Roll Call*, November 8, 2004.

8. Elisabeth Bumiller, "Turnout Effort and Kerry, Too, Were G.O.P.'s Keys to Victory," *New York Times*, November 4, 2004.

9. From Associated Press, "Kerry Assures Democratic Colleagues He'll Compete in South," posted on www.cnn.com/2003/ALLPOLITICS/03/27/kerry.ap, March 27, 2003.

10. Ibid.

11. Wire Reports, "As Bush Launches Campaign, Focus Turns to Key 2000 States," March 4, 2004. Accessed at www.eagletribune.com/news/stories/20040304/FP_005.htm, December 22, 2004.

12. In the end, Edwards did little to help in the South, losing even his native state of South Carolina, which he had carried in the Democratic presidential primary, and his home state of North Carolina.

13. North Carolina is in the group of occasional visits (defined as 1–10 visits). Nine of the ten visits to the state were from the Edwardses, who live there.

14. National polls repeatedly showed that Americans in general viewed Ms. Bush more favorably than Ms. Kerry.

15. Judy Keen and Richard Benedetto, "Laura Bush Raises Her Voice (a Bit)," *USA Today*, June 29, 2004.

16. Chuck Todd, "A Provisional Post-Mortem," *National Journal*, November 3, 2004.

17. Republicans won the registration game in Florida as well, having registered more voters since 2000 than the Democrats. It was only through the frenzied registration efforts of 527 groups like MoveOn.org and America Coming Together that Florida Democrats nearly caught up with the Republicans in numbers registered since the 2000 election.

18. Overall, the 2004 presidential election was the first in modern history with an equal turnout of Democrats and Republicans. Elisabeth Bumiller, "Turnout Effort and Kerry, Too, Were G.O.P.'s Keys to Victory," *New York Times*, November 4, 2004.

19. Jim Kane quoted in Laura Parker, "Democrats Fail to Get More of Their Voters Out," *USA Today*, November 4, 2004. For a similar account of the GOP volunteer strategy's success in Ohio, see Paul Farhi and James V. Grimaldi, "GOP Won With Accent on Rural and Traditional," *Washington Post*, November 4, 2004, p. A01.

20. Peggy Noonan, "So Much to Savor," *Wall Street Journal*, November 4, 2004.

21. Thomas B. Edsall and James V. Grimaldi, *Washington Post*, December 30, 2004, p. A01.

22. Ibid.

23. Ibid.

24. An analysis of voting patterns in Congress in 2003 by *National Journal* rated Kerry more liberal than Kennedy.

25. Respondents to the exit poll were asked: Which ONE issue mattered most in deciding how you voted for president? (Check only one): Health Care, Moral Values, Economy/Jobs, Terrorism, Iraq, Education, or Taxes?

26. Arkansas, Georgia, Kentucky, Mississippi, Montana, North Dakota, Ohio, Oklahoma, and Utah. The other two were blue states (Michigan and Oregon).

27. At a July fund-raiser in New York City, Kerry referred to anti-Bush celebrities, some of whom had called the president a liar or a thug, as "the heart and soul of America."

28. Steven Thomma, "Election Reveals America Leans Moderate to Conservative," *Miami Herald*, November 4, 2004.

29. Poll conducted by the Pew Forum on Religion and Public Life. Cited in Dana Milbank, "For The President, A Vote of Full Faith and Credit," *Washington Post*, November 7, 2004, p. A07.

30. Some, like Carroll Doherty, a pollster for the Pew Research Center, call it the "observance gap." See Jim Remsen, "Bush Overwhelmingly Captures Catholic Vote," *Philadelphia Inquirer*, November 7, 2004.

31. Terry Eastland, "The Moral Majority," *Wall Street Journal*, November 5, 2004, p. W17. It may have been the most critical in Ohio where an estimated 54,000 new voters registered to vote for traditional marriage (David Broder, "Perspective: The Democratic Process Has Spoken," *Washington Post*, November 5, 2004.)

32. Columnist Suzanne Fields, "Why America Chose Bush," *Washington Times,* November 5, 2004.

33. Married women with kids were also quite concerned about terrorism; they were the "security moms."

34. Cf. Michael Gonzalez, "Hispanics For Jorge," *Wall Street Journal*, November 8, 2004, p. A15.

35. David Broder, "Perspective: The Democratic Process Has Spoken," *Washington Post*, November 5, 2004.

36. The first ad initially ran in three states (Ohio, West Virginia, and Wisconsin) but ended up running in many more when the attention it received drew in $7.5 million in contributions over the Internet and $2 million from direct mail. The group raised money from more than 100,000 individual donors from all 50 states. In the final three weeks of the campaign, the Swift Boat Veterans for Truth spent $6.3 million on TV advertising, much of it in Ohio. See Tyler Whitley, "Group Glories in Kerry's Defeat," *Richmond Times-Dispatch*, November 8, 2004; and Eliza Newlin Carney, "The 527 Phenomenon: Big Bucks for Upstarts," NationalJournal.com, December 13, 2004. The ads accomplished what they had set out to do: They undermined Kerry's "positioning vis-à-vis President Bush on key issues such as handling the War in Iraq, the War on Terrorism, National Defense, and who is perceived as a 'strong leader.'" Fabrizio McLaughlin & Associates, "Public Release of Battleground States Survey Results: 'Swift Boat Veterans for Truth' Attacks More Than Just Flesh Wounds for Kerry," August 23, 2004, p. 2.

37. Michael Janofsky, "Advocacy Groups Spent Record Amount on 2004 Election," *New York Times*, December 17, 2004.

38. http://www.washtimes.com/national/inpolitics.htm, accessed December 17, 2004.

39. There were also open U.S. Senate seats in North Carolina and Georgia, but they were less competitive and were in states where terrorism was not ranked as the No. 1 issue.

40. Respondents to the exit poll were asked: "Which ONE candidate quality mattered most in deciding how you voted for president? (Check only one): He has clear stands on the issues; He will bring about needed change; He is intelligent; He is a strong leader; He is honest and trustworthy; He has strong religious faith; or He cares about people like me."

41. Jill Lawrence, "Campaign Hindsight is also 20/20," *USA Today*, November 4, 2004.

42. "Issue: Jobs," *Online News Hour*, the web site of "The NewsHour with Jim Lehrer," http://www.pbs.org/newshour/vote2004/issues/issue_jobs.html, accessed December 30, 2004.

43. Organizations labeled "527s" got the name from the section of the IRS tax code that regulates them. It gives the organizations the authority to raise unlimited sums of money outside the campaign-donations restrictions laid out in the McCain-Feingold Act.

44. *National Journal*, "Poll Track," November 4, 2004.

45. Floyd Norris, *New York Times* News Service, "Election 2004: Economy Was Not Major Issue for Most Voters," *Naples Daily News*, November 4, 2004.

46. Jeffrey M. Jones, "Different Influences Found for Bush, Kerry Voters," The Gallup Organization, December 16, 2004, p. 2.

47. Kathy Kiely and Mimi Hall, "Losses Leave Dems Pondering the Future," *USA Today*, November 4, 2004, p. 6A.

48. Peter S. Canellos, "Win Shows 'Red States' on the Rise," *Boston Globe*, November 4, 2004.

49. The Associated Press, "Open States of West and South Lead in Growth of Population," posted on *New York Times* web site, December 22, 2004.

50. It would result in a net gain of two for the red states. Red-state gainers: Arizona, Florida, Texas, and Utah—one seat each; red-state losers: Iowa and Ohio—one seat each; blue-state losers: New York and Pennsylvania. G. Scott Thomas, American City Business Journals, "GOP-Leaning States to Gain Seats in Congress," posted on MSNBC.com, December 22, 2004.

51. Donna L. Brazile, "In Rebuilding Party, Democrats Need to Start from Scratch," *Roll Call*, November 4, 2004.

52. Nicholas D. Kristof, "Living Poor, Voting Rich," *New York Times*, November 3, 2004.

53. Democratic Leadership Council founder Al From and President Bruce Reed, quoted in Donald Lambro, "Some Democrats blame the Liberals," *Washington Times*, www.americasnewspaper.com/middle.shtml, accessed December 31, 2004.

54. Martin Frost, quoted in Donald Lambro, "Some Democrats blame the Liberals," *Washington Times*, www.americasnewspaper.com/middle.shtml, accessed December 31, 2004.

55. David Gergen, quoted in Jann S. Wenner, "Why Bush Won: A Look at the Numbers, What They Really Mean and What Happens Next," *Rolling Stone,* posted November 17, 2004, www.rollingstone.com/politics/story/_/id/6635544?rnd=1104513296437&has-player=false.

56. Ibid.

CHAPTER SEVEN

Swift Boats and Tax Hikes: Campaign Advertising in the 2004 Election

Paul Freedman

DEPARTMENT OF POLITICS, UNIVERSITY OF VIRGINIA

Campaign 2004 was, like all presidential election campaign bat-tles, fought on two fronts: in the air and on the ground. The ground war was particularly intense in 2004, with unprecedented efforts to mobilize old and new voters alike, undertaken by parties and independent groups drawing on new technologies and sophisticated databases (Bai 2004, 2004a). In the end, these efforts paid off hand-somely, as voter turnout was up significantly over 2000 with an esti-mated 60 percent of eligible voters casting a ballot (McDonald 2004).

But it was in the air that the most important battles for the hearts and minds of American voters were fought. The air war in 2004 started early, was especially hard-fought, and brought to the fore some of the most important themes and messages of the cam-paign (in spots that often recalled some of the most memorable ads in recent presidential history). The air war of 2004 also highlighted the role played by independent organizations known as "527" groups (after the controlling section of the U.S. tax code). In the end, the efforts of one such group, the Swift Boat Veterans for Truth, may have had a decisive impact on the outcome of the race.

THE AIR WAR

The 2004 presidential election was the most expensive in history: A record $2.2 billion was spent by the candidates, parties, and independent groups, and the spending was relatively evenly matched: President Bush and his supporters outspent the Kerry forces by only $60 million, $1.14 billion to $1.08 billion (Edsall and Grimaldi 2004). Of this, an estimated $1.6 billion was spent on television advertising, more than double estimates for the 2000 election (Memmott and Drinkard 2004). The general election air war started unusually early.[1] On March 4, just after it became clear that Senator John Kerry would be the Democratic nominee, the Bush campaign launched a series of positive ads that focused on themes of leadership, strength, and values. "What sees us through tough times?" asks the voice-over in "Tested," "Freedom, faith, families and sacrifice." The ad concludes, "President Bush: steady leadership in times of change."[2] A second spot, "Safer, Stronger" (which also appeared in a Spanish-language version) featured video of firefighters pulling a flag-draped body from the rubble at the World Trade Center after the September 11 attacks. (It was sharply criticized by some families of 9/11 victims who protested what they saw as the exploitation of personal tragedy for political purposes.)

Bush's third ad was an upbeat, 60-second spot called "Lead"

that featured the President, First Lady, and images of a strong and prosperous America reminiscent of Ronald Reagan's classic 1984 "Morning in America" re-election ad.

If the President's campaign started out with a positive message, it didn't stay with it for long. By the end of the month he had run a spot entitled "100 Days," claiming that if elected, John Kerry would raise taxes by $900 billion in his first 100 days in office, and would weaken America. "John Kerry," the ad concludes, "Wrong on taxes. Wrong on defense." A second spot, "Wacky," suggested that Kerry supported a fifty-cent per gallon gas tax. "If Kerry's gas tax increase were law," the ad suggested, "the average family would pay $657 more a year." The ad concluded by implying that Kerry was an out-of-touch elitist: "Maybe John Kerry just doesn't understand what his ideas mean to the rest of us."

Throughout the campaign, Bush's ads sought to portray the President as a strong, resolute leader in times of crisis, while painting John Kerry as out of touch and inconsistent. In a spot that recalled the famous Dukakis tank ad of 1988 (in which the Massachusetts Governor was pictured riding around in a tank while an announcer listed the weapons systems he had opposed), the Bush campaign released a spot in late September that featured actual footage of John Kerry windsurfing. The text says it all:

In which direction would John Kerry lead? Kerry voted for the Iraq war, opposed it, supported it and now opposes it again. He bragged about voting for the $87 billion to support our troops before he voted against it. He voted for education reform and now opposes it. He claims he's against increasing Medicare premiums, but voted five times to do so.

John Kerry. Whichever way the wind blows.

For his part, John Kerry was forced to begin his general election advertising by responding to Bush's charges. His first spot, "Misleading America" began by stating that "John Kerry has never called for a 900 billion dollar tax increase," and asked, "Doesn't America deserve more from its president than misleading negative ads?" Toward the end of the month, Kerry made a more proactive appeal, emphasizing what would become the central themes of his campaign: "John Kerry," the ad concluded. "The military experience to defend America. A new plan to create jobs and put our economy back on track."

In early May, Kerry launched a three-week, $25 million campaign to "reintroduce" himself with a pair of 60-second biographic spots to be broadcast in 19 "battleground" states. The ads, "Lifetime" and "Heart," featured testimony from veterans who served with him in Vietnam and, in one of the spots, from Vanessa and Teresa Heinz Kerry. Both ads closed with the same simple message: "A lifetime of service and strength. John Kerry for president."

This is by no means to imply that Kerry's ads didn't also accentuate the negative. On health care, on the economy, on Iraq, Kerry could be just as hard-hitting, just as direct as Bush. "How out of touch is George Bush with Ohio?" asked one ad. Another began, "We see it for ourselves: the mess in Iraq created by George Bush. Over 1,000 U.S. soldiers killed. Kidnappings. Americans held hostage. Bush sees nothing wrong. It's time for a fresh start."

But if the candidates could get down and dirty, the real negative heavy lifting in 2004 was taken on by the 527s. Groups like MoveOn.org, the Media Fund, and the Progress for America Voter Fund produced serious (although occasionally humorous) attacks on both candidates. One Progress for America spot featured images of Osama bin Laden and Mohammed Atta and asked, "Would you trust Kerry against these fanatic killers?" It was compared to 1988's "Willie Horton" ad by FactCheck.org. (Kerry fired back with an ad of his own stating, "It's time to stop dividing America and stop playing politics with the war on terror.")

But without a doubt, the most important 527 organization was made up of a group of veterans who claimed to be standing up for the truth.

SWIFT BOAT VETERANS FOR TRUTH

On August 5, less than a week after a Democratic Convention that had highlighted John Kerry's heroic Vietnam war record, a little-known 527 group called Swift Boat Veterans for Truth aired a 60-second spot challenging Kerry's war story. The initial ad buy was a relatively small bomb—only $550,000 to air the ad in a handful of media markets—but the explosion was huge. The ad, entitled, "Any Questions?" pulled no punches. It featured veterans who claimed to have served with Kerry in Vietnam, accusing the candidate of lying about his war record, of having illegitimately received his Bronze Star and one Purple Heart, and having "betrayed the men and women he served with in Vietnam." "He dishonored his country," concludes one veteran, "he most certainly did." (See Appendix for full text).

Reaction to the Swift Boat ad was, well, swift. Within days, significant numbers of Americans had seen the ad—which was replayed regularly on cable news channels—or had heard about it on talk radio. The National Annenberg Election Study (NAES) at the University of Pennsylvania interviewed 2,209 Americans between August 9 and August 16, and found that, despite the relatively modest initial ad buy, a third of respondents (33 percent) had seen the spot and another 24 percent had heard something about it within the first two weeks of the initial broadcast (NAES 2004). Among heavy cable news viewers (those watching five to seven days a week), a full 48 percent reported having seen the ad.[3]

In the face of these charges, many of which were effectively debunked in the media (FactCheck.org 2004c) John Kerry was strangely silent. His campaign did not fire back with an ad challenging the attacks, nor did he address the Swift Boat charges directly for a full two weeks. Finally, on August 19, Kerry told a gathering of firefighters in Boston, "more than thirty years ago, I learned an important lesson—when you're under attack, the best thing to do is turn your boat into the attacker. That's what I intend to do today. Over the last week or so," Kerry explained, "a group called Swift Boat Veterans for Truth has been attacking me. Of course, this group isn't interested in the truth—and they're not telling the truth." Kerry went on to call the group "a front for the Bush campaign. And the fact that the President won't denounce what they're up to tells you everything you need to know—he wants them to do his dirty work." (Kerry 2004).[4]

It was arguably too little too late. The NAES study found that 46 percent of the ad's viewers found its claims "very" or "somewhat" believable (NAES 2004), and by August 19, the day of Kerry's address to the firefighters, thirty percent of Americans believed that the candidate "did not earn" all of his war medals (NAES 2004a). Moreover, the very next day, on August 20, the Swift Boat Veterans fired back with a new 60-second ad. This spot, entitled "Sellout" featured John Kerry's 1971 testimony before the

United States Senate. Because it used Kerry's own words, in his own voice, the ad was most likely more believable and more effective in portraying Kerry as having betrayed his fellow soldiers after, if not during, the war. Along with several other ads sponsored by Swift Boat Veterans for Truth that aired on national cable and in selected markets through September, these ads likely reinforced doubts that already existed about Kerry's record, and forced the candidate into a defensive posture during the critical period between the Democratic and Republican conventions.

THE IMPACT OF ADVERTISING IN 2004

What effect, if any, might campaign advertising have had on voters in the 2004 election? Recent scholarship suggests that campaign ads can play an important role in creating an informed electorate. A recent study of the 2000 election showed that ads served as "information supplements" for citizens: People who saw more ads in 2000 were, all else equal, more informed about the candidates and their policy positions (Freedman, Franz and Goldstein 2004). But the 2004 election suggests that campaign advertising has the potential to mislead, as well as inform. If voters learn from ads, are they learning the wrong lessons?

The National Annenberg Election Study interviewed 1,026 adults between April 15 and May 2, 2004 (NAES 2004b). These respondents lived in the 18 "battleground" states in which the Bush and Kerry campaigns had been advertising most heavily.[5] NAES presented respondents with a series of statements appearing in Bush and Kerry ads and identified by FactCheck.org (their fellow Annenberg organization) as being substantially false or misleading.[6] For example, FactCheck.org found that a Kerry ad released April 1 entitled "10 Million Jobs" falsely claimed that the President said that sending jobs overseas "makes sense" for America. The same day, the Bush campaign released an ad entitled "Troubling" which asserted that Kerry had supported higher taxes "over 350 times" and repeated the charge that his tax plan would "raise taxes by at least $900 billion."

All three statements, FactCheck.org found, were false or misleading. The President had never made the statement attributed to him by the Kerry ad (FactCheck.org 2004) and "the 350-vote figure is so off base that it actually counts some Kerry votes for tax cuts as votes for 'higher taxes.'" (FactCheck.org 2004a, 2004b). Still, the Annenberg survey found that 61 percent of respondents in the 18 battleground states believed that the President "favors sending American jobs overseas," and 56 percent believed that Kerry had "voted for higher taxes 350 times." People were more skeptical about the alleged $900 billion tax increase: only 34 percent thought the claim by Bush was "definitely true" or "probably true." But a full 72 percent accepted as true a Kerry ad claim (similarly criticized as misleading by FactCheck.org) that 3 million jobs had been lost during the Bush presidency (NAES 2004).

Annenberg found intriguing, if not surprising, partisan patterns in credulousness, with Democrats and Republicans each more likely to believe claims made by their own candidate. Sixty-five percent of Democrats in battleground states but only 36 percent of Republicans (and 55 percent of Independents) believed that Bush favored sending American jobs overseas, for example. Conversely, 60 percent of Republicans but only 44 percent of Democrats (and 53 percent of Independents) believed that Kerry had voted to raise taxes 350 times.

There are, of course, a number of important caveats to keep in mind. The NAES study includes no measure of actual ad exposure, and no comparison group. Instead, it is a general-population survey of voters in states (not markets) where advertising was relatively heavy. The results are suggestive, not conclusive, that citizens can learn—or "mislearn"—from campaign ads, and that if ads can inform and clarify they can also obfuscate.

Beyond learning, a second—and for the candidates, more important—potential effect of campaign advertising is *persuasion*: To what extent did campaign ads in 2004 affect the horse race? Demonstrating the independent effect of any one communication stream in the context of an election campaign is notoriously difficult. Isolating the impact of campaign ads from that of speeches, appearances, debates, and media coverage is extremely challenging, to say the least. Nevertheless, the general dynamics of campaign 2004 suggest that advertising may have played at least some role in shaping the horse race. As seen in Figure 1, which reports Gallup data from early March to the end of October, the Bush-Kerry contest was relatively tight for much of the campaign. Bush gained a slight advantage after launching his first round of ads in early March, but the race remained roughly even (with Bush enjoying a slight advantage) until the beginning of May, when Kerry launched his own ad blitz, ushering in a period in which Kerry enjoyed a modest advantage through the beginning of July when, after announcing Edwards as his vice-presidential pick, his lead expanded to eight points (with Kerry hitting the 50 percent mark, the first time for either candidate).

Kerry was unable to build on his lead coming out of the Democratic Convention in Boston. Although Kerry did see improvements

FIGURE 1
2004 Presidential Horse Race

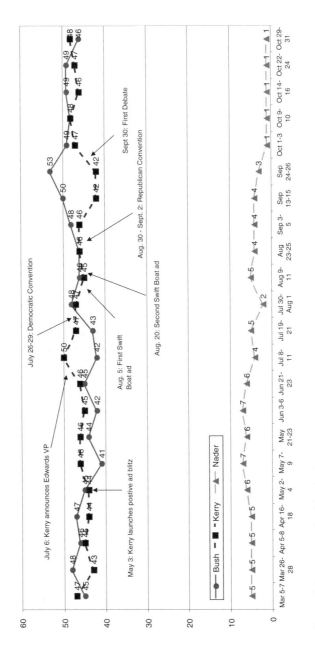

Source: Gallup surveys of registered voters.

with respect to evaluations of him as a candidate along a range of issues, it was essentially an "invisible bounce" that did not translate into a horse-race advantage. Moreover, the month of August was dominated by the Swift Boat controversy, which effectively denied Kerry any upward movement in the polls (arguably undermining the strength of his support among key groups while galvanizing his opponents). The result was that Bush was well-positioned to come out of the Republican Convention in New York with a spring in his step and a bounce in his numbers, enjoying an advantage that continued to grow until the first presidential debate.

Once again, it is not clear that advertising made a decisive difference—or even any difference at all. But the horse-race data are consistent with the claim that the Swift Boat controversy effectively held Kerry back and kept him bogged down during a critical period when he could have otherwise been making his case and building support.

The ad war in 2004 started early, stayed intense, and reflected the most important themes and messages of the campaign. To understand the fundamental dynamics of modern presidential elections, scholars and citizens alike must look to the air.

Paul Freedman is an Associate Professor of Politics at the University of Virginia.

REFERENCES

Bai, Matt. 2004. "The Multilevel Marketing of the President." *New York Times Magazine*. April 24, p.43.

Bai, Matt. 2004a. "Who Lost Ohio?" *New York Times Magazine*. November 21, p.67.

CNN Special Report: America Votes 2004, Campaign Ads. http://www.cnn.com/ELECTION/ 2004/special/president/campaign.ads/ (accessed February 8, 2005).

Edsall, Thomas B. and James V. Grimaldi. 2004. "On Nov. 2, GOP Got More Bang for its Billion, Analysis Shows." *Washington Post*, December 30, p.A1.

FactCheck.org. 2004. "Outsourcing Jobs: The PRESIDENT said that?" April 3. http://www.factcheck.org/ article168.html (accessed February 8, 2005).

____2004a. "Bush Accuses Kerry of 350 Votes for 'Higher Taxes.' Higher than What?" March 24. http://www.factcheck.org/article159.html (accessed February 8, 2005).

____2004b. "Bush Ad Is "Troubling Indeed." April 7. http://www.factcheck.org/article167.html (accessed February 8, 2005).

____2004c. "Republican-funded Group Attacks Kerry's War Record." August 22. http:// www.factcheck.org/article231.html (accessed February 8, 2005).

Freedman, Paul, Michael Franz and Kenneth M. Goldstein. 2004. "Campaign Advertising and Democratic Citizenship." *American Journal of Political Science* 48(4):723–41.

Katz, Adam (with Amanda Fuchs). 2004. "The Road to the Presidency: A Timeline of the 2004 Presidential Campaign." Institute of Politics, Kennedy School of Government, Harvard University.

Kerry, John. 2004. "Speech to the International Association of Fire Fighters." Boston, August 19. http://www.johnkerry.com/pressroom/speeches/spc_2004_0819.html (accessed February 8, 2005).

McDonald, Michael P. 2004. "Up, Up and Away! Voter Participation in the 2004 Presidential Election." *The Forum*. 2(4). http://www.bepress.com/forum/vol2/iss4/art4/ (accessed February 8, 2005).

Memmott, Mark and Jim Drinkard. 2004. "Election Ad Battle Smashes Record in 2004." *USA Today*. November 26, 2004.

National Annenberg Election Study. 2004. "Cable and Talk Radio Boost Public Awareness of Swift Boat Ad." August 20. http://www.annenbergpublicpolicycenter.org/naes/2004_03_swiftboat-ad_ 08-20_pr.pdf (accessed February 8, 2005).

____2004a. "Pluralities of Public, Independents Believe Bush Campaign Is Behind Swift Boat Veterans' Ads." August 27. http://www.annenbergpublicpolicycenter.org/naes/2004_03_Kerry-Vietnam_ 08-27_pr.pdf (accessed February 8, 2005).

____2004b. "Americans Say They Don't Learn from Ads But They Believe Strained Campaign Ads Anyway." May 12. http://www.annenbergpublicpolicycenter.org/naes/2004_03_%20kerry-and-bush_ 05-12_pr.pdf (accessed February 8, 2005).

National Journal, "Ad Spotlight." http://nationaljournal.com/members/adspotlight/.

APPENDIX

Text of Swift Boat Veterans for Truth "Any Questions?" Ad

John Edwards: "If you have any questions about what John Kerry is made of, just spend 3 minutes with the men who served with him."

(On screen: Here's what those men think of John Kerry)

Al French: I served with John Kerry.

Bob Elder: I served with John Kerry.

George Elliott: John Kerry has not been honest about what happened in Vietnam.

Al French: He is lying about his record.

Louis Letson: I know John Kerry is lying about his first Purple Heart because I treated him for that injury.

Van O'Dell: John Kerry lied to get his bronze star...I know, I was there, I saw what happened.

Jack Chenoweth: His account of what happened and what actually happened are the difference between night and day.

Admiral Hoffman: John Kerry has not been honest.

Adrian Lonsdale: And he lacks the capacity to lead.

Larry Thurlow: When the chips were down, you could not count on John Kerry.

Bob Elder: John Kerry is no war hero.

Grant Hibbard: He betrayed all his shipmates...he lied before the Senate.

Shelton White: John Kerry betrayed the men and women he served with in Vietnam.

Joe Ponder: He dishonored his country...he most certainly did.

Bob Hildreth: I served with John Kerry...

Bob Hildreth (off camera): John Kerry cannot be trusted.

Source: FactCheck.org (2004c)

NOTES

1. For an unusually detailed timeline of the 2004 campaign, see Katz (2004).

2. Text of ads taken from *National Journal*'s "Ad Spotlight."

3. Even among people who never watched cable news, more than a fifth (22 percent) recalled having seen the ad, further evidence of its reach.

4. In fact, media accounts documented the links between the Republican fundraisers and the Swift Boat Veterans, and on August 25, Ben Ginsberg, a legal advisor to the Bush campaign, resigned after it was revealed that he had provided legal counsel to the Swift Boat group (FactCheck.org 2004c, Katz 2004).

5. The states included Arizona, Arkansas, Delaware, Florida, Iowa, Maine, Michigan, Missouri, Minnesota, Nevada, New Hampshire, New Mexico, Ohio, Oregon, Pennsylvania, Washington, West Virginia, and Wisconsin.

6. Many of the charges made in ads on both sides in 2004 were misleading—or downright false—and 2004 was the year in which ad watches became front-page news. Perhaps the most prominent ad-watching organization was FactCheck.org, based at the Annenberg Public Policy Center at the University of Pennsylvania. Propelled by a public mention by Dick Cheney during the vice-presidential debate (unfortunately he got the URL wrong, referring to "FactCheck.com") the web site was inundated with visitors and media attention.

CHAPTER EIGHT

A New Media

Vaughn Ververs
THE HOTLINE

For all the stories, events and trends that impacted the 2004 presidential election, the media itself has to rank near the top. Perhaps like never ever before, the press became an issue in the race and impacted it in critical ways at critical times. And the fallout will certainly change the way in which the fourth estates interact with politics for many years to come.

The mainstream media—consisting largely of the television networks, news magazines and major daily papers—has long helped to set the agenda and backdrop of campaigns. Its focus on one issue or event over another can dominate long periods of a cycle and push other issues to the background. And the narratives they create can color both the election and its aftermath. We remember Willie Horton and patriotism from the 1988 campaign. In 1992, it was the "desire for change." Before the recount that defined 2000, it was earth tones, alpha males and DUI's.

Losing campaigns tend to decry the lack of focus on what they

179

see as the real issues (the ones that may have benefited them). Partisans cry "bias" and find insidious connections that worked against them or blame the press for shallowness or laziness. Members of the media gather at conferences or roundtables to echo those calls, gaze into their own navels and emerge with pledges to correct their mistakes the next time.

But years of these exercises have now combined with an explosion of technology, a non-stop news cycle and increasing partisan divides within the press itself to turn the old media order upside down. The mainstream has splintered into tributaries, each with a current of its own. They may flow in the same general direction, but how a certain story is covered by the likes of the *New York Times* or NBC News can be quite different than how it's played on the Fox News Channel or the Internet.

Bloggers, talk radio and cable news now maintain a never-ending flow of news and commentary. With such a full menu of choices, news consumers and voters are increasingly choosing to get their information from outlets they feel comfortable or in-tune with. And the differences, even when nuanced, in how stories are played from one outlet to another only bolsters charges of bias and make the media itself an issue.

CAMPAIGN INTERRUPTED

While 2004 marked the end of the mainstream media era in some ways, old trends die hard, something that was clear in the early part of the year. Having struggled to define the Democratic field throughout 2003, that year ended with a consensus narrative and

Howard Dean was declared the clear frontrunner. The designation was not off base. Dean had raised more money than any other previous Democratic candidate in the year prior to the election (a distinction that had always before predicted the nominee), he seemingly had set the grassroots on fire, and he had double-digit leads in Iowa and New Hampshire.

All that set the stage for a classic feeding frenzy by the media, and the first example of how the press impacted the campaign. Having been the prohibitive favorite just days earlier, Dean's third-place finish in the Iowa caucuses was a bruising defeat. Addressing his supporters that night, Dean tried to rally the troops with a throaty admonition that became known as the "Dean scream."

Anyone who paid any attention whatsoever to the campaign is familiar with the episode, having seen or heard it ad nauseam on cable TV and radio for months afterwards. For those in the room at the time, Dean's performance wasn't even noticed. The loud crowd made it necessary for the candidate to project. But to anyone else, and that included most of the media, who watched it on television, Dean came across as a ranting madman not fit for the presidency.

In retrospect, popular history has decided that "the scream" cost Dean the nomination. In reality, his disappointing finish in the caucuses (which came before the scream) was the real trouble. The "scream"—and its constant refrain in the media—did not finish his candidacy, but it made it impossible for him to ever mount a comeback in subsequent contests. What perhaps was one of the final great examples of the media's feeding frenzy soon gave way to an ever-widening divide within the media itself.

SETTING THE STAGE

Even before John Kerry had a lock on the nomination, the media's forces were at work attempting to set up the narrative for the campaign. Only this time, there were two competing narratives to choose from. Not unlike the president's own declaration, the press was either with the administration or against it.

For months leading up to the invasion of Iraq in the spring of 2003, the press as a whole was, if not entirely supportive of the goals, at least excited about the prospect of going to war. The Pentagon's unprecedented "embed" program had put visions of glory—and ratings—into the heads of executives, anchors and reporters who dreamt of previously unheard-of access and coverage. Those feelings lasted throughout the initial invasion and when Saddam Hussein's statue fell on live TV, it appeared to be justified. But as 2003 dragged on, the initial euphoria turned sour, at least among the tradition media.

As it became increasingly apparent that the primary justification for war—Iraq's possession of weapons of mass destruction—was flawed, the mainstream media's initial excitement turned sour. The prison scandal, the continuing violence and the growing body count caused many to turn away. The *New York Times* issued an apology for even tacitly supporting the war and it was followed in an aggressive manner by other organizations that felt betrayed and were determined to make it up in their coverage.

By the time of the New Hampshire primary, many in the media had turned sour on the campaign in Iraq. The pictures had turned from those initial glorious days to a seemingly unending flow of horror. Escalating casualties gave way to the Abu Ghraib prison scandal. And suddenly, there were two very different ways of looking at this war.

On the one side were the networks, ABC, CBS and NBC, joined by the coverage in the *New York Times, Washington Post, Los Angeles Times* and many more. These outlets would daily document the failures of the administration and its policy. On the other side, suddenly nearly equal in reach, could be found the Fox News Channel, talk radio, Internet news sites and a smattering of local outlets. The lines were drawn, a division which set the stage for the campaign.

SWIFT, YET SLOW

A final division occurred just after the Democratic convention when the Swift Boat Veterans for Truth surfaced as the biggest non-reported influence in modern political history. This low-funded ad campaign, designed to refute Kerry's war-hero status using fellow veterans, at first appeared to be a drop in the bucket in the midst of the most expensive campaign in American history. In the final analysis, even Democratic partisans admit it had a devastating effect.

The Swift Boat effort kicked off with a relatively modest-sized ad buy in swing states and was bolstered by the release of a book detailing the veterans' complaints about the accepted claims of Kerry's service. Hardly any of the old mainstream news organizations provided coverage of the claims. The *Times* and the *Post* may have ignored them, but they became a firestorm nonetheless.

What couldn't be found in the traditional news suddenly was the only topic addressed everywhere else. On talk radio—from Rush Limbaugh and Sean Hannity to hundreds of imitators—to the Fox News Channel, Internet weblogs and even CNN and MSNBC. The

Swift Boaters became the elephant in the room, ignored by the powers-that-be but talked about by the masses. For the first time, the agenda was set not by the traditional media, but by the new media.

In nearly every post-election recap, the Swift Boaters come up as one of the deciding factors of the election. Many, if not most, continue to cast doubt about the authenticity of their claims. That is for others to decide. But there is no doubt that the ad campaign they launched, and the manner in which it was covered, marked a sea change in the way politics will be covered in this country for decades to come.

BIAS IS AS BIAS DOES

Although division has existed for years, the final blow to the monolithic media occurred in the fall of 2004, when CBS's "60 Minutes Wednesday" aired a report claiming that President Bush had gotten special treatment to get into the Texas Air National Guard and had not fulfilled his service once there. The story, based on apparently false or forged documents, would lead to the downfall of CBS News, once the epitome of mainstream media.

This was not only a tale of the downfall of a giant; this episode marked the end of an era. Since the invention of television and the proliferation of it into American homes, the three broadcast networks ruled the agenda. Once Walter Cronkite was the "most trusted man in America." Now his network—and his own successor, Dan Rather—have signaled the end of the reign of anchor-kings.

Beyond the documents in question, CBS's actions were telling on other levels. First, this story line was not new. Bush's acceptance into, and performance once in the National Guard, had been written about, talked about and insinuated about since the 2000 presidential campaign. On and off, various news organizations would raise the subject once again with some new question or vague document as if it proved the president's version wrong. The dogged pursuit of this line by CBS in and of itself was enough to convince Bush partisans that the network was out to get their man, as they suspected all along. Add to that the willingness to go forward with less-than-solid evidence and the suspicions became fact.

Second, the arrogance demonstrated by taking such a weak story to air demonstrated that the network was either out of touch with the current media landscape or simply ignorant of it. Within hours of the "60 Minutes" broadcast Internet bloggers had dissected the documents and raised enough questions about their authenticity (simply from what was presented on the air) to throw an entire network into a tailspin.

Finally, the timing of the broadcast, coming within several weeks of the election, led to few other explanations other than CBS and Rather were trying to affect the outcome of the election. Why else go to air with a story that the network now acknowledges had plenty of question marks? For decades now, even since Richard Nixon held the White House, Republicans have accused Rather and CBS of actively working against them. After this episode, could they be wrong?

CBS wasn't the only outlet where bias could be found, or at least seen. The Fox News Channel, since its inception openly suspected of conservative bias, had its own problems. FNC's chief political correspondent Carl Cameron filed a faux story on Kerry that made fun of the candidate's lifestyle by commenting on how well his fingernails looked. That report ended up being posted on the network's web site and proved to FNC's critics all they suspected and claimed in the first place. Meanwhile, ABC's political director circulated an internal memo leading many critics to believe he was advocating harsher coverage of the Bush campaign. Critics on both sides jumped and made more of these episodes than was probably deserved.

A NEW DAY

Weblogs, cable news and talk radio have inalterably transformed the face of today's media, especially where political matters are concerned. It's important to remember that this is not a landscape made overnight. It is one shaped by years of shifting winds and remains unstable today. But it is, perhaps, a more accurate reflection of the nation's sentiment than we have ever seen. Prior to so many outlets, so many sources of instant information and commentary, consensus was easy to find and it was found by the broadest common denominator. Society is segmented in so many ways today, the media was sure to follow, and 2004 marked the year in which it did.

How the media goes forward is much less predictable. In a world in which news consumers have such a wide menu of choices, will information now become a la carte, take-what-fits? Will conservatives rely on certain outlets, liberals on others, and everything in-between with still others? Will all sides devolve into a battle to discredit the rest?

Most importantly, what in the future will serve as the commonly accepted narrative? Which media outlets will be perceived as setting the stage for the debates and arguments of the day? Which will we look toward for what is news and what is posturing? Who will be the arbiter of the "truth?"

These are the questions left from the 2004 presidential election. Whether or not the Iraq war was right, whether or not one bought the accusations of the Swift Boat Veterans, regardless of whether CBS News and Dan Rather pursued an agenda, matters not. What matters is where credibility will ultimately lie. Will it be blogs? Cable news? Network news? Major daily papers? Talk radio? Judging by the past campaign, it certainly can't be all.

Vaughn Ververs is Editor of *The Hotline*.

CHAPTER NINE

The Impact of the New Campaign Finance Law on the 2004 Presidential Election

Michael Toner

FEDERAL ELECTION COMMISSION

The 2004 presidential election was the first election waged under the McCain-Feingold law, which made the most significant changes to the federal election laws in a generation. The McCain-Feingold legislation has three key components, all of which had a major impact on how the Bush-Kerry race was fought. Under McCain-Feingold:

- The national political parties, including the Republican National Committee ("RNC") and Democratic National Committee ("DNC"), were barred from raising and spending any soft money for any purpose;

- The individual contribution limit to presidential candidates doubled from $1,000 to $2,000, and the amount individuals could give to the national parties increased by 25%; and

- Corporations and labor unions were restricted in how they financed television and radio advertisements depicting or referring to presidential candidates within 30 days before a primary and 60 days before the general election.

President Bush, Senator Kerry, the political parties, and outside interest groups were forced to adapt their campaign strategies to these major changes in the nation's campaign finance laws. In this chapter I will focus primarily on the impact of the first two sets of legal changes on the 2004 presidential campaign. More than ever before, presidential campaign strategy in 2004 was infused, and in some instances driven, by legal considerations. The legalization of presidential politics is likely to continue on the road to the White House in 2008.

THE SOFT MONEY BAN AND THE RISE OF 527 ORGANIZATIONS

Under the McCain-Feingold law, the national political parties are prohibited from raising and spending soft money for any purpose.[1] Prior to the McCain-Feingold legislation, the Democratic National Committee and Republican National Committee spent hundreds of millions of dollars of soft-money funds each election cycle on issue advertisements attacking and promoting presidential candidates, as well as on partisan get-out-the-vote operations.[2] This soft-money spending was a key part of the campaign support the Democratic and Republican parties historically provided to their presidential nominees and often played a role in determining which candidate was victorious on Election Day.

With the national parties subject to the soft-money ban for the 2004 presidential race, soft-money spending migrated from the national political parties to a number of prominent Section 527 organizations. Section 527 organizations get their name from the section of the federal tax code under which they operate. Under the tax code, groups may organize under Section 527—and therefore shield many of their activities from taxation—if their exempt function is "influencing or attempting to influence the selection, nomination, election, or appointment of any individual to any Federal, State, or local public office or office in a political organization, or the election of Presidential of Vice-Presidential electors."[3] 527 organizations are partisan political organizations as a matter of law.

Early in the 2004 election cycle, several prominent Democratic 527 organizations contended that, despite the soft-money ban that applied to the national political parties, they remained legally able to continue raising and spending soft money. The Democratic 527s contended that they were legally able to spend unlimited soft-money funds on issue advertisements promoting and attacking the presidential candidates and on partisan voter registration and get-out-the-vote activities, provided their public communications did not contain express advocacy, and they did not coordinate their operations with any candidate or political party.

Many Democrats believed it was critical for 527 groups to play an aggressive role because they feared that President Bush, who had already raised record sums of money in the 2000 presidential race, and was unopposed in the Republican primary in 2004, would substantially outspend the Democratic nominee, particularly in the key time between March of the election year, when each party's presumptive nominee emerges, and the summer nominating conventions.

Accordingly, several prominent Democratic 527 groups began spending tens of millions of soft-money funds during the spring and summer of 2004 on hard-hitting issue ads attacking President Bush and on extensive voter-registration and get-out-the-vote operations. The biggest Democratic 527 group, Americans Coming Together ("ACT"), reportedly spent $76 million on a wide range of voter-registration and GOTV activities during the 2004 election cycle.[4] According to published reports, ACT deployed up to 2,500 canvassers to register approximately 500,000 voters.[5] Moreover, the Media Fund, a Democratic 527 run by Harold Ickes, who was Deputy Chief of Staff under President Clinton, reportedly spent approximately $55 million on anti-Bush advertising.[6] In addition, the Moveon.org Voter Fund reportedly spent approximately $21 million.[7]

Republican strategists initially contended that the soft-money spending of the Democratic 527 groups was illegal and urged the Federal Election Commission ("FEC") to require the groups to register with the FEC and abide by the hard-dollar limits of federal law. In May 2004, the FEC rejected proposed regulations that would have subjected certain 527 groups to hard-dollar limits, and announced that it would not issue any regulations governing 527 organizations for the 2004 election.[8]

Following the FEC's decision, Republican operatives quickly began raising and spending soft-money funds through 527 organizations on the same kinds of activities that the Democratic 527s were undertaking. The largest Republican 527 was the Progress for America Voter Fund ("PFA"), which reportedly spent more than $35 million on a wide range of political activities.[9] PFA sent out millions of direct-mail pieces and aired hard-hitting issue ads attacking Senator Kerry and promoting President Bush that were targeted to battleground states.[10] However, perhaps the most memorable and effective Republican 527 in 2004 was the Swift Boat Veterans for Truth, which spent more than $20 million on a series of ads attacking Senator Kerry's Vietnam War record.[11]

All told, 527 groups reportedly raised and spent approximately $409 million on activities designed to influence the 2004 presidential race.[12] Of this amount, Democratic-oriented 527s reportedly spent $266 million, for 65% of the total, and Republican groups spent $144 million, for 35% of the total.[13] However, Republican-oriented 527s reportedly outspent their Democratic counterparts during the closing weeks of the campaign.

To put the scope of 527 spending in perspective, President Bush and Senator Kerry were each limited to spending only $75 million during the entire general election phase of the campaign.

Individual donors donated staggering sums of money to 527 groups. The top 15 donors to 527s gave $125 million to the groups combined, accounting for about 25% of their total funding.[14] Democratic donors were the most prolific givers: George Soros was the biggest 527 contributor, at $23.7 million, followed by Peter Lewis ($23.3 million), Stephen Bing ($13.7 million), and Herb and Marion Sandler ($13 million).[15] On the Republican side, Bob and Doylene Perry reportedly donated $9.6 million to 527 groups, and Alex Spanos and Dawn Arnall each gave $5 million.[16]

Moreover, six of the top 10 donors to 527 groups were billionaires who were on the *Forbes Magazine* list of the richest Americans.[17] Published reports indicate that $8 out of every $10 collected from individuals by Democratic-oriented 527s came from donors who gave at least $250,000 each.[18] On the Republican side, the amount was $9 out of $10.[19] The Swift Boat Veterans for Truth reportedly was able to finance the bulk of its activities from just four contributors, who gave the group over $12.7 million.[20] To put these multi-million dollar donations to 527 groups in perspective, individuals may only give $25,000 a year to the DNC and the RNC.

Although Democrats were the first to make major use of 527 groups as soft-money vehicles, Republicans quickly matched and even exceeded the Democrats, at least in the final stages of the election. Moreover, the Republican Swift Boat Veterans for Truth emerged as the most influential 527 group during the 2004 election. For Democrats in terms of 527 groups, the old adage was fitting—he who lives by the sword can die by it.

McCAIN-FEINGOLD'S HIGHER CONTRIBUTION LIMITS TRIGGERED RECORD FUNDRAISING BY PRESIDENTIAL CANDIDATES AND PAVED THE WAY FOR THE NOMINEES OF BOTH MAJOR PARTIES TO DECLINE MATCHING FUNDS

Beginning with the 2004 election cycle, the McCain-Feingold law doubled the amount of money individuals could contribute to all federal candidates, including presidential candidates, from $1,000 to $2,000 per election. The new law also increased the amount of money that individuals could give to national political parties—from $20,000 to $25,000 per year—and doubled what each person could give to state parties, from $5,000 to $10,000 per year. The only important contribution limit that did not increase was the amount that individuals could give to multi-candidate political action committees ("PACs"), which remained at $5,000 per year.

The increased contribution limits, combined with a highly competitive presidential race, led presidential candidates in 2004 to raise unprecedented sums of money for the primaries. These factors also resulted in both major party nominees, for the first time, declining matching funds and operating outside of the presidential public financing system during the primaries.

Under the presidential public financing system, candidates can receive matching funds from the government up to $250 for each individual contribution they receive.[21] To be eligible to receive matching funds, candidates must raise $5,000 in 20 or more states from individuals in amounts of $250 or less. In 2004, each presidential candidate could receive a maximum of approximately $19 million in matching funds. However, candidates electing to receive matching funds for the 2004 race were subject to a nationwide spending limit of approximately $45 million, as well as state-by-state spending limits based on the population of each state.[22] Under the federal election laws, the primary season runs from the time a person legally becomes a candidate for the presidency through the national nominating conventions, which can last 18 months or longer. The primary spending limits apply throughout this period of time. Candidates who decline to take matching funds are not subject to any spending limits during the primary period, and may raise as much money as they want, subject to the contribution limits.

The general election period legally begins for candidates when they are nominated at their national conventions and runs through Election Day in November. Candidates can legally opt out of the public financing system during the primaries, but opt for public money for the general election. The general-election public grant for major party candidates in 2004 was approximately $75 million. Candidates who accept a public grant for the general election are subject to a national spending limit of the same amount and are prohibited from raising private contributions, except for separate funds to pay for legal and accounting expenses.[23] No major party candidate has ever declined public funds for the general election.

In 2000, George W. Bush raised approximately $100 million during the primaries—which was the greatest amount of money ever raised by a presidential candidate at the time—and became the first person to decline matching funds to win the presidency. In 2004, fueled by the increased contribution limits, President Bush again opted out of public financing during the primaries and raised a record-breaking $270 million.[24] This total was more than six times the $45 million spending limit that would have applied if the President had opted for matching funds.

Senator John Kerry also raised extraordinary sums of money and likewise opted out of public financing during the primaries. Kerry raised approximately $235 million during the primary phase of the campaign, which was more than five times the spending limit.[25] President Bush and Senator Kerry combined raised over $500 million for the primaries; if they had participated in the public financing system, they would have been limited to spending only approximately $90 million.[26]

Overall, all the presidential candidates running in 2004 raised $673.9 million combined.[27] This aggregate total was 92% higher than the $351.6 million that all the presidential candidates raised during the 2000 election cycle.[28] It also represented a staggering 172% increase over the total amount that presidential candidates raised in 1996.[29] In light of this data, there is no question that McCain-Feingold's higher contribution limits greatly strengthened the fundraising abilities of presidential candidates from both major parties in 2004.

The law's increased contribution limits also helped spur increased fundraising by congressional candidates during the 2004 election cycle. Congressional candidates participating in the 2004 general election raised a combined $985.4 million from January 1, 2003, through Election Day, which was a 20% increase over the comparable period in the 2002 election cycle.[30] House candidates participating in the 2004 general election raised a total of $613.8 million, which was 14% higher than the aggregate total raised for the 2002 election cycle.[31] Moreover, Senate candidates participating in the 2004 general election raised a combined $371.6 million, which was 32% higher than their counterparts raised during the 2002 cycle.[32]

NATIONAL PARTY FUNDRAISING

McCain-Feingold's increased limits to the national political parties helped the Democratic National Committee and Republican National Committee raise unprecedented amounts of hard money for the 2004 election. For the 2000 election, when it was still legal for the national parties to raise and spend soft money, the DNC collected a total of $260 million of hard and soft money combined. For the 2004 election, the DNC raised more hard money than the combined hard and soft money it had raised for the 2000 election. The DNC raised a total of $391 million for the 2004 election, which was a 150% increase in hard-dollar receipts compared to the 2000 election.[33] The RNC likewise raised more hard money for the 2004 race than the total amount of hard and soft money it had collected in 2000. The RNC raised $384 million during the 2004 election cycle, which represented a 69% increase in hard-dollar receipts.

However, perhaps the most surprising development in 2004 was that the DNC outraised the RNC for the first time in decades. The RNC pioneered and perfected direct-mail, small-dollar fundraising during the late 1970s and 1980s, which helped provide the RNC with a clear hard-dollar fundraising edge over the DNC for more than two decades. The RNC's hard-dollar edge ended in 2004. The RNC raised a total of $384.3 million during the 2004 election cycle.[34] However, the DNC raised a total of $391.2 million.[35]

The DNC's efforts to expand and enhance its low-dollar fundraising programs through Internet and direct-mail appeals played a major role in its historic fundraising success.[36] In 2000, the DNC raised a total of $58.8 million in contributions from individuals in amounts of $200 or less per year. For the 2004 cycle, the DNC nearly tripled this amount, raising $165.2 million of low-dollar contributions.[37] The RNC also raised record sums of contributions from individuals under $200 a year, with its aggregate total increasing from $88.2 million in 2000 to $153.9 million in 2004.[38]

Although low-dollar donations were an important part of the DNC's and RNC's record fundraising in 2004, high-dollar contributions also played a major role in each party's success. The McCain-Feingold legislation increased the individual contribution limit to the national parties from $20,000 to $25,000 per year. This 25% increase in the national-party contribution limit did not receive nearly as much attention as the law's doubling of the candidate-contribution limits to $2,000 per election. However, both national committees capitalized on the increased limits.

For the 2000 election, the DNC received $10.9 million in contributions from individuals giving the maximum $20,000 contribution, which accounted for 9.9% of the total receipts the DNC raised.[39] For the 2004 cycle, the DNC raised nearly four times as much money from maxed-out donors, receiving $43.5 million from individuals giving the maximum $25,000 contribution, which accounted for 12.2% of the DNC's total receipts.[40] The RNC also greatly increased the amount of money it raised from contributors giving the legal maximum. For the 2000 cycle, the RNC raised $12.7 million from maxed-out donors, which accounted for 6.8% of its total receipts.[41] During the 2004 election cycle, the RNC increased that figure more than four-fold, raising $60.8 million from maxed-out contributors, who comprised 17.7% of its fundraising total.[42]

In light of the foregoing, it is clear that the increased contribution limits were a major ingredient in the ability of the DNC and RNC to raise record sums of money for the 2004 election, surpassing even the combined amount of hard and soft money the two committees raised during 2000. Some analysts feared that McCain-Feingold's soft-money ban would weaken and even cripple the national parties. In 2004, the national parties were more than able to off-set the loss of soft-money funds by targeting low-dollar donors and taking full advantage of the increased contribution limits.

The RNC and DNC spent their funds, as in past election cycles, on a wide range of voter registration, voter identification, and get-out-the-vote programs. The vast majority of these voter mobilization activities took place in the 18–20 states that were targeted by the presidential campaigns. Under federal law, each national party also may make coordinated expenditures on behalf of their presidential nominees. Coordinated expenditures permit the parties, in full consultation with their nominees, to pay for any campaign expenses they choose—including radio and television advertisements, polling services, and campaign staff salaries. In 2004, each national party could make up to $16.25 million of coordinated expenditures on behalf of their nominees.

THE RISE OF INDEPENDENT PARTY SPENDING

Under Supreme Court precedent, political parties have a constitutional right to make unlimited independent expenditures on behalf of federal candidates.[43] Independent expenditures are public communications that expressly advocate the election or defeat of a clearly identified candidate. Under FEC regulations, for any entity, including a political party, to legally make an independent expenditure on behalf of a federal candidate, the expenditure must not be made "in cooperation, consultation, or concert with, or at the request or suggestion" of the candidate.[44] The expenditure also must be paid for entirely out of hard dollars raised subject to the prohibitions and limitations of federal law.

During the 2004 election cycle, the national parties significantly increased the amount of independent expenditures that they made on behalf of their presidential nominees as compared to previous election cycles. The DNC spent approximately $120 million on independent expenditures on behalf of Senator Kerry.[45] Much of the DNC's independent expenditures were made during August and early September, while Senator Kerry was attempting to conserve general election funds for the fall campaign.[46]

The RNC reported making $18.2 million of independent expenditures on behalf of President Bush.[47] The RNC also spent $45.8 million on media advertisements that contained joint campaign messages on behalf of both President Bush and the Republican ticket.[48] The cost of these joint advertisements was split between the Bush-Cheney Campaign and the RNC.[49]

2004 saw a remarkable surge in the amount of independent expenditures that the national political parties made on behalf of congressional candidates. The National Republican Senatorial Committee ("NRSC") made no independent expenditures on behalf of Republican Senate candidates during the 2002 election cycle and only $267,600 during the 2000 cycle.[50] However, during the 2004 campaign, the NRSC made $20.1 million in independent expenditures on behalf of Republican Senate candidates across the country.[51] The growth of independent spending was even more dramatic for the National Republican Congressional Committee ("NRCC"). The NRCC made only $1.2 million of independent expenditures on behalf of Republican House candidates in 2002. For the 2004 election, the NRCC spent nearly 40 times more money on independent expenditures, with a total of $46.9 million.[52]

The Democratic congressional committees likewise dramatically increased their independent expenditures in 2004. Like the NRSC, the Democratic Senatorial Campaign Committee ("DSCC") made no independent expenditures during the 2002 election cycle and only $133,000 in the 2000 cycle.[53] However, during the 2004 cycle, the DSCC made $18.7 million of independent expenditures.[54] The surge in independent expenditures was even more dramatic for the

Democratic Congressional Campaign Committee ("DCCC"). The DCCC made only $1.1 million in independent expenditures during the 2002 election cycle. For the 2004 campaign, the DCCC's independent expenditures increased 36-fold, totaling $36.1 million.[55]

The notable increase in the amount of independent expenditures made by the national parties in 2004 is potentially significant in at least two respects. First, the independent expenditure programs were fueled and made possible only because the national parties broke all hard-dollar fundraising records. Although political parties have a constitutional right to make unlimited independent expenditures on behalf of their candidates, they are only legally able to do so if they have sufficient hard dollars to pay for the advertising.

Second, and more importantly, independent expenditures may be one way that the national parties are adapting to the soft-money prohibition under the McCain-Feingold law. Prior to McCain-Feingold, the national parties used hundreds of millions of dollars of soft-money funds to help underwrite issue ads attacking and promoting federal candidates. With the national parties barred from spending soft money for the 2004 election, the parties channeled tens of millions of hard dollars into independent advertising, and thereby maintained an active presence on the nation's airwaves on behalf of their candidates. In this respect, the 2004 election may have ushered in a new era in campaign finance with the rise of independent party spending.

Michael Toner is Vice Chairman of the Federal Election Commission.

NOTES

1. "Soft money" is defined as funds raised and spent outside of the prohibitions and limitations of federal law. Soft money includes corporate and labor union general treasury funds and individual donations in excess of federal limits. Funds raised in accordance with federal law come from individuals and federally registered political action committees and have historically been harder to raise; hence, these funds are known as "hard money."

2. "Issue advertisements" are public communications that frequently attack or promote federal candidates and their records, but which refrain from expressly advocating the election or defeat of any clearly identified federal candidate, which is referred to as "express advocacy." "Vote for Bush" and "Vote Against Gore" are examples of express advocacy. The Supreme Court established the express advocacy standard in *Buckley* v. *Valeo*, 424 U.S. 1 (1976).

3. See 26 U.S.C. §527(e)(2).

4. Kenneth P. Doyle, "Section 527 Groups Raised $500 million in '04 Race, Had Big Impact on Campaign, Studies Say," *BNA Money & Politics Report*, December 20, 2004.

5. Ibid. Glen Justice, "Advocacy Groups Reflect on Their Role in the Election," *New York Times*, November 5, 2004. ACT also "made 16 million phone calls, sent 23 million pieces of mail and delivered 11 million fliers door to door. On Election Day, [ACT] fielded as many as 70,000 paid workers and volunteers to get people to the polls."

6. Kenneth P. Doyle, "Section 527 Groups Raised $500 million in '04 Race, Had Big Impact on Campaign, Studies Say," *BNA Money & Politics Report*, December 20, 2004.

7. Center for Public Integrity, "527s in 2004 Shatter Previous Records for Political Fundraising" (report released December 16, 2004).

8. The author co-sponsored the proposed 527 regulations. The 6-member FEC declined to adopt the proposed regulations by a vote of 4-to-2.

9. Center for Public Integrity, "527s in 2004 Shatter Previous Records for Political Fundraising" (report released December 16, 2004).

10. Glen Justice, "Advocacy Groups Reflect on Their Role in the Election," *New York Times*, November 5, 2004.

11. Eliza Newlin Carney, "Rules of the Game: The 527 Phenomenon: Big Bucks for Upstarts," Nationaljournal.com, December 13, 2004.

12. Ibid.

13. Ibid.

14. Kenneth P. Doyle, "Section 527 Groups Raised $500 Million in '04 Race, Had Big Impact on Campaign, Studies Say," *BNA Money & Politics Report*, December 20, 2004.

15. Michael Janofsky, "Advocacy Groups Spent Record Amount on 2004 Election," *New York Times*, December 17, 2004; Center for Public Integrity, "527s in 2004 Shatter Previous Records for Political Fundraising" (report released December 16, 2004).

16. Michael Janofsky, "Advocacy Groups Spent Record Amount on 2004 Election," *New York Times*, December 17, 2004; James V. Grimaldi and Thomas B. Edsall, "Super Rich Step Into Political Vacuum," *Washington Post*, October 17, 2004, p. A01.

17. Ibid.

18. Ibid.

19. Ibid.

20. Kenneth P. Doyle, "Section 527 Groups Raised $500 million in '04 Race, Had Big Impact on Campaign, Studies Say," *BNA Money & Politics Report*, December 20, 2004.

21. PAC contributions are not matchable.

22. The state spending limits in some of the most important early primary and caucus states were very low. For example, the spending limit in Iowa was only $1.3 million. *FEC Record* (November 2003) at 9. The spending limit for the New Hampshire primary was even lower, at $730,000. Ibid.

23. These accounts are known as General Election Legal and Accounting Compliance Funds ("GELACs"). GELAC funds are subject to the same $2,000 per-person limit as applies to primary campaign accounts.

24. "2004 Presidential Campaign Financial Activity Summarized," FEC Press Release (February 3, 2005).

25. "2004 Presidential Campaign Financial Activity Summarized," FEC Press Release (February 3, 2005).

26. Even Governor Howard Dean, who dropped out of the presidential race in March 2004, raised approximately $51 million, which was 113% of the primary spending limit. "2004 Presidential Campaign Financial Activity Summarized," FEC Press Release (February 3, 2005).

27. "2004 Presidential Campaign Financial Activity Summarized," FEC Press Release (February 3, 2005).

28. Ibid.

29. Ibid.

30. *FEC Record* (November 2003) at 8–9.

31. Ibid.

32. Ibid. It should be noted that some of the increase in Senate candidate receipts may be attributable to the fact that there were Senate campaigns in several mega-states in 2004 that typically are more expensive. California, New York, and Pennsylvania had incumbents seeking re-election in 2004, and Illinois and Florida had open-seat races.

33. "Party Financial Activity Summarized," FEC Press Release (December 14, 2004).

34. Ibid.

35. Ibid.

36. The DNC reportedly expanded its list of direct-mail prospects from one million to 100 million and its Internet contacts from 70,000 to one million. Davis S. Broder, "A Win for Campaign Reform," *Washington Post*, February 3, 2005, p. A27.

37. Ibid.

38. Ibid.

39. "Party Financial Activity Summarized," FEC Press Release (December 14, 2004).

40. Ibid.

41. Ibid.

42. Ibid.

43. See *Colorado Republican Federal Campaign Committee v. FEC*, 518 U.S. 604 (1996).

44. 11 C.F.R. §100.16.

45. "2004 Presidential Campaign Financial Activity Summarized," FEC Press Release (February 3, 2005).

46. Candidates who opt for public funds for the general election under the presidential public financing system become general-election candidates when they receive their party's nomination at the national convention. Once candidates enter the general-election phase, they are required to defray all of their campaign expenses out of public funds and are prohibited from raising or spending private contributions, other than to cover certain legal and accounting expenses. Senator Kerry was nominated during the last week of July and began the general election at that time. President Bush was not nominated until the first week of September, which legally allowed the President to continue using private contributions to defray campaign expenses throughout August.

47. "2004 Presidential Campaign Financial Activity Summarized," FEC Press Release (February 3, 2005).

48. Ibid.
49. Ibid.
50. "Party Financial Activity Summarized," FEC Press Release (December 14, 2004).
51. Ibid.
52. Ibid.
53. Ibid.
54. Ibid.
55. Ibid.

CHAPTER TEN

Going Broadband, Getting Netwise: The Cyber-Education of John Kerry and Other Political Actors

Michael Cornfield

PEW INTERNET & AMERICAN LIFE PROJECT

CLIMBING ABOARD THE LEARNING CURVE

On December 1, 2002, John Kerry appeared on the television program "Meet The Press" to announce that he would form a presidential exploratory committee in the week ahead. It was a traditional, almost ritualistic, maneuver. Kerry used the program to inform its audience of five million political *cognoscenti* that he was going to run for president in 2004. A loud and broad negative reaction to his announcement or to his responses to the notoriously tough questions posed by the show's host, Tim Russert, might have given Kerry pause, prompting a delay or even a change in plans. A positive review to his performance would have enhanced his stature as a likely front-runner in the race.

Nearly two years later, when he conceded defeat to George W. Bush, Kerry again appeared on television, delivering an address from Faneuil Hall in his home town of Boston. But this time Kerry also sent a textual version of his remarks, under the heading "A Sincere Thank You," to the 2.7 million subscribers on his campaign email list. A transcript of the concession speech appeared on his campaign web site, which had been visited by twenty million adult Americans.

Like many other people, John Kerry had become politically net-wise in the intervening months. He had learned what the internet could do for his campaign at a time when it was becoming a popular medium for activists and close observers of public affairs. Had his campaign been netwise in December 2002, it might have inspired some of the people who liked what they saw and heard on "Meet The Press" to visit the campaign web site. Some of those visitors might have signed up to receive email from the campaign, and volunteered to work for the campaign, both online and off. In other words, Kerry's online network might have been larger, earlier.

Kerry's inner circle might have also noticed something that didn't surface in newspaper accounts of his appearance. The press stitched together quotes of Kerry's positions on current issues with basic facts about his life and career, the nomination process, and the latest polls. But in the conservative regions of that constellation of individual web sites known as the blogosphere, the following summary of one exchange between Kerry and Russert popped up.

NBC's Tim Russert: "Senator…should we freeze or roll back the Bush tax cut?" Kerry: "Well, I wouldn't take away from people who've already been given their tax cut....What I would not do is give any new Bush tax cuts...." Russert: "So the tax cut that's scheduled to be implemented in the coming years...." Kerry: "No new tax cut under the Bush plan....It doesn't make economic sense." Russert: "Now, this is a change, because let me show you what you said in September of 2001 when I asked you the very same question." (NBC's "Meet The Press," December 1, 2002)

This chunk of text resurfaced repeatedly online for the duration of the campaign. It was held up as an example of what would soon be termed a Kerry "flip-flop." Had the Kerry campaign monitored the online reaction to the interview, it would have noticed that the candidate had a budding consistency problem.

The price of not being attuned to the blogosphere would prove even greater in August 2004, when the Kerry campaign waited for poll results to come back before responding in full to attack ads by the ad hoc advocacy group Swift Boat Veterans for Truth. Part of the rationale for not responding was that the ads had only aired in a few small television markets. But they were also online. Conversations about the ads were online. By the time polling confirmed a threat to Kerry's stature, the drop was considerable.

By August 2004, however, the Kerry campaign had learned another advantage of online campaigning. Together with the Democratic National Committee, it would collect a record $122 million in contributions through the internet in 2004. Much of that money was raised through appeals the campaign made; some of it came at donors' initiatives. Kerry was eligible to receive that amount because he had opted out of public financing the previous fall, in order to try and keep pace with the fundraising prowess of his Democratic rival Howard Dean.

Dean, the front-runner in the race for much of 2003, relied on the internet not just for money, but also for grassroots organizing, message dissemination, and tactical intelligence. The Dean campaign learned from the progressive online advocacy group MoveOn.org and went beyond them, even as MoveOn.org continued to innovate and evolve. Meanwhile, the Bush-Cheney reelection campaign and the Republican National Committee (RNC) teamed up with advocacy groups to use the internet to help implement what RNC Chairman Ed Gillespie justifiably called, in *his* post-election thank you email to over 7 million subscribers, "the most sophisticated voter contact strategy in campaign history."

The numbers of Americans receiving presidential campaign emails and watching Sunday morning politics programs were roughly comparable in the 2004 election cycle. There was probably considerable congruency between these internet and television audiences. But the internet is quite different from television, and every other political medium for that matter. First, the internet allows campaigners to avoid the press and speak directly to cognoscenti, without having to pony up big bucks for a thirty-second advertising spot. Second, the internet is bi-directional, allowing members of a campaign audience to send back comments, dollars, subscription addresses, and pledges of volunteer time. On the internet, every audience member is also, potentially and simultaneously, an activist. Third, the online channels which connect campaigns with cognoscenti are embedded in a network which allows both ends to talk laterally as well: among themselves, to members of other circles, to the world at large, and to posterity. The blogosphere has emerged as a symbol of this talk-laden region of the internet, but email, chat groups, and message boards are also important online forums for political discourse.

No medium matches television's reach to the politically inattentive. But no medium matches the internet for tactical versatility and democratic accessibility. The 2002–2004 election cycle marks the point in history when presidential campaigns figured out how to make some of the internet's distinctive qualities pay off on a continual and systematic basis. Equally important, campaigns recognized that they had to develop an internet strategy, and keep up with the latest developments in online techniques and technologies, because whatever happened online was an integral part of public life.

The campaigners' climb onto the internet learning curve was the psychological equivalent of the move internet users make when they switch from a dial-up to a broadband connection. "Going broadband," in the vernacular, means taking advantage of all the things you can do with a super-fast, always-on, high-volume link to the internet. Campaigners still have much to learn about the internet. (Neither Kerry nor Bush nor any other seriously considered presidential candidate, including Howard Dean, knew how to blog in the 2004 cycle.) But political professionals now realize that they must make the commitment to keep learning. Once you go broadband, you can't stop trying to get netwise—because too many other people who are important to your campaign are doing the same.

DEAN FOR PRESIDENT: THE CAMPAIGNERS' WAKE-UP CALL

One month after Kerry's quasi-announcement, as 2003 began, the Howard Dean for President campaign had $157,000 cash on hand, seven paid staff, 432 identified supporters nationwide, and no offices other than its headquarters in Burlington, Vermont. A year later, 400 paid staff occupied offices in 24 states. More than 280,000 people had donated $40 million to the campaign, a little more than half of its 552,930 identified supporters. (The average donation was just over $100.) Three national labor unions, thirty members of Congress, and the party's 2000 nominee, Al Gore, had endorsed Dean. "Just imagine," read the campaign web site posting for January 1, 2004, after ticking off many of these statistics, "what 2004 can bring."

Few among the cognoscenti imagined that the Dean campaign had recently passed its apogee of strength, and was headed for a rapid descent. Yet despite its collapse, this long-shot to front-runner campaign stands out as the best example to date of what a netwise operation can achieve. The internet was not the only factor behind Dean's rise; his feisty opposition to the Iraq war galvanized progressives, giving them a leader to rally around. But Dennis Kucinich opposed the war, too. Dean's ascent benefited from his hiring of campaign manager Joe Trippi, who possessed a rare combination of expertise in both presidential politics and high-technology enterprise. Together, they created a campaign team eager to experiment with the internet. The discoveries they made together with the hundreds of thousands of Americans who became active in the Dean network during 2003 amount to a veritable textbook in online campaigning. Five innovations stand out:

1. *News-pegged fundraising appeals.* Campaigns typically play to three motivations when they solicit donations. Potential contributors want access to decision-makers, to please a friend (or get rid of a pest), and to advance shared policy goals. The Dean campaign, taking a cue from Moveon.org, demonstrated that candidates can raise

money a fourth way, on the strength of the internet's instant turnaround capacity: by promulgating short-term goals which immediate donations can help the campaign attain.

Such goals often flow out of a campaign's daily battles to win media attention. Contributions are sought to finance ads that will let a campaign respond fast and prominently to an opponent's assertion, or to stage an event that will attract news coverage. The campaign can then thank the donors with evidence of the media play their dollars made possible. And it can count on the ensuing week to bring fresh news and new goals to set.

For example, in July 2003 the Dean campaign took advantage of news reports about an upcoming $2,000-a-plate Republican luncheon featuring Vice-President Cheney. Up, out, and around the Dean network went word of "The Cheney Challenge"—could Dean supporters raise more money than the luncheon by the time it took place?—accompanied by a web video of the candidate munching on a "three-dollar" turkey sandwich. Cheney's lunch raised $250,000 from 125 guests. The online fundraising gimmick netted the Dean campaign $500,000 from 9700 people, and great publicity about its grassroots enthusiasm and prowess.

Before long, every television appearance by a presidential candidate, from the Sunday talk shows to the conventions and debates, was seen by netwise campaigns as an opportunity to rake in money. In July 2004, Kerry asked his online supporters to make a statement to the nation on the day he accepted the party nomination, and pulled in $5.6 million.

2. *"Meetups" and other net-organized local gatherings.* Early in 2003, Trippi put a link on the home page of the Dean campaign to the web site of MeetUp.com, a company which helps individuals arrange to get together with others in their area who share an interest in something. The something can be a hobby, sports team, television program, or a campaign, as the Dean team discovered to its delight. The Dean Meetup population eventually constituted a virtual mid-size city, with several hundred thousand activists situated across the nation and beyond. Monthly Meetups among Dean campaign veterans were still attracting people in January, 2005.

3. *Blogging.* A blog is an online diary posted in reverse chronological order, sometimes with room for reader comments, usually with links to blogs run by people the reader may also find interesting. The social bonding and grassroots organizing which occurs in and around Meetups also occurs through clusters of blogs. In 2003, the Dean campaign posted 2,910 entries on its "Blog for America" and received 314,121 comments, which were also posted there. As the result of one of those comments, 115,632 handwritten letters were sent from supporters to eligible voters in the upcoming Iowa caucuses and New Hampshire primary. (MeetUp captains were issued lists, stamped envelopes, and a sample text for the letterwriters to follow.) A blogger also came up with the Cheney Challenge.

4. *Online referenda.* When the Dean campaign considered opting out of public financing, it decided to put the question to its network for an online vote. The overwhelming

positive response affirmed to the Dean supporters and the political world that the move was worth it; indeed, those who voted "yes" received back a thank-you email with a request for money. Two other 2003 online referenda provided its backers with political cover, resources, and momentum: the drive to recall California Governor Gray Davis, and the draft Wesley Clark for President movement.

Technically speaking, these were not actual referenda; no one was legally bound to follow the majority. Verification and privacy issues make actual online voting problematic. These aggregations of opinions weren't scientific enough to pass muster as polls, either. But as a tool to engage support, online referenda can be handy to campaigns regardless of how much is known about the participants, and how the voting population is constructed.

5. *Decentralized decision-making.* Dean's slogan was "You have the power." His campaign put something behind the rhetoric (populist, but also libertarian) through the four techniques listed above, and more generally by leaving local supporters to campaign as they saw fit. Balancing the positive energy flow of a movement with the precision of an organization presents the next generation of campaigners with perhaps their greatest challenge. The internet makes this a matter of software configuration as well as political management.

At the end of June 2003, Dean won the "money primary" constituted by the reporting of fundraising totals to the Federal Election Commission for the second quarter of 2003. George W. Bush had burst to the front of the Republican pack in the comparable report in 1999. Now it was Dean's turn. The internet was rightly seen as the primary instrument through which his political power was accruing. If one had to single out a mass moment of realization among political actors that they had to climb aboard the online learning curve, this was it.

The big question for emulators of the Dean campaign is: did these innovations prefigure the campaign's failure as well as its success? Dean and Trippi both say no, and, as with the rise, there are non-internet explanations for the fall. The candidate was not ready, and perhaps not entirely willing, to perform before a mass audience as a presidential front-runner. Several of his competitors, notably Kerry, picked up his anti-war message, and as they did the liberal blogosphere and Democratic activists elsewhere turned what was once an insiders' consideration into a voters' issue: "electability." However, there was something flawed about the Dean campaign's net-heavy organization. The Bush-Cheney campaign corrected one of those flaws in a way that worked spectacularly for them, and so became part of the ever-expanding textbook of online campaigning.

TARGETED GRASSROOTS: GOTV GOES DIGITAL

After decades of mass-media domination, interpersonal campaigning underwent a renaissance in the early years of the millennium. The so-called "ground war" entails canvassing citizens to discern their preferences, engaging them to persuade and mobilize supporters, and finally, getting out the vote (GOTV), both on election day and before through programs aimed at taking advantage of the burgeoning early and absentee voter programs in many states. All told, nearly two-thirds of the adult population (64%) was contacted directly by political actors in the final two months of the 2004 campaign. Republicans and Democrats reached roughly the same number of people, and relied on the four same interpersonal channels in about the same proportions: regular (or "direct") mail remained the top channel of contact (reaching 49% of the public), with phone calls second at 40%, emails at 14%, and home visits at 9%. But these numbers say nothing about the efficacy of the contacts. The internet made a difference in helping campaigns decide who to contact, what to say, when to say it, and, crucially, who to send to say it. This is where the Republicans shone.

While the Democrats had more activists in their field operation, the Republicans did a better job of integrating computer power and internet communication into theirs.

The Bush-Cheney campaign (or BC04, as it was known) gained proficiency in internet campaigning from the mundane but vital advantage of having its team in place before the Democratic candidates began competing with each other, let alone with the Republican nominee. For example, the campaign's e-campaign director, Chuck DiFeo, started working at the RNC in April 2002, and at BC04 when it commenced operations in June 2003. To be sure, longevity is not an asset unless the personnel are good. They were.

With fundraising not a necessity, and grassroots organizing a perceived need for improvement dating back to the 2000 campaign, BC04 planned, tested, refined, and committed itself and its allies to a program which fused the basics of old-fashioned canvassing, marketing, and proselytizing with the latest in data acquisition, analysis, and distribution. Call it targeted grassroots. The campaign determined which segments of the voting population it wanted to contact, installed a rewards program to motivate volunteers (notably, choice seats at events featuring the president), equipped volunteers with customized talking points and contact lists so as to make the most of existing relationships (and supplied home door-knockers with downloadable maps spelling out estimated walking times), and kept track of every action taken to increase efficiency and output.

The House Party for the President initiative constituted one aspect of this targeted grassroots operation. Starting on April 29, 2004, the BC04 campaign relied on the internet to organize and coordinate simultaneous team-building sessions across the country—Meetups without the company as middleman. The July 15, 2004 parties featured a 30-minute conference call with Laura Bush, who answered six questions selected earlier from submissions and then brought her husband to the phone for a surprise cameo finish. There were 6,920 parties that day; in all, over 30,000 would be held, with over 350,000 participants.

Democrats mounted a targeted grassroots which matched the Republicans in sophistication, but not in cohesiveness or effectiveness. They started later. Like Dean, they hired recruits and bussed college students to faraway states, where the GOP relied more on the stronger ties inherent to local congregations, neighborhoods, and (under the aegis of the "Prosperity Project" spearheaded by BIPAC, the Business-Industry Political Action Committee) employer-employee and business-stakeholder relations. The Democratic field team was also hampered more by the rules of the recently enacted Bipartisan Campaign Reform Act. Under its restrictions, field operatives working for one of the 527 groups could neither coordinate with the Kerry campaign, nor advocate voting for him.

In the end, the Democrats mustered what was probably the second best GOTV operation in modern campaign history. Ed Gillespie had it right.

CONCLUSION: THE RIPENING OF THE ONLINE CITIZENRY

Did internet use make a difference in the 2004 presidential race? Yes. The most successful campaigns relied on it to gain advantages over their competitors. And the numbers of adult Americans who relied on the internet to get interested in the campaigns, to help make up their minds, to help others make up theirs, and to register and vote is simply too large relative to the final margin to think otherwise.

Interest in the presidential election was up through all media, as might be expected for a race regarded as close and crucial. But internet use for political news and information grew 83% between 2000 and 2004. Tens of millions of Americans had gone broadband before the election caught their attention, and once it did, broadband carried more of it to them, and more of them into it, than had ever been seen in this country. The number of eligible voters looking online for news and information about the campaigns doubled from 34 to 63 million, representing 31% of the U.S. adult population. Those getting election news and information on a daily or more frequent basis reached 20 million by election day. About 42 million people said they used email to discuss politics. About 13 million people used the internet to donate money, volunteer, or learn about events to attend. All told, 75 million Americans did something online pertinent to the 2004 elections. This engorged constituency for online politics guarantees that, no matter how exciting or dull the 2006 and 2008 elections turn out to be, campaigns will benefit from having an online component to everything they do.

John Kerry has certainly grasped this. He has moved to the forefront in political internet use with an innovation he calls the first online Congressional hearing. In January 2005, he set up a system through his web site and email list to collect telephone "testimony" about the need for legislation to provide health care to uninsured children. Phone messages are recorded, and some are posted to the site for listening. Citizens can also sign up to "cosponsor" Kerry's "Kids First" bill. This venture may work as public lobbying; it may work to keep Kerry's nationwide network alive and growing—who knows. The point is, he's netwise—or, at the least, netwiser.

Michael Cornfield is a Senior Research Consultant at PEW Internet & American Life Project and also an adjunct professor at The George Washington University.

[NOTE: Bibliographic references and survey data cited in this essay may be found at www.pewinternet.org starting at the author's biographical page.]

CHAPTER ELEVEN

Religion in the 2004 Presidential Election

Russell Muirhead, Nancy L. Rosenblum,
Daniel Schlozman, Francis X. Shen
HARVARD UNIVERSITY

"One cannot be President of our great country without a belief in God; without the truth that comes on one's knees."[1]

INTRODUCTION

America has been aptly called "God land."[2] Relative to other western democracies, a vastly greater proportion of Americans profess faith and join religious groups.[3] In the United States, not only is the number of religions dizzying (America is "the most profusely religious nation on earth"[4]) but religious groups of every stripe are politically active. The climate for this activity is hospitable. Political positions and public policies are regularly justified by religious as well as civic arguments,[5] and popular opinion across the political and religious spectrum supports personal religious identification by candidates and political organization by religious groups.[6] No candidate today feels compelled to repeat John F. Kennedy's cautious1960 statement: "I believe in an America where the separation of church and state is absolute—where no Catholic prelate would tell the President…how to act, and no Protestant minister would tell his parishioners for whom to vote."[7] Observers of the 2004 election were primed for religion to play a central role in the campaign and in the electoral outcome.

Religion in fact did play the dominant rhetorical role and key mobilizing role it was expected to play in the 2004 campaign. George W. Bush understood the persuasive and organizational power of religion in politics. He also appreciated the countervailing fact that even ecumenical appeals to religion could be divisive. Thus, Bush showed himself willing to use religion forcefully to sharpen partisan divisions and highlight his own qualities as a leader. But on matters of national security and the war in Iraq, which required national unity, his appeals to religion were more constrained. For his part, John Kerry was alert to the parties' so-called "religion gap." Although his campaign eventually responded to Bush in religious kind, Kerry and the Democratic Party faced obstacles in using religious rhetoric, in appealing to religion to underscore his qualities as a leader, and in benefiting from the political organization of religious groups. Religion was at the heart of the campaign, and this essay shows in what precise ways religion figured, and why. Despite that, the religious vote was *not* the key to the electoral outcome. Religion functioned as a resource for Bush especially—both in the standard political sense, by providing a basis for political organization, and in the rhetorical sense, by allowing Bush to frame, justify, and connect his various proposals and convictions. Ultimately, however, religious mobilization and religious rhetoric has to be managed so that the candidate appeals to voters who do not put religion first when thinking about politics.

RELIGION IN AMERICAN POLITICS: THE BASELINE

In western democracies today, religion—particularly Islam adhered to by recent immigrants to Europe—has created social upheaval and political conflict. In the United States, by contrast, the politically salient religious divisions are long-standing and home-grown, and arise chiefly within Christianity. In the background of the 2004 election, which has been slowly shaped over more than 20 years, two developments stand out.

The first is a change in politically salient religious divisions. Analysts who use survey data to study the electorate have expanded the list of relevant religious groups from the conventional five— White Evangelical Protestants, Black Protestants, Mainline Protestants, Catholics, and Jews—to as many as 18. One categorization consists of traditional, centrist, and modernist Evangelical Protestants; traditional, centrist, and modernist Mainline Protestants; Latino Protestants; Black Protestants; Other Christians; Other Faiths (including Muslims); Jews; and three classes of Unaffiliated: Unaffiliated Believers, Seculars, and Atheist/Agnostics.[8] These refined categories reflect the fact that in contrast to the situation fifty years ago, when white Protestants voted predominantly Republican while Catholics voted Democratic, and religious cleavages generally followed ethnic, racial, and socio-economic cleavages, the correlation between denominational membership and political alignments is no longer so simple.[9] Several denominational shifts are well established: the loss of membership by mainline Protestants (in Jerry Falwell's words, "from Mainline to sideline"[10]), and their shift from the GOP to the middle; the rise of membership in white Evangelical groups that became predominantly Republican by 1988; the weakening of long-standing white Catholic support for Democrats with a small shift to Republican and to the middle (in 2004 Catholics favored Bush over Kerry by 52% to 47%, a switch from 50% for Gore in 2000).[11] The stability of Jewish Democratic partisanship is clear. Hispanics, now the largest minority group, and in particular Hispanic Catholics, will be increasingly important as they begin to turn out in large numbers. At the same time, the number of adults without any religious identification has doubled in just over a decade, from 14.3 million (8%) in 1990 to 29.4 million (14%) in 2001.[12]

We also know that today, the most salient political divisions occur *within* rather than among denominations. Robert Wuthnow's name for this nondenominational cleavage is "the restructuring of American religion."[13] A conservative-liberal split now takes place within denominations, so that for instance, conservative Jewish voters have more in common with conservative Christian voters than with liberal Jews. What matters is not simply whether one is "evangelical," to take another example, but what *kind* of evangelical one is. Seven of ten traditionalist Evangelicals were Republicans, for example, but only three of ten modernist Evangelicals.[14] William Galston refers to this as "the traditionalist entente"; it has also been called the "ecumenism of orthodoxy."[15]

Refining things further, what appears to matter most in electoral politics is neither denomination nor whether one is conservative or liberal within the denomination, but how regularly one attends religious services. Religious observance as measured by church attendance is the best predictor of voter participation. It is also a predictor of partisan voting. Voters who fall into the category of intense religiosity also describe themselves as politically conservative and vote predominantly Republican. Voters who are less regularly observant or secular describe themselves as liberal and vote predominantly Democratic. Against this textured background, it is not hard to see that viewing Election 2004 as a crude contest between the secular and the religious misunderstands religion, politics, and the evolving relation between the two.

TABLE 1
Presidential Vote by Church Attendance

	BUSH	KERRY	NADER	BUSH IN 2000
More than weekly (16%)	64%	35%	1%	63%
Weekly (26%)	58	41	0	57
Monthly (14%)	50	49	0	46
A few times a year (28%)	45	54	0	42
Never (15%)	36	62	1	32

Source: CNN.com

The second long-term background development is a product of direct political activity: the organization and mobilization of religious voters by clergy and lay activists. The relation between religion and political attitudes is not direct but mediated by the experience of religious association and the political norms of the religious group.[16] The organization of the "Christian Right" in the 1980 and 1984 elections marked the start of the contemporary wave of religious mobilization: registering and turning-out church members to vote, creating a parallel media and popular culture that could be put to political use; networking with other churches, including non-Evangelical ones. This activity is on the rise. The Southern Baptist Convention led its first voter registration drive in 2004. This is not to say that white Evangelicals are the only organized religious group: political action has been a feature of black Protestant churches going back to the Civil Rights Movement. In contrast, both moderate religionists who are not as deeply rooted in the organizational matrix of a religious community and secular voters are less easily mobilized.

In addition to voter mobilization, the political landscape is marked by the multiplication of religious advocacy groups that lobby officials and support or oppose candidates (albeit indirectly): groups like Focus on the Family and the Family Research Council.[17] New associations have formed to counter these groups on the religious right, such as Americans United for the Separation of Church and State, People for the American Way, and Mobilization 2004. The newly formed Interfaith Alliance objected to "politicizing religion," sent out Voter Guide Warning Letters, and urged that "thoughtful and prayerful involvement" be connected to *civic* participation.[18] The proliferation of groups in contest with one another has become a familiar part of the electoral landscape: "Redeem the Vote" was a response to MTV's "Rock the Vote."

In the wake of these developments, political commentators seem to be inexorably drawn to the misleading idea of a "culture war" between religious traditionalists on the one side and seculars on the other.[19] In this militant, polarizing formulation, religious moderates, centrists, and all those with an ambivalent appreciation of one or another of these extremes drop out of the picture. This image serves the interests of extremists on both sides as well as a media eager to spice up its stories with a narrative of conflict. The notion of a "culture war" acquiesces, for instance, in the conservative complaint that America has become a "culture of disbelief, that secularists seek freedom *from* religion, that public discourse is hostile to reasoning rooted in faith, and that religious organizations are treated unfairly in public policy. In Ronald Reagan's words, "Morality's foundation is religion...We have begun to make great steps toward secularizing our nation and removing religion from its honored place...Religion needs defenders."[20] During the campaign, Bush too said that his faith-based initiative would require "changing the culture," by which he meant the secular policy culture of Washington, D.C.[21]

Yet to suppose that America as a whole is beset by "culture wars" is simply wrong. Only some candidates and only some issues divide along anything resembling religious lines. On most issues that are divisive, polarization is not rooted in religion. Indeed on race, gender, and crime issues, "the general public has gravitated toward a liberal consensus."[22] Moreover, even on religiously divisive issues most Americans have not taken sides; they are pulled in competing directions. The middle is generally sympathetic to religion, but also wary of religious authority and cautious about justifying public policy in religious terms. For them, Alan Wolfe has argued, the culture war is not carried on between distinct groups but goes on within, personally and individually.[23] Americans may be ambivalent, but they are not extremists. Nonetheless, the notion that religion and people of faith are embattled continues to be fueled by political activists who reap the benefits of alarmism; in 2004 the international distress call was incorporated into the title of a new conservative religious advocacy group, "Mayday for Marriage." Invoking grievances and representing their followers as victims, these activists are "increasingly adept at refining the religious content of political messages, at modeling righteous behavior, and at dismissing or scapegoating the unrighteous."[24] Perhaps the most effective result of these political efforts has been to persuade many Americans and many in the press that the Republican Party is more friendly to religion than are the Democrats, who are portrayed as secularists, and that conservatives are more friendly to religion than are liberals.[25] For their part, not only secular citizens but many religious moderates as well are alarmed by what they see as decidedly non-ecumenical, crusading religious convictions and a readiness to abandon, not just relax, separation of church and state. It serves political mobilization, and makes good press, to cast Bush as a theocrat and Kerry as a Godless secularist.

ELECTION IN THE SHADOW OF 2000

Bush failed to win the popular vote in 2000, the electoral vote was disputed, and the outcome was decided by the Supreme Court. The tight election of 2000 compelled both parties to do everything conceivable to increase turnout. Religion helped Republicans accomplish this goal more than it helped Democrats.

The aim of Republican activists was to increase the turnout of supporters by "mobilizing the base": the goal for 2004 was 4 million more Evangelical voters. Ralph Reed, former Executive Director of the Christian Coalition and the Bush-Cheney campaign's southern coordinator spoke of the "evolution of the conservative faith vote: 'In the past, we left a pretty good chunk of votes to other people to turn out. We're not doing that anymore.'"[26] An example of the campaign's aggressive outreach effort was the call for churches to send their membership lists to state Bush-Cheney headquarters; it was abandoned after a public outcry. Congressional Republicans also tried unsuccessfully to pass a "safe harbor" bill for churches, which would have allowed them to engage in partisan politics and endorse candidates without losing the tax benefits that are conditional on distance from political campaigns.

The parties' capacity to mobilize an increase in turnout was not symmetrical. Mobilization is not just a matter of ideology, but of social organization. Republicans had an advantage insofar as "intensely religious" voters are tied into the institutional matrix of churches and allied voluntary associations. The Democrats' principal institutional support came from black churches and unions. The Democratic party had difficulty identifying established organizations that could be effective counterweights to religious groups organized in support of conservative policies and candidates. Both parties ramped up door-to-door efforts by volunteers and paid canvassers, but Democrats were more dependent on these "grass roots" get-out-the-vote drives. Turn-out efforts directed at individuals are more labor- and information-intensive than mobilization via established social and religious groups, and, lacking roots in stable institutions, they are less likely to persist beyond a particular campaign.

Another shadow Election 2000 cast over 2004 was the phenomenon that goes by the name "moral values." In 2004, 22% of the electorate cited "moral values" as the most important consideration in casting their vote (and 4/5 of these people voted for Bush). The relation between values and religion is ambiguous: not all moral conviction is rooted in religion, nor does religion have a monopoly on "moral values." Yet the tendency to identify moral values with religion only underscores the Republicans' success in representing their party, candidates, and signature issues as uniquely concerned with "moral values," with the implication that secular and amoral are paired.

If we look at specific issues, however, we see that things are more complex. One illustration is same-sex marriage, which was guaranteed a central place in the campaign by the 2003 ruling by the Massachusetts Supreme Judicial Court that the state constitution required licensing same-sex marriage. The issue was given a religious halo, captured by the notion of a "sacred" marital bond, and conservative religious groups got prohibition of same-sex marriage on the ballot in 11 states. But we know that opposition to same-sex marriage was neither exclusively religion-based nor politically conservative. Democrats who favored civil unions for gays, including Kerry, opposed it. Some of the strongest arguments against same-sex marriage were political, not religious, based on the tradition of state control of marriage and on objections to courts making a decision that is better left to democratic majorities. The referenda solidly won in all 11 states with support ranging from 57% to 77%. The figures show that their success relied on more than religiously based or conservative voting. The referenda do not appear to have boosted relative conservative turnout in those states above the overall national increase to any substantial extent.[27] Probably aided by strong get-out-the-vote operations in Ohio and Oregon, Democratic turnout increased almost as much in the 11 states with same-sex marriage referenda on the ballot as did Republican turnout. In short, the effects of the referenda were neither large nor one-sided.

The most notable change from 2000 with regard to "moral values" is that the range of values issues was enlarged. In previous election cycles, the phrase had referred to a small subset of issues: vouchers for religious schools and the pledge of allegiance, and of course abortion, which was given added impetus by the possibility that new appointments to the Supreme Court might overturn *Roe v. Wade*. In 2004 a related issue came to the fore: embryonic stem-cell research. More important, "moral values" were extended into entirely different political areas. Bush presented his faith-based initiative not just as another way of providing needed social services but as a better way: "Faith-based programs are only effective because they practice faith....I have asked Congress not to fear faith."[28] In addition, "values" were extended to national security, war and peace. The terrorist attack on September 11 and the war in Iraq made national security and foreign policy the most important issues of the election, and the biggest "religion" story of the campaign was how national security was tied to faith either directly or via "moral values."

THE 2004 CAMPAIGN: PIETY AND POLICY

Historically, American foreign policy has often been framed in religious terms; anticommunism for example combined ideological opposition with resistance to the scourge of atheism. In the 2004 campaign, Bush did more than ritualistically invoke perennial phrases like America as a "city on the hill" and "the sacred cause of freedom." He cast the moment of crisis created by the September 11th attack on the country in spiritual if not sectarian terms, describing the global conflict as good versus evil. Bush also characterized the American response to 9/11 as a matter of spiritual as well as military self-defense. He credited his faith for firm decision-making, and steadfastness, and he linked both his understanding of America's purpose in the world and his ability to understand the nature of the terrorist threat to religion. Bush forcefully fused faith and the cause of human freedom: "Freedom is on the march, and America and the world are more secure because of it. I believe in my heart of hearts that every person in the world wants to live in a free society. I believe this because I understand that freedom is not America's gift to the world; freedom is the Almighty God's gift to each man and woman of this world."[29]

Although Bush was careful to put the response to 9/11 and the Iraq war in ecumenical rather than narrowly Christian terms, and that Islam had been "hijacked by terrorists," still, his words were open to sectarian interpretation. Among other things, there was Bush's frequent incorporation of scripture in his speeches. During the course of the campaign, some officials spoke openly of a Christian crusade. Undersecretary of Defense Lt. General William Boykin denounced Muslims for belief in a false God, and suggested that Islamic terrorists attacked the United States "because we're a Christian nation, because our foundation and our roots are Judeo-Christian."[30] Our "spiritual enemy will only be defeated," Boykin said, "if we come against them in the name of Jesus [sic]."[31] It is not surprising that Muslim organizations protested the "crusade-esque feel" of the administration, and what they feared was a global "war of civilizations" between the West and Islam.[32] They interpreted public remarks in the context of the administration's homeland security policy, which involved dragnets of Muslim men and civil rights violations, and led Muslim groups to oppose Bush's reelection. Although Bush repudiated Boykin's comments and insisted that "our war is not against the Muslim faith," his steady identification of God's purposes with America's foreign policy left room for such misunderstandings.[33] In saying "God is not neutral," Bush did not refer explicitly to the God of Christianity only, or point to warring religious camps, but his remark was open to such a reading.[34]

The Democrats faced two choices in 2004. One choice was whether to answer Bush's exhibition of personal religiosity in kind. The other was how to forge links of their own among religion, "moral values," and policy. Kerry prided himself on religious reserve and on separating his religious beliefs from his decisions in public life—so much so that a Pew poll in July, 2004 found that only 43% of Catholics knew Kerry was Catholic.[35] Over the course of the campaign, at first mainly during appearances in black churches, Kerry set out to establish his credentials as a man of religion. He referred increasingly to his own religious experiences, injected God in stump speeches, and blessed America on every occasion; his campaign hired a "religion outreach" director. Still, pundits charged that like many Democrats, Kerry was "tone deaf" to religion and described his expressions of faith as "sub par."[36] Observers tended to view these efforts cynically: the Democrats "still think of religion mostly as a constituency problem…how many Catholic votes in the Rust Belt they can get by employing a certain strategy."[37] No matter that Kerry's beliefs were sincere and that public statements about them were efforts to educate the public about him, the Democratic candidate was at a disadvantage.

One source of weakness came in the circumstances of being a liberal Catholic. Kerry identified with a religion that is explicitly doctrinal and whose hierarchical leadership imposes a claim to obedience. Bush in contrast did not identify himself with any particular religious community or precise religious doctrine.[38] He spoke generally of "faith" as inspiration but not of its specific demands. By emphasizing his own personal religious experience over his identity as a Methodist, Bush resembled—and represented—the post-denominational non-doctrinaire Protestantism widespread in contemporary America. But Kerry, by virtue of his Catholicism, was vulnerable to criticism by the hierarchy on doctrinal grounds: that because of his support for abortion rights and civil unions, he was not a "good Catholic." The dictates of a few Catholic bishops that Kerry should be denied communion (and that Catholics who voted for Kerry would lose their good standing in the Church) was exploited by other Christian conservatives. A telling quip heard throughout the campaign was that if John F. Kennedy was too Catholic for the nation, John Kerry was not Catholic enough. Ironically, the image of Kerry picking and choosing occasions for obedience to religious mandates, amplified the often repeated Republican charge that he was a political opportunist.

But the religious challenge for Democrats ran deeper than Kerry's personal beliefs. They had to decide *how* to bring religion to bear on policy in the absence of a long Democratic tradition of relating religious understanding to values and to specific issues. For more than 20 years Republicans have linked "life" and "family values" to both religious belief and conservative policies (criminalizing abortion or tax credits for personal dependents, for example). A bumper sticker in the 2004 campaign read "GOP: God's Official Party." Democrats challenged this monopoly. John Edwards insisted, "we cannot concede values to this president, because I think we win a values debate with this president...."[39] But the Democrats entered the faith and values fray without the benefit of decades of political spade-work connecting their policies and promises with communities of faith.

The associations Democrats began to forge among religion, values, and policy were noticeably different from Bush's. For Bush, faith is the key to correctly diagnosing the country's ills, it is the best means to combat those ills, and faith reveals America's highest purposes. Bush spoke in individualist terms of changing America "one heart and soul at a time." Kerry challenged this in religious terms by drawing a contrast between faith and deeds. He appealed repeatedly to the Book of James: "It is not enough, my brother, to say you have faith when there are no deeds....Faith without works is dead." Where Bush emphasized the insufficiency of good will in the absence of faith, Kerry emphasized the insufficiency of faith in the absence of sound and effective commitments. Where Kerry's rhetoric suggested that the problems of America stem from inadequate judgment, Bush argued that our problems stem from a deficit of faith.

Voters attuned to religion in politics were offered a choice. But despite Democratic efforts, there was an asymmetry between the parties. Democrats connected "family values" to issues like raising the minimum wage and improving health care, and "moral values" like stewardship to environmentalism. But Republicans had a head start in creating and fixing mental associations among religion, moral values, and policy. Moreover, the institutional matrix is crucial to framing issues effectively. A religious frame for issues is potent when organized groups are primed to accept them and stand ready to lobby on behalf of these issues. In 2004 the groups that advocated progressive health care reforms or environmental protection were not identified with religious communities. Catholic voices were not as prominent on behalf of social justice issues promoted by Democrats as they were on behalf of Republican stands on abortion.

In the decisive matter of national security and the war in Iraq, this partisan difference in connecting piety and policy loomed large. Kerry invoked God's blessing on America and its troops, but his challenges to Bush's foreign policy were political. Because he did not argue that Bush's foreign policy and the war were unjust, Kerry could not benefit from religious opposition to the war by the National Council of Churches or by Catholics who employed just war theory to condemn the American intervention in Iraq. His criticism was aimed at Bush's political judgment—at the President's misrepresentations and mismanagement of the conflict—rather than at his moral justifications. Kerry promised "a more effective, more thoughtful, more strategic, more proactive, more sensitive war."[40] "Who has the right plan," Kerry asked, "to win the war on terror?" Transparent facts and thoughtful plans, not faith, were the core of his promise. Kerry delivered a religious punch only once, to point out Bush's unreasonable certitude: "I don't want to claim that God is on our side. As Abraham Lincoln told us, I want to pray humbly that we are on God's side."[41] If we cannot be certain that God approves of American policy, Kerry could not use religious understanding to justify America's engagement or his own policy prescriptions. Bush, in contrast, put the struggle for freedom at the center of a story that links divine purpose with national purpose, and both with his leadership. Bush's faith translated into war against the enemy as "evil." Kerry's religious style translated into a less gripping preoccupation with "managing" security.

CONCLUSION

Religion was at the heart of political rhetoric and voter mobilization in Election 2004. We have pointed to three asymmetries between the parties. Republicans had the advantage of many years of work forging connections in the public's mind among faith, moral values, and conservative policies. These links were called upon when the events of 9/11 and the war in Iraq required not just a justification for specific decisions but a compelling narrative account of American purposes. Republicans also had the advantage of religious institutions that had served for some time as the basis for political organization and voter mobilization. Finally, Bush was able to frame his predominantly religious-based appeals in a way that did not scare off voters who were not intensely religious, and who may not have been attracted to religious arguments at all.

The election brought out new voters; a 16% rise from roughly 105 million in 2000 to 122 million in 2004, an increase from 54% to 60% of age-eligible citizens. The Republican increase was roughly from 50.5 million in 2000 to 61.7 million in 2004; the Democratic rise was from 51 to 58.5 million. How much of the Republican increase was white Evangelical and fundamentalist Christians? Estimates are 4.5 to 5 million, an estimate muddied by changes in the exit-poll question that counted them more broadly. Two facts put these increases in perspective. First, only 35% of Bush voters in 2004 described themselves as white Evangelicals. Second, those who attended church weekly or more constituted exactly the same share of the electorate in 2004 as in 2000, 42%; similarly those who attend church monthly (14%) and those who attend seldom or never (42%) were also an unchanged share of the electorate.

Bush's increased share of the vote did not come mainly from intensely religious voters, in short. Decomposing Bush's gains by church attendance makes the same point. He picked up only 0.4% in share of the total electorate among those who attend church weekly or more. His increase in the share of those who attend monthly was 0.6%. His increase of those who attend seldom or never was the greatest: 1.6%. That is, almost two-thirds of Bush's gains came among infrequent worshippers or nonreligious voters.[42] The candidate who laced his rhetoric with religion and who mobilized supporters with the help of religious organizations won by virtue of garnering a greater share of the nonreligious vote than he had in the last election.

Bush and the Republicans were able to call on religious organizations and to use religious rhetoric more effectively than Kerry and the Democrats. In doing so, they were able to amplify their support among intensely religious voters, and to attract moderately religious voters. They were also able to avoid repelling both those for whom religion is not a monthly or weekly activity and nonreligious voters. They drew on the political resources religion offers without losing support from voters at the religious center or voters whose political considerations were purely secular. Bush expressed and represented contemporary post-denominational religiosity, which takes faith seriously yet is not doctrinaire. At the same time, he used religious language to invoke qualities of character that would appeal to the center, often for purely secular reasons. In this way, religion framed the presentation of character and the description of policies and issues in campaign 04. But this does not mean that most votes were critically informed by religious considerations, much less that every vote was a vote for or against religion. Religion was at the center of the campaign but the religious vote was not the decisive factor in the outcome.

Russell Muirhead is an associate professor of government at Harvard University.

Nancy L. Rosenblum is Senator Joseph Clark Professor of Ethics in Politics and Government and Chair of the Department of Government at Harvard. She is the author of *Membership and Morals: The Personal Uses of Pluralism in America* (Princeton University Press, 1998), which was awarded the David Easton Prize by the Foundations of Political Theory section of the APSA in 2002. She is editor and contributor to *Obligations of Citizenship and Demands of Faith: Religious Accommodation in Pluralist Democracies* (Princeton University Press, 2000); co-editor with Robert Post of *Civil Society and Government* (Princeton University Press, 2001); editor and contributor to *Breaking the Cycles of Hatred: Memory, Law, and Repair*, a collection on interpersonal and intergroup violence (Princeton University Press, 2002). She is currently working on a theoretical study of political parties.

Daniel Schlozman is a doctoral student in Government and Social Policy at Harvard University.

Francis X. Shen is a joint J.D./Ph.D. candidate in Harvard Law School and Government Department.

NOTES

1. Clinton, William J. *Remarks at a Prayer Breakfast in Houston*, 28 Weekly Comp. Pres. Doc. 1460 (Aug. 20, 1992).

2. O'Brien, Conor Cruise. (1988). *God Land: Reflections on Religion and Nationalism*. Cambridge, MA: Harvard University Press.

3. In 2001, 81% of the adult population identified with a religion. Kosmin, Barry A., Mayer, Egon, & Keysar, Ariela. (2001). *American Religious Identification Survey*. New York: The Graduate Center of the City University of New York, p. 10. This report is herein referred to as ARIS.

4. Eck, Diana. (2001). *A New Religious America: How a "Christian country" has now become the world's most religiously diverse nation*. San Francisco: Harper San Francisco, p. 5.

5. This explains the renaissance of study of religion and politics in the United States. See: Leege, David C., Kellstedt, Lyman A., Eds. (1993). *Rediscovering the Religious Factor in American Politics*. Armonk, NY: M.E. Sharpe.

6. Though there is a fall-off of support for endorsement of candidates by churches and clergy (*GOP The Religion Friendly Party*. Retrieved on August 31, 2003 from The Pew Research Forum on Religion and Public Life web site: http://pewforum.org/docs/index.php?DocID=51). At the same time, a separate PEW study finds that only about a fifth say they frequently rely on their religious beliefs to help them decide how to vote. (*Religion and Politics: Contention and Consensus*. Retrieved on August 24, 2004 from The Pew Research Forum on Religion and Public Life web site: http://pewforum.org/docs/index.php?DocID=26.)

7. Address of Senator John F. Kennedy to the Greater Houston Ministerial Association, September 12, 1960, Rice Hotel, Houston, Texas. Retrieved on August 24, 2004 from John F. Kennedy Library and Museum web site: http://www.jfklibrary.org/j091260.htm.

8. Green, John C. *The American Religious Landscape and Political Attitudes: A Baseline for 2004*. Retrieved on August 24, 2004 from The Pew Research Forum on Religion and Public Life web site: http://pewforum.org/publications/surveys/green-full.pdf. Green judges that the three sets of religious traditionalists groups were majority Republican and Centrist Protestants and Other Christians were plurality Republican. Seven religious groups were majority Democratic, including Modernist Christians, Atheist/Agnostic, and minority religious groups (at 9).

9. Manza, Jeff & Brooks, Clem. (1997). "The religious factor in U.S presidential elections, 1960–1992." *American Journal of Sociology*, Vol. 103, Issue 1, p. 73: "Far from approaching the point of insignificance predicted by the "declining cleavage" thesis, the religious cleavage appears to be nearly twice the magnitude of the more widely debated class cleavage."

10. Woodward, Kenneth L., with Patricia King, Peter McKillop, and Anne Underwood. "From 'Mainline' to Sideline," *Newsweek*, Dec. 22, 1986, p. 54.

11. 2000 and 2004 exit polls; source: cnn.com.

12. ARIS at 10–11 (see note 3).

13. Wuthnow, Robert. (1990). *The Restructuring of American Religion: Society and Faith since World War II*. Princeton, NJ: Princeton University Press.

14. Green (2004) at 7.

15. Galston, William A. (2004) at 4. "Religious pluralism and the limits of public reason," Paper: "How Naked a Public Square? Reconsidering the Place of Religion in American Public Life," Princeton University, October 22, 2004. Accessed online in November 2004 at: http://web.princeton.edu/sites/jmadison/events/conferences/conferences.htm. Fowler, Robert B. & Hertzke, Allen D. (1995) *Religion and Politics in America: Faith, Culture, and Strategic Choices*. Boulder, CO: Westview Press, p. 50.

16. Wald, Kenneth D. (2003). *Religion and Politics in the United States* (Fourth Edition). New York: Rowman and Littlefield, at 197.

17. In this election, proliferation was encouraged by campaign finance reform and 527s.

18. Interfaith Alliance. Retrieved on Nov. 1, 2004 from: www.interfaithalliance.org/news.

19. The phrase is James Davison Hunter's. Hunter, James D. (1991). *Culture Wars: The struggle to define America*. New York: BasicBooks.

20. *President Reagan's Remarks at an Ecumenical Prayer Breakfast*, Dallas, Texas, August 23, 1984. Retrieved on August 24, 2004 from the Ronald Reagan Presidential Library web site: http://www.reagan.utexas.edu/resource/speeches/1984/82384a.htm.

21. "President Bush: America's Strength Found in Hearts and Souls of Our Citizens," Speech given at Union Bethel AME Church, New Orleans, January 15, 2004. Retrieved on August 24, 2004 from: http://www.georgewbush.com/News/Read.aspx?ID=2165.

22. Dimaggio, Paul, Evans, John, & Bryson, Bethany, "Have Americans' Social Attitudes Become More Polarized," in Rhys H. Williams, Ed., *Cultural Wars in American Politics* (New York: Aldine de Gruyter, 1997) at 77; John H. Evans, "Have Americans' Attitudes Become More Polarized—An Update," Princeton University Center for Arts and Cultural Policy Studies Working Paper #24, Spring 2002; Fiorina, Morris P., with Samuel J. Abrams and Jeremy C. Pope (2005). *Culture War?: The Myth of a Polarized America*. New York: Pearson Longman.

23. Wolfe, Alan. (1998). *One Nation After All: What Middle-class Americans Really Think about God, Country, and Family, Racism, Welfare, Immigration, Homosexuality, Work, the Right, the Left, and Each Other*. New York: Viking.

24. Leege, David C., "Methodological Advances in the Study of American Religion and Politics," Paper presented at the 100th Annual Meeting of the American Political Science Association, August 28, 2003, Chicago, IL, p. 20.

25. *Religion and Politics: Contention and Consensus*. Retrieved on August 24, 2004 from The Pew Research Forum on Religion and Public Life web site: http://pewforum.org/docs/index.php?DocID=26. Linking the polarizing ideological labels "conservative" and "liberal" to religious traditionalism and secular progressivism respectively. Miller, Alan S., & Hoffmann, John P., "The Growing Divisiveness: Culture Wars or a War of Words," *Social Forces* (December 1999) 78(2): 721–752.

26. Cited in Cooperman, Alan, "Evangelical Leaders Appeal to Followers to Go to the Polls," *Washington Post*, Friday, October 15, 2004.

27. In states with gay-marriage referenda, the share of age-eligible citizens voting Republican increased by 5.16% between 2000 and 2004, compared to a national increase of 4.76%. However, the proportion of citizens voting Democratic in states with gay-marriage referenda rose by 3.88% while the national increase was only 2.98%. An unweighted average of the eleven states with same-sex marriage referenda shows increases of 4.6% of voting-age population for Republicans and 2.81% for Democrats. Data on voting-age population from Gans, Curtis, "Voter Turnout in Election 2004," accessed December 10, 2004, at www.fairvote.org. Election results from www.uselectionatlas.org, accessed December 10, 2004. Also, using turnout data from Professor Michael P. McDonald at George Mason University, we found no statistically significant correlation between Bush's share of the vote and the presence of

gay-marriage referenda on the ballot, or between change in voter turnout from 2000 and the presence of gay-marriage referenda on the ballot. Some individual states with referenda saw a large increase in turnout (such as Georgia and Ohio, each with over a 9% increase), while others did not (such as Montana, with a 2.4% increase). Meanwhile some states without referenda had a large increase in turnout, such as Arizona, Colorado, Florida, Nevada, New Mexico, and South Dakota, all with over a 9% increase from 2000.

28. "President Bush: America's Strength Found in Hearts and Souls of Our Citizens," Speech given at Union Bethel AME Church, New Orleans, January 15, 2004. Retrieved on August 24, 2004 from: http://www.georgewbush.com/News/Read.aspx?ID=2165.

29. "President Bush in Wisconsin: Progress Depends on Safety of American People," Brown County Veterans Memorial Complex, Ashwaubenon, Wisconsin, Saturday, October 30, 2004. Retrieved on November 1, 2004 from: http://www.whitehouse.gov/news/releases/2004/10/20041030-5.html.

30. Quoted in: "Rumsfeld defends general who commented on war and Satan," Associated Press, Friday, October 17, 2003.

31. Graham, Bradley, "General Rebuked for Talk of God," msnbc.com, October 17, 2003, story ID 215186886.

32. Press Release, "Arab Americans Endorse Sen. Kerry," October 6, 2004. Retrieved on October 30, 2004 from: http://www.aapac.org.

33. Press conference by the President, October 28, 2003. Retrieved August 28, 2004 from www.whitehouse.gov.

34. President Bush, "Our Mission and Our Moment," Joint Session of Congress, September 20, 2001. Retrieved on August 24, 2004 from: http://www.whitehouse.gov/news/releases/2001/09/20010920-8.html.

35. Wilgoren, Jodi & Keller, Bill, "Kerry and Religion," *New York Times*, October 7, 2004.

36. Perlstein, Rick, "The Politics of Piety," *Los Angeles Times*, July 11, 2004.

37. Sullivan, Amy. "Preach It, Brother: Why did Kerry stop talking about faith?," in *Gadflyer*. Retrieved on August 24, 2004 from: http://gadflyer.com/articles/?ArticleID=147.

38. He is a member of the mainline Protestant United Methodist Church.

39. Edwards, John, Interview with Fox News Sunday, Dec. 28, 2003. Retrieved on August 24, 2004 from: http://www.foxnews.com/story/0,2933,106812,00.html.

40. Remarks of Senator John Kerry at the UNITY 2004 Conference, August 5, 2004. Retrieved on August 24, 2004 from: http://www.johnkerry.com/pressroom/speeches/spc_2004_0805.html. This remark was mocked by Vice-President Cheney for its mention of "sensitivity," as revealing a soft-hearted rather than ruthless and tough-minded approach to foreign policy.

41. Speech to the 2004 Democratic National Convention, July 29, 2004. Retrieved on August 24, 2004 from: http://www.johnkerry.com/pressroom/speeches/spc_2004_0729.html.

42. These are our calculations from the 2000 and 2004 exit polls, available at cnn.com. They concur with the post-election poll and analysis done by America Coming Together, which holds that religious voters were not the basis of Bush's victory in Ohio; see Rosenthal, Steve, "Okay, We Lost Ohio; the Question is Why?" *Washington Post*, December 5, 2004, p. B3.

CHAPTER TWELVE

The 2004 Congressional Elections

Bruce A. Larson

FAIRLEIGH DICKINSON UNIVERSITY

INTRODUCTION

The presidential contest was clearly the main attraction of the 2004 elections, but the congressional elections certainly added some drama. The big winners in this year's House and Senate contests were incumbents of both parties—nearly all of whom won reelection—and Republicans, who increased their majorities in both chambers. Senate Republicans had a particularly momentous showing, sweeping five Democratic-held open seats in the South and ousting Senate Democratic Leader Tom Daschle in South Dakota. Senate Democrats averted total disaster only by capturing Republican-held open seats in Illinois and Colorado. But the GOP's net gain of four seats gives them a solid 55–44 advantage over Democrats in the Senate.[1]

In the much larger U.S. House, the GOP's net gain of four seats was considerably more modest—and attributable entirely to the mid-decade Texas redistricting engineered by GOP House Majority Leader Tom DeLay. Outside of Texas, House Republicans actually registered a net *loss* of two seats. All told, and despite the millions of dollars spent, most House contests were characterized by the status quo, thanks to the enormous number of gerrymandered congressional districts drawn to give one party or the other a virtually insurmountable advantage.

Republican gains in the House and Senate should make it easier for the GOP to push through its agenda in the 109th Congress. Yet the ability to pass the party's legislative program will be more complicated in the Senate, where Senate Republicans remain five seats short of a filibuster-proof majority (60), than in the House, where a simple majority wins the day. With retirements and defeats further depleting the already dwindling ranks of political moderates, the 109th Congress promises a continuation of the intense partisan polarization and rancor that have characterized Congress for the past two decades. This is especially true in the House, where heavily partisan districts offer few rewards for compiling a politically moderate record and where the majority party can use procedural rules to steamroll the minority party.

The 109th Congress will set the stage for the 2006 midterm elections. In the House, the heavily gerrymandered districts all but guarantee a stable, if modest, Republican majority for 2006—and probably for the remainder of the decade, when the decennial redistricting process unfolds again. In the Senate, Democrats will face another uphill battle, defending more seats than Republicans and needing an improbable six-seat gain to win a majority.

THE SETTING

Voters generally hold the president's party in Congress responsible for bad news, and the news in 2004 was certainly not good. Job creation was modest, gas prices were high, budget deficits soared, and—at least by the public's assessment—the war in Iraq was going poorly.[2] To make matters worse, the 9/11 Commission's conclusion that Iraq played no role in the September 11, 2001, terrorist attacks, as well as chief U.S. Weapons Inspector Charles A. Duelfer's conclusion that Iraq had not had a viable weapons of mass destruction program for more than a decade, undermined the Bush administration's chief reasons for invading Iraq.[3] Then in October, only two weeks before Election Day, news surfaced that nearly 380 tons of explosives had vanished from a supposedly safe storage area in Iraq.[4] Not surprisingly, polls showed that many voters thought the nation was on the wrong track, and President Bush's approval ratings were relatively low for an incumbent facing reelection.[5] With the GOP holding the presidency and both houses of Congress, Democrats tried to pin the blame for the nation's woes on Republicans. Democratic leaders insisted that the spate of bad news provided an electoral tailwind for the party's congressional candidates.[6]

In the term leading up to the 2004 election, partisan vitriol on Capitol Hill never seemed far from boiling over. With the House and Senate almost evenly divided between Republicans and Democrats, both parties would do nearly anything to gain even the slightest edge. Examples abound. When considering the Medicare prescription drug legislation on November 22, 2003, House Republican leaders kept the final floor vote open for an unprecedented three hours while they twisted enough arms to pass the bill. Afterwards, House Democrats called on the House Ethics Committee to investigate Majority Leader Tom DeLay's tactics in securing votes for the measure. A year later, the House Ethics Committee formally admonished DeLay for his heavy-handed maneuvering.[7] In the Senate, meanwhile, Majority Leader Bill Frist ratcheted up partisan hostilities by breaking with custom and actively campaigning against his Democratic counterpart Tom Daschle in Daschle's home state of South Dakota.[8] Even member-versus-member lawsuits weren't off limits for partisans looking to score political points. When Louisiana Representative Rodney Alexander made a last-minute switch to the GOP in August 2004, several House Democrats threatened to sue Alexander if he didn't return the campaign contributions they had given to him during the past four years. The suit was averted only when Alexander promised to return the contributions by Election Day.[9] At times, the norms of civility between Democrats and Republicans completely broke down in the 108th Congress, as when Representatives Pete Stark (D-Calif) and Scott McInnis (R-Colorado) exchanged heated words during a July 2003 House Ways and Means Committee meeting. The brief squabble began when Stark objected to a procedural motion designed to move along the bill:

> **Stark:** Objection.
>
> **McInnis:** Shut up.
>
> **Stark:** Are you big enough to make me, you little wimp? Why don't you come over here and make me; I dare you. You little fruitcake. You little fruitcake.[10]

The meeting ended with committee Chair Bill Thomas (R-Calif) summoning the Capitol Hill Police to have Democrats evicted from the committee chambers.

But the apogee of raw partisan politics in the 108th Congress was no doubt the mid-decade remap in Texas engineered by GOP Majority Leader Tom DeLay (R-Texas). Unhappy with the 2002 midterm election results in Texas, and bolstered by new GOP majorities in the Texas statehouse, DeLay pushed for a second round of redistricting to replace the court-drawn congressional map produced after the 2000 census. The result was a highly contentious *re-redistricting* process during which several Democratic state lawmakers fled to neighboring Oklahoma and New Mexico to deny the state legislature a quorum. In the end, the GOP won the standoff, ramming through a district map that Republicans hoped would yield as many as seven new GOP seats in the Texas delegation. Indeed, Texas Democrats lost two seats even before a single election was held, as 80-year-old Ralph Hall switched parties and Democrats failed to even run a candidate in Texas's newly redrawn 10th district.

DeLay's bold tactics, which incensed Democrats and raised eyebrows even among a few Republicans, prompted yet another Ethics Committee investigation. Responding to a complaint filed by Representative Chris Bell—a one-term Democrat crushed in a primary in Texas's newly redrawn 9th district—the House Ethics Committee unanimously admonished DeLay on October 6, 2004, for allegedly trading legislative favors for campaign contributions and dispatching federal officials to locate the Texas lawmakers who fled the state during the redistricting battle.[11] Democrats moved quickly to exploit DeLay's troubles for their own political gain. "Mr. DeLay has proven himself to be ethically unfit to lead his party," declared House Democratic Leader Nancy Pelosi (D-Calif).[12]

Partisan vitriol only heightened the general tension created by the lingering threats of terrorist attacks on Capitol Hill. With the

Hart Senate Office building the target of an anthrax attack in October 2001, and with traces of the deadly chemical ricin discovered in the Dirksen Senate Building in February 2004, security officials were concerned that terrorists might attempt to disrupt the election by waging a direct attack on Congress. Most members took the security threats in stride, but Senator Mark Dayton (D-Minn) took the unusual step of closing his Washington office three weeks prior to the election in order to protect his staff.[13] Dayton claimed he had a moral responsibility to protect his staff; others claimed he had overreacted. Either way, Dayton's actions added to the tensions leading up to Election Day and reminded observers of how life had changed in post-9/11 America.

THE HOUSE CONTESTS

The outcomes of two special elections early in 2004 seemed to bode well for House Democrats. In Kentucky's 6th district, Democrat Ben Chandler, who had earlier lost Kentucky's race for governor to Republican House member Ernie Fletcher, handily defeated Republican state senator Alice Forgy Kerr, 55 to 43 percent, in a February 2004 special election to replace Fletcher. Then, in a June 2004 special election in South Dakota, Democrat Stephanie Herseth defeated Republican former state senator Larry Diedrich by fewer than 3,000 votes (51 to 49 percent) in a race to succeed Representative Bill Janklow, who had stepped down following a manslaughter conviction in an automobile accident. GOP leaders played down the defeats, insisting that they were a function of purely local circumstances and had no national implications. But Democrats claimed that the two victories reflected a national mood swing in favor of

Democrats and that the results were a harbinger of good things to come in November. Some Democrats even went as far as to suggest that November would bring about the reversal of the Republican tsunami of 1994, which itself began with two special election victories.[14] But even the most optimistic Democrats acknowledged that it wouldn't be easy. Democrats would still need a net gain of 11 seats to capture the House majority in November.

It was not to be. Any Democratic hopes of significant gains in the House were dashed by the Texas remap and, in many states, by congressional districts that were carefully drawn (in many cases by Republican-controlled legislatures) to lock in the status quo.[15] As Election Day neared, election forecasters showed only a handful of competitive districts. In its final pre-election analysis, for example, *Congressional Quarterly* rated only 35 (8 percent) of the 435 House races as highly competitive ("leans" or "no clear favorite")—down from 48 in 2002 and 54 in 2000.[16]

The 2004 House election results, summarized in Table 1, reaffirmed the near absence of electoral competition. All told, two incumbents were defeated in the primaries and another seven in the general election, adding up to an overall incumbent reelection rate of 98 percent.[17] The average incumbent, moreover, garnered 70 percent of the vote—a landslide by most standards—with only 34 incumbents (8 percent) receiving 55 percent or less of the vote.[18] What's more, 62 incumbents—34 Republicans and 28 Democrats— had no major-party opposition at all. As Table 2 shows, even open-seat contests were strikingly one-sided, with both parties successfully defending most of the seats they held going into the election. The overall results in Table 3 show that, all in all, it was a status quo election in the House. When all the votes were tallied,

Republicans scored a modest net gain of four seats, and those gains can all be attributed to DeLay's mid-decade remap in Texas. Outside of the Lone Star state, House Democrats actually scored a net gain of two seats.

Among the few incumbent defeats, most were not surprises. The loss of six Texas Democratic incumbents—two in the primaries and four in the general election—was all but guaranteed by the 2003 Texas remap. What *was* surprising in Texas is that veteran Democrat Chet Edwards, running in a district that included only about a third of his previous constituents, survived to serve yet another term in Congress. Edwards garnered 51 percent of the vote against Republican State Representative Arlene Wohlgemuth in Texas's 17th district—which, ironically, includes President Bush's Crawford ranch. The incumbent losses outside of Texas were not shockers either. In Georgia's 12th, Republican Max Burns lost to Democrat John Barrow in a district drawn for Democrats. (Democrats had lost the seat in 2002 only after the emergence of unfavorable, late-breaking news about their nominee, Charles Walker, Jr., propelled Burns to victory.) In Indiana's 9th district, three-term Democrat Baron Hill succumbed to the district's Republican leanings and to a strong challenger, Mike Sodrel, who had given Hill a serious run for his money in 2002. And in Illinois's 8th district, Republican Philip Crane, a 17-term incumbent who battled an alcohol addiction in 2000, was defeated in his rematch with Melissa Bean, an energetic 42-year-old high-tech consultant who hammered home the theme that Crane had lost touch with his district. Bean, who was 7 years old when Crane first won election to the House in 1969, continuously referred to Crane as the "junket king." Even a heavily Republican district couldn't save Crane in his second tussle with Bean.[19]

TABLE 1
Outcomes in 2004 House Contests Featuring an Incumbent

Incumbent reelection rate [a]	98%
Incumbents unopposed	62
Average incumbent vote share	70%

[a] Includes two Democratic incumbents defeated in the primaries.

TABLE 2
Outcomes in the 2004 House Open-Seat Contests[a]

	REPUBLICANS	DEMOCRATS
Open seats successfully defended	17 of 20	10 of 12
Open seats captured from the opposition party	2 of 12	3 of 20
Open seats from newly created districts [b]	3 of 4	1 of 4

[a] Two Democratic incumbents were defeated in the primaries; the districts in which they lost are defined as open seats.

[b] New districts created by the Texas remap in which no incumbent ran in the general election.

TABLE 3
Outcomes in the 2004 House General Elections

	REPUBLICANS	DEMOCRATS
Incumbent victories	207	186
Challenger victories	3	2
Open-seat victories	22	14
Partisan balance in 109th Congress (2005–06)[c]	232	202
Net gain or loss from 108th Congress (2003–04)	+4	-4

[c] Totals add up to 434 because there is one independent in the House (Representative Bernard Sanders of Vermont).

To be sure, a few House incumbents survived unexpectedly close races. In Connecticut's 4th district, for example, a surprisingly strong challenge by Democrat Diane Farrell, a Westport selectwoman, nearly cost GOP maverick Christopher Shays his seat. Shays' 52-percent showing in the race was by far the worst of his 17-year House career. But most incumbents enjoyed predictably easy victories, as the parties narrowed their playing fields to focus on the handful of contests that remained too close to call. Indeed, House Democrats eventually even abandoned their one-time star challenger Steve Broznak—the only House challenger featured at the Democratic National Convention—when it became clear that he had no chance of unseating Republican Mike Ferguson in New Jersey's 7th district.[20]

The lack of electoral competition in the 2004 House elections can be attributed to the post-2000 round of redistricting, in which state mapmakers drew districts with an eye for protecting one party or the other. Indeed, while the nationwide two-party vote for U.S. House candidates in 2004 was closely divided between Republican and Democrats, the two-party vote in most House districts was anything but even. Democrats who won their districts in 2004 garnered, on average, 73 percent of the two-party vote, while Republican victors amassed an average of 70 percent of the vote. And these numbers reflect more than the usual incumbency advantage. Even Democratic and Republican *open-seat* winners defeated their opponents by 24 and 34 percentage points, respectively. The redistricting that followed the 2000 census simply left very few districts in play—a fact that will minimize electoral competition in House races for the rest of the decade and likely guarantee a Republican majority for the foreseeable future.

THE SENATE CONTESTS

Senate Democrats entered the 2004 elections confronting a severe challenge. Of the eight open seats created by retirements, five were held by Democrats—and all five were in the South, where the GOP had been gradually establishing itself as the dominant party over the past two decades. The Republicans, meanwhile, would only need to defend open seats in Colorado, Illinois, and Oklahoma.

Senate contests are typically more competitive than House races. (As a *Wall Street Journal* editorial joked, senators haven't yet figured how to gerrymander states.[21]) But as Table 4 illustrates, the 2004 Senate contests were more one-sided than usual: 25 of 26 incumbent senators (96 percent) were reelected, and the average incumbent received 64 percent of the vote. The only incumbent to lose was in South Dakota, where, in a hard-fought and closely watched battle, former House member John Thune defeated Senate Democratic leader Tom Daschle by only 4,534 votes, ending Daschle's 18-year career in the Senate. As Minority Leader, Daschle was in the unenviable position of being chief obstructionist of the Bush agenda while hailing from a state that gave the president a 22-percentage point victory over Democratic presidential candidate John Kerry. In the Senate, Daschle's defeat was as much of a blow to Democrats as it was an enormous psychological victory for the GOP.

TABLE 4
Outcomes in 2004 Senate Contests Featuring an Incumbent

Incumbent reelection rate	96%
Incumbents unopposed	0[a]
Average incumbent vote share	64%

[a]Senator Michael Crapo of Idaho, who received 99.5 percent of the two-party vote, was all but unopposed.

A few other Senate incumbents had close calls. In Pennsylvania, GOP Senator Arlen Specter narrowly turned back a primary challenge by conservative House member Patrick Toomey before going on to defeat Democrat Joe Hoeffel in the general election. And in Kentucky, GOP Senator Jim Bunning barely squeaked by after a last minute surge from Democrat state Senator Daniel Mongiardo, who exploited several bizarre statements Bunning made late in the campaign. Bunning may well owe his slim victory to the gay marriage measure on Kentucky's ballots, which brought conservatives out to the polls.[22] In Alaska, after battling three primary opponents, Senator Lisa Murkowski eked out a razor-thin victory against former two-term Democratic Governor Tony Knowles. Murkowski's problems began in 2002, when, in a controversial move, her father, Governor Frank Murkowski, appointed her to serve out the remainder of his U.S. Senate term when he won the governorship. Other than these close calls, however, Senate incumbents mostly had an easy time of it. Of the 25 Senate incumbents up for reelection, 17 improved on their 1998 vote margins.[23]

The real action was in open-seat Senate contests, and the big news there was the GOP's sweep of the South. In three of the states, the contests were close. In Florida, Republican and former Housing and Urban Development Secretary Mel Martinez squeaked by former state education commissioner Betty Castor, 49 to 48 percent, with south Florida's Cuban population giving Martinez the edge. In North Carolina, Representative Richard Burr defeated President Bill Clinton's former chief of staff Erskine Bowles by a margin of 52 to 47 percent. This was Bowles' second statewide loss in two years, having lost to Elizabeth Dole in 2002. And in Louisiana's Election-Day primary, House member David Vitter garnered 51 percent against a pack of Democrats, avoiding a December runoff. Republican victories were considerably more lopsided in South Carolina, where Representative Jim DeMint handily defeated state school superintendent Inez Tenenbaum, and in Georgia, where Representative Johnny Isakson trounced House member Denise Majette. Republicans also easily kept Oklahoma in their column, with former House member (and ultra-conservative) Tom Coburn handily defeating Democratic Representative Brad Carson, 53 to 41 percent.

TABLE 5
Outcomes in the 2004 Senate Open-Seat Contests

	REPUBLICANS	DEMOCRATS
Open seats successfully defended	1 of 3	0 of 5
Open seats captured from the opposition party	5 of 5	2 of 3

TABLE 6
Outcomes in the 2004 Senate General Elections

	REPUBLICANS	DEMOCRATS
Incumbent victories	12	13
Challenger victories	1	0
Open-seat victories	6	2
Seats not up in 2004	36	29
Partisan balance in 109th Congress (2005–06)[a]	55	44
Net gain or loss from 108th Congress (2003–04)	+4	-4

[a]Totals add up to 99 because there is one independent in the Senate (Senator Jim Jeffords of Vermont).

Having been utterly swept in the South, Senate Democrats could take some solace in Illinois and Colorado, where they captured Republican-held open seats. In Illinois, state Senator Barack Obama walloped Republican Alan Keyes, 70 to 27 percent. The GOP imported Keyes, a former ambassador and presidential candidate, from Maryland when the Party's initial nominee, Jack Ryan, withdrew from the contest following public disclosure of his sex club visits.[24] Obama, a rising star whose speech at the Democratic National Convention electrified Democrats, will be the Senate's only African American in the 109th Congress (and only the third to be elected to the Senate since Reconstruction). Democrats enjoyed a narrower victory in Colorado, where Democratic state Attorney General Ken Salazar defeated beer executive Peter Coors by 3 percentage points (50 to 47 percent). Salazar's victory was the second for his family on Election Day; his brother, John, narrowly won the open-seat contest in Colorado's 3rd District.

Republicans finished the day with a net gain of four seats in the U.S. Senate, giving them 55 seats for the 109th Congress and holding Democrats, with 44 seats, to their lowest numbers in the U.S. Senate since Herbert Hoover was president.[25] What's more, Republican domination of the South is near complete. Republicans will hold 22 of the South's 26 U.S. Senate seats in the 109th Congress, with Democrats remaining only in Florida (Bill Nelson), Louisiana (Mary Landrieu), and Arkansas (Blanche Lincoln and Mark Pryor). Louisiana elected its first Republican senator *ever*, and South Carolina will have two GOP senators for the first time since Reconstruction.[26] The "solid" appellation is once again appropriate for the South, but now it's the solid *Republican* South.

CAMPAIGN FINANCE

The 2004 elections were the first to play out under the new campaign finance regulations put in place by the 2002 Bipartisan Campaign Reform Act (BCRA). This legislation affected the flow of money in the 2004 congressional elections in several critical ways.[27] For starters, BCRA raised individual contribution limits from $1,000 to $2,000 per candidate, per election.[28] Second, through the so-called "Millionaires' Amendment," BCRA set contribution limits three to six times higher for candidates facing opponents who exceed a threshold amount of self-financing.[29] Third, BCRA prohibited the national parties from raising and spending unregulated soft money. State parties could still raise soft money to pay for get-out-the-vote efforts, but such funds were limited to $10,000 per source and could be raised only if permitted by state law.[30] Finally, BCRA prohibited the use of unregulated union or corporate money to finance "electioneering communications" broadcast within thirty days of a primary election or sixty days of a general election.[31] However, the ban on such communications did not extend to so-called 527 groups—independent non-profit partisan groups—and in May 2004, the Federal Election Commission (FEC) declined to bring such groups under the law.[32] Not surprisingly, 527s flourished.[33] As the Court wrote in *McConnell v. the Federal Election Commission* (2003), "Money, like water, will always find an outlet."[34]

BCRA surely didn't slow the flow of campaign money in the 2004 congressional elections. All told, spending by Senate candidates was up 32 percent from 2002, and spending by House candidates had increased by 10 percent.[35] Table 7 shows that, as usual, House and Senate incumbents significantly out-raised and outspent challengers. Not shown in the table is that House and Senate incumbents had more cash-on-hand in their campaign accounts than challengers *had even spent*. In open-seat races, where there was no incumbent to corner the political money market, candidates of each party raised and spent substantial sums of campaign money—though GOP open-seat House and Senate candidates had a clear financial advantage. The averages presented in Table 7, of course, obscure the priciest contests. The most expensive Senate race was in South Dakota, where Senate Democratic Leader Tom Daschle had spent $19,739,259 to his GOP challenger John Thune's $14,332,983. With 391,093 votes cast in the race, the two South Dakota candidates spent a combined $87.12 per voter. The most expensive House contest was the incumbent-versus-incumbent contest in Texas's 32nd district, in which Republican Pete Sessions had spent $4,466,337 and Democrat Martin Frost had spent $4,623,104. BCRA's increased contribution limits for Senate candidates facing wealthy self-financed opponents were triggered in at least one contest—the Illinois Democratic primary in which securities trader Blair Hull sank more than $29 million of his own money into the race.[36]

When BCRA was passed in 2002, some political analysts worried that the bill's soft money prohibition would sideline the national parties in federal elections. But true to form, the national parties adapted to the new regulations and played a significant role in financing the 2004 elections. As Table 8 shows, all four of the party congressional campaign committees were able to hold their own even without soft money by increasing substantially the sums of hard dollars they raised. Indeed, the National Republican Congressional Committee (NRCC) raised nearly as much in hard dollars in 2003–04 as it raised in hard and soft dollars *combined* in

TABLE 7
Average Major-Party Candidate Receipts and Expenditures
in the 2004 House and Senate Elections[†]

	HOUSE		SENATE	
	AVERAGE RECEIPTS	AVERAGE EXPENDITURES	AVERAGE RECEIPTS	AVERAGE EXPENDITURES
DEMOCRATS				
Incumbents	$1,001,092	$881,901	$7,426,543	$7,324,347
Challengers	$284,914	$278,684	$1,571,396	$1,541,373
Open seats	$958,346	$916,188	$7,887,551	$7,636,368
REPUBLICANS				
Incumbents	$1,194,587	$1,043,747	$5,548,553	$5,440,377
Challengers	$248,930	$241,841	$3,228,501	$3,047,974
Open Seats	$1,344,686	$1,239,948	$8,156,210	$7,718,387

[†]Through December 31, 2004.
Source: Federal Election Commission data.

TABLE 8
Congressional Campaign Committee Receipts, 2003–04 and 2001–02

	HARD MONEY RECEIPTS, 2003–04 (IN MILLIONS)[†]	HARD AND SOFT MONEY RECEIPTS, 2001–02 (IN MILLIONS)		
	HARD	TOTAL	HARD	SOFT
DEMOCRATS				
DCCC	$93.17	$102.89	$46.44	$56.45
DSCC	$88.66	$143.44	$48.39	$95.05
REPUBLICANS				
NRCC	$185.72	$193.30	$123.62	$69.68
NRSC	$78.98	$125.59	$59.16	$66.43

[†]Through 20 days prior to the election.
Source: Federal Election Commission, "Party Financial Activity Summarized for the 2004 Election Cycle," Press Release (March 2, 2005).

TABLE 9
Independent Expenditures Made by the Congressional Campaign Committee Receipts, September 1 Through October 28

	INDEPENDENT EXPENDITURES IN SUPPORT OF CANDIDATES	INDEPENDENT EXPENDITURES AGAINST CANDIDATES
DEMOCRATS		
DCCC	$29,522,143	$4,652,086
DSCC	$2,484,192	$5,566
REPUBLICANS		
NRCC	$11,329,618	$36, 898,297
NRSC	$1,271,908	$16,226,412

Source: Campaign Finance Institute, "Party Independent Spending Soars," Press Release (November 5, 2004).

2001–02. The soft money ban in the 2002 BCRA also prompted the national parties to make significant hard-money independent expenditures. Such party spending is unlimited provided it is done independently of the party's candidates. Table 9 presents the sums of independent expenditures made by the party congressional campaign committees between September 1st and October 28th. The NRCC's efforts were particularly impressive, spending more than $36 million against Democratic House candidates in the final months of the campaign.

Members of Congress themselves also did their part. In 2004, House and Senate incumbents in safe seats contributed substantial sums of campaign money to candidates in tight contests and to the party congressional campaign committees. For example, House Ways and Means Chair Bill Thomas (R-Calif) contributed $228,000 to Republican congressional candidates from his leadership PAC (Congressional Majority Committee), another $35,000 to

GOP candidates from his reelection account, and $425,000 to the NRCC from his reelection account. Meanwhile, Thomas's Democratic counterpart on Ways and Means, ranking member Charles Rangel (D-NY), gave $340,500 to Democratic congressional candidates from his leadership PAC (National Leadership PAC), $65,000 to Democratic candidates from his reelection account, and $440,000 to the DCCC from his reelection account. Two Senate Democrats—Charles Schumer of New York and Harry Reid of Nevada—each made $1 million contributions to the DSCC. Contributions from incumbents to the congressional campaign committees helped the party committees offset the loss of soft money prohibited by BCRA; incumbent donations also provided essential support for needy candidates. Running in Texas's 32nd district, for example, GOP House member Pete Sessions received $337,991 directly from his Republican colleagues in Congress. Party leaders lean hard on safe incumbents to share their campaign resources, and during the past decade especially, incumbents have become an integral part of each party's fundraising machinery.37

Interest groups were also heavily involved in the financing of congressional elections. The FEC had not yet released final PAC data for the 2003–04 election cycle at the time of this writing, but in a report released on September 1, 2004, the Commission reported that PAC contributions to House candidates for the first 18 months of the cycle were up by 21 percent compared with the similar 18-month period in 2001–02; PAC contributions to Senate candidates had increased by 20 percent.38 By June 30, 2004, PACs had already contributed more than $203 million to congressional candidates. Many PACs also spent substantial sums of hard money independently of candidates; between October 19th and 24th, for example, the American Medical Association made $282,196 in hard-money independent expenditures in support of Louisiana GOP Senate winner David Vitter, and the National Rifle Association spent $135,788 in support of Florida GOP Senate victor Mel Martinez. Finally, scores of so-called 527 groups spent substantial sums of unregulated money on voter mobilization efforts and issue ads—ads that praise or criticize a candidate's record without expressly advocating the election or defeat of the candidate.[39]

CONCLUSION: TOWARD THE 109TH CONGRESS AND THE 2006 MIDTERM ELECTIONS

Congress watchers can expect familiar patterns in the 109th Congress. Led by Speaker Dennis Hastert (R-Illinois) and iron-fisted Majority Leader Tom DeLay, House Republicans will continue to use their substantial procedural prerogatives to steamroll House Democrats and ram through the GOP's conservative agenda. Democrats, led by one of the House's most liberal members—Representative Nancy Pelosi of San Francisco—will respond as they have since 1994, launching vitriolic partisan assaults from the back benches. The heavily partisan districts drawn in the post-2000 redistricting, which offer few rewards to members who compile politically moderate records, will only exacerbate the intense partisan rancor that has characterized the House in the past two decades. More than ever, compromise will be synonymous with treason in the House.

The picture is more complex in the Senate, where minority party members enjoy more power than in the House and where, even after the GOP's southern sweep, both parties still contain a few political moderates. Although the Senate GOP's majority was bolstered considerably by the 2004 elections, Republicans remain five seats short of a filibuster-proof majority of 60. To be sure, Daschle's defeat will never be far from the minds of Bush-state Democrats up for reelection in 2006, and they will be understandably nervous about obstructing the GOP agenda. But moderates in the Republican Party—notably Olympia Snowe and Susan Collins of Maine and Lincoln Chafee of Rhode Island—are by no means automatic votes for the GOP agenda, and the Senate GOP leadership must treat them fairly, lest they follow Senator Jim Jeffords's (I-Vermont) path out the door.[40] In the Senate, then, at least some members still have an incentive to look for common ground with their colleagues across the partisan isle. The near certain retirements of several Supreme Court Justices can be expected to provide a high-profile display of the Senate's partisan and ideological divisions, as it fulfills its constitutional responsibility of confirming President Bush's nominees for the Court.

All of this, of course, will take us to the 2006 midterm elections. Since World War II, midterm elections during a president's second term have typically produced losses for the president's Party. Yet there are good reasons to believe that this pattern won't hold in 2006. In the House, the preponderance of politically one-sided districts will make it difficult for *either* party to add seats. Indeed, the electoral maps in most states ensure that even a sizable public opinion shift in favor of Democrats would do little to alter the House's partisan composition. And while the federal courts are still scrutinizing Texas's new district map—a judicial invalidation would certainly help Democrats—the courts have upheld even the most egregious of partisan gerrymanders as long as they comply with voting rights standards.[41] In short, then, the House electoral map all but guarantees a stable, if modest, Republican House majority after the 2006 elections—and probably for the remainder of the decade, when the decennial redistricting process unfolds again.

In the Senate, Democrats will need a six-seat net gain to capture a majority in 2006—a most improbable scenario. For one, Democrats will again be defending more seats than Republicans in 2006, including five in states won by President Bush in 2004: Florida, Nebraska, New Mexico, North Dakota, and West Virginia. Of course, Democrats enjoy favorable odds of retaining these seats as long as the current incumbents run for reelection. (It's difficult to conceive of Senator Robert Byrd *ever* losing in West Virginia.) But exceptionally strong GOP challengers or incumbent retirements in any of these states could spell deep trouble for Democrats. Democrats could also face formidable challenges in Michigan and Washington, where Senators Debbie Stabenow and Maria Cantwell each won narrow victories in 2000, and in Wisconsin, where Senator Herb Kohl has hinted at retirement. Senate Republicans are not without their own potential vulnerabilities, of course. Pennsylvania Senator Rick Santorum is decidedly more conservative than his politically moderate state, and Rhode Island Senator Lincoln Chafee will be vulnerable as long as he remains a Republican in a highly Democratic state. One can even imagine a strong challenge to Virginia GOP Senator George Allen by popular Democratic Governor Mark Warner.[42] Still, Senate Democrats would appear to be facing greater challenges than Republicans as we head toward 2006. In the end, only time will tell what's in store for the 2006 elections, as events play out, the parties jockey for position, and incumbents decide whether to seek another term.

Bruce Larson is an assistant professor of American Government and Politics at Fairleigh Dickinson University.

NOTES

1. Independent Jim Jeffords of Vermont, who bolted the GOP in 2001, votes largely with Democrats.

2. Gary C. Jacobson and Samuel Kernell, *Strategy and Choice in Congressional Elections*, 2nd ed. (New Haven, CT: Yale University Press, 1983). John R. Hibbing and John R. Alford, "Electoral Impact of Economic Conditions: Who is Held Responsible?" *American Journal of Political Science* 25 (August 1981): 423–439. On public opinion regarding the Iraq war, see the *New York Times/CBS* poll conducted from October 28–30, 2004, showing that 50 percent of registered voters believed the war was going badly or somewhat badly, whereas only 47 percent believed it was going well or somewhat well. The results for likely voters were only slightly more positive. *The Polling Report*, accessed online at www.pollingreport.com on November 6, 2004.

3. National Commission on Terrorist Attacks Upon the United States, *The 9/11 Commission Report* (New York: W.W. Norton, 2004), pp. 66, 228–229. David Johnston, "Saddam Hussein Sowed Confusion About Iraq's Arsenal as a Tactic of War," *New York Times* (October 7, 2004), accessed online at www.nytimes.com on December 10, 2004.

4. James Glantz, William Broad, and David E. Sanger, "Huge Cache of Explosives Vanished From Site in Iraq," *New York Times* (October 25, 2004), accessed online at www.nytimes.com on December 10, 2004.

5. In national polls conducted between October 15 and 22, 2004, an average of 54 percent believed the nation was on the wrong track. *RealClearPolitics*. Accessed online at www.realclearpolitics.com on October 28, 2004. Similarly, in national polls conducted between October 18 and 25, 2004, an average of 50 percent approved of President George W. Bush's performance. *RealClearPolitics*. Accessed online at www.realclearpolitics.com on October 28, 2004.

6. Lauren W. Whittington, "Matsui Sees Potential for Big Win," *Roll Call* (October 26, 2004), accessed online at www.rollcall.com on October 27, 2004. Carl Hulse, "For Democrats, a Whiff of Victory," *New York Times* (May 28, 2004), p. A17. Chris Cillizza, "Democrats Tout Generic Ballot," *Roll Call* (May 24, 2004), accessed online at www.rollcall.com on May 26, 2004. Lauren W. Whittington, "Trash Talk Precedes Election," *Roll Call* (October 28, 2004), accessed online at www.rollcall.com on December 9, 2004.

7. Mary Agnes Carey, "Medicare Deal Goes to Wire in Late-Night House Vote," *Congressional Quarterly Weekly* (November 22, 2003), pp. 2879–2883. Delay allegedly tried to induce Representative Nick Smith (R-Michigan) to support the bill by offering to provide campaign assistance to Smith's son, who was running in a primary to replace the retiring Smith. Susan Ferrechio with Alan K. Ota, "Delay's Third Ethics Rebuke Threatens Potential Rise to Speaker," *Congressional Quarterly Weekly* (October 9, 2004), pp. 2369–2371. Carl Hulse, "House Ethics Panel Says DeLay Tried to Trade Favor for a Vote," *New York Times* (October 1, 2004), accessed online at www.nytimes.com on October 1, 2004.

8. Paul Kane, "Frist Going to Daschle's Turf," *Roll Call* (April 12, 2004), accessed online at www.rollcall.com on April 12, 2004.

9. Erin P. Billings, "Hoyer Close to Suing Switcher," *Roll Call* (October 6, 2004), accessed online at www.rollcall.com on October 6, 2004. Erin P. Billings, "Alexander Cuts Checks With Suit Looming"

Roll Call (October 12, 2004), accessed online at www.rollcall.com on October 12, 2004.

10. Nicole Duran, "Not Your Typical Markup: Democratic Walkout Prompts Threats, Taunts, and Police Response," *Roll Call* (July 18, 2003), accessed online at www.rollcall.com on November 22, 2004; Alan K. Ota, Liriel Higa, and Siobhan Hughes, "Fracas in Ways and Means Overshadows Approval of Pension Overhaul Measure," *Congressional Quarterly Weekly* (July 19, 2003), p. 1822.

11. Sheryl Gay Stolberg, "After Ethics Rebukes, DeLay's Fortunes May Now Lie With His Party's," *New York Times* (October 7, 2004). Ben Pershing, "DeLay Keeps Support," *Roll Call* (October 12, 2004), accessed online at www.rollcall.com on October 13, 2004.

12. David Stout, "Ethics Rebuke to Delay Prompts Democratic Calls for Ouster," *New York Times* (October 7, 2004), accessed online at www.nytimes.com on October 7, 2004.

13. Paul Kane, "Security Threat Prompts Dayton to Shutter Office," *Roll Call* (October 12, 2004), accessed online at www.rollcall.com on October 12, 2004.

14. Jennifer Mock, "Parties Spin the National Implications of Democrats' Special-Election Win," *Congressional Quarterly Weekly* (June 5, 2004), pp. 1342–1343. Stephen Kinzer, "Both Parties Seek National Momentum in South Dakota Race," *New York Times* (May 20, 2004), p. A16. Carl Hulse, "For Democrats, a Whiff of Victory," *New York Times* (May 28, 2004), p. A17.

15. Sam Hirsch, "The United States of Unrepresentativeness: What Went Wrong in the Latest Round of Congressional Redistricting," *Election Law Journal* 2 (Number 2, 2002): 179–216.

16. Peter E. Harrell, "Dearth of Close Races Makes Status Quo a Best Bet," *Congressional Quarterly Weekly* (October 23, 2004), pp. 2506–2511.

17. Counting the two incumbents defeated in the primaries, 404 incumbents sought reelection in 2004; 395 of those incumbents were successful.

18. This figure includes incumbents with no major-party opposition.

19. *Washington Post* Staff Writers, "New Representatives: Profiles of Non-Incumbent Winners," accessed online at www.washingtonpost.com on November 10, 2004. Peter E. Harrell, "Dearth of Close Races Makes Status Quo a Best Bet," *Congressional Quarterly Weekly* (October 23, 2004), p. 2514.

20. Suart Rothenberg, "Steve Brozak: Hot Commodity? Or Exaggerated Threat?" *Roll Call* (July 26, 2004), accessed online at www.rollcall.com on July 26, 2004.

21. Editorial, "No Contest," *Wall Street Journal* (November 12, 2004), p. A12.

22. James Dao, "Same-Sex Marriage Issue Key to Some G.O.P. Races," *New York Times* (November 4, 2004), p. 4.

23. These figures don't include Murkowski, who was appointed in 2002.

24. Lauren Whittington, "Ryan Quits Bid for Illinois Senate Seat." *Roll Call* (June 25, 2004), accessed online at www.rollcall.com on June 25, 2004.

25. That was in the 71st Congress (1929–31). The U.S. Senate, "Party Division in the Senate, 1789–Present," www.senate.gov/pagelayout/history/one_item_and_teasers/partydiv.htm, accessed on December 5, 2004.

26. Gregory Giroux, "Sweeping the New South," *Congressional Quarterly Weekly* (November 6, 2004), pp. 2602–2604. By comparison, Democrats held 17 of the 26 southern U.S. Senate seats after the 1988 elections. See Gregory Giroux, "Red States, Blue States—or Shades of Violet?," *Congressional Quarterly Weekly* (November 27, 2004), p. 2777.

27. For an excellent comprehensive treatment of BCRA, see Michael Malbin, ed., *Life after Reform: When the Bipartisan Campaign Reform Act Meets Politics* (Lanham, MD: Rowman & Littlefield, 2003).

28. The new limits are indexed for inflation.

29. For an excellent treatment of the Millionaires' Amendment, see Jennifer A. Steen, "The Millionaires' Amendment," in Michael Malbin, ed., *Life After Reform: When the Bipartisan Campaign Reform Act Meets Politics* (Landham, MD: Rowman & Littlefield, 2003).

30. The Supreme Court upheld the right of political parties to make independent expenditures in *Colorado Republican Federal Campaign Committee v. Federal Election Commission* 116 S. Ct. 2309 (1996). The 2002 BCRA initially required party committees to choose between making limited hard-money expenditures in coordination with their candidates or unlimited hard-money expenditures independently of their candidates. But the Supreme Court struck down those provisions in *McConnell v. the Federal Election Commission* (No. 02–1674, 2003).

31. Electioneering communications are defined as those which mention a specific federal candidate, reach the candidate's electorate, and are broadcast within 30 days of a primary or 60 days of a general election.

32. Glen Justice, "F.E.C. Declines to Curb Independent Fundraisers," *New York Times* (May 14, 2004), p. A14. John Cochran, "First Big Test of Campaign Finance Law Has Both Sides Girding for Next Round," *Congressional Quarterly Weekly* (May 29, 2004), pp. 1282–1283.

33. Chris Cillizza, "527s Bedevil Hill Hopefuls," *Roll Call* (August 31, 2004), accessed online at www.rollcall.com on August 31, 2004. Glen Justice, "Republicans Rush to Form New Finance Groups," *New York Times* (May 29, 2004), accessed online at www.nytimes.com on May 29, 2004.

34. *McConnell v. the Federal Election Commission* (No. 02–1674, 2003).

35. Federal Election Commission, "Congressional Campaigns Spend $711 Million through Pre-Election Period" (October 28, 2004), accessed online at www.fec.gov on December 6, 2004.

36. Lauren Whittington, "Hull Goes for Broke," *Roll Call* (February 25, 2004), accessed online at www.rollcall.com on December 10, 2004. Increased contribution limits were nearly triggered in a few general election contests, such as the race between Democrat Russ Feingold and Republican Tim Michels in Wisconsin. Nicole Duran, "Will Michels Trigger Millionaires' Provision in Wisconsin Senate Race?," *Roll Call* (October 7, 2004), accessed online at www.rollcall.com on November 5, 2004.

37. Larry J. Sabato and Bruce A. Larson, *The Party's Just Begun: Shaping Political Parties for America's Future*, 2nd ed. (New York: Longman, 2002), pp. 84–88.

38. Federal Election Commission, "PAC Activity Increases at 18-Month Point in 2004" (September 1, 2004), accessed online at www.fec.gov on December 6, 2004.

39. Center for Responsive Politics, accessed online at www.opensecrets.org/527s/527cmtes.asp on December 6, 2004. See also David Nather, "The $4 Billion Campaign: Better, or Just Louder?" *Congressional Quarterly Weekly* (October 30, 2004), pp. 2546–2550.

40. Complaining about the treatment he received from GOP conservatives, Jeffords quit the Party in the summer of 2001 and became an independent, shifting control of the Senate to Democrats for the balance of the 107th Congress.

41. Texas's new congressional map initially survived scrutiny by a special three-judge federal panel in Austin in January 2004. Then in October 2004, the U.S. Supreme Court ordered the lower court to revisit the case in light of ruling it had handed down in an April 2004 redistricting case (*Vieth v. Jubelirer*, 2004). The lower court's reconsideration is likely to come sometime in early 2005. As of this writing, Georgia's GOP-controlled state legislature had just passed its own mid-decade remap, which promises to bolster the state's Republican Congressional delegation.

42. Sabato's Crystal Ball, Volume II, Issue 48, accessed online at www.centerforpolitics.org/crystalball on November 9, 2004.

CHAPTER THIRTEEN

Conclusion

William Saletan
SLATE.COM

What was the 2004 campaign all about? What place will it occupy, and what watersheds will it mark, in the history of presidential elections? Here are eight educated guesses.

1. It was the first presidential election of the age of terrorism—and Democrats failed the test. In the latter third of the 20th century, Democrats won the presidency just three times: once in 1976 after Watergate, and twice in 1992 and 1996. Bill Clinton's victories raised Democratic hopes that the country was returning to a progressive era. Al Gore's capture of the popular vote in 2000 kept those hopes alive.

Two schools of thought predicted opposite outcomes in 2004. One school said Sept. 11 had changed everything. The other said it was the economy, stupid, and the economy was too weak to reelect an incumbent. The first school turned out to be roughly correct, but not exactly. Sept. 11 turned out to be not so much the dawn of a new political world as the return of an old one: a world dominated by national security and foreign policy.

In retrospect, the elections of 1992, 1996, and 2000 marked a lull between the era of communism and the era of terrorism. National security faded as a voting issue, and Democrats, liberated from the burden of being less trusted with the nation's safety, successfully exploited their advantages on health care, entitlements, and other domestic issues. Now the psychology of the Cold War has returned. The elections of 2002 tested whether, during the lull, the Democratic Party had effectively used its control of the presidency to regain the public's trust on national security. And the answer was no.

2. It crushed the illusion that Democrats could win by relying on their base. For decades, Democrats have clashed over the merits of playing to the center or the left. In the 1990s, centrists argued that Clinton's success demonstrated the wisdom of moving the party to the middle on balanced budgets and welfare reform. Liberals countered that Clinton got more political juice from exciting the party's base as he defended entitlements and fought for a higher minimum wage.

Gore's ambiguous result in 2000—winning the popular vote but losing the Electoral College—allowed both schools to claim vindication. Centrists accused Gore of blowing an easy win by abandoning Clinton's moderation and turning to insurrectionist populism. Progressives countered that Gore owed his surge in the final days to an outpouring of blacks, union members, and other traditional Democratic constituencies. In the 2004 primaries, liberals rallied behind Howard Dean as he promised to reclaim the White House by following the base-turnout strategy that had worked for Gore. They told themselves and each other that Democrats could swamp the GOP at the polls by mobilizing millions of nonvoters and disenchanted voters on the left.

The 2004 returns destroyed that fantasy. Democrats succeeded wildly in boosting turnout for their presidential nominee, from 51 million votes in 2000 to 59 million in 2004. But they were blown out of the water by turnout for George W. Bush, which ballooned from 50.5 million in 2000 to 62 million in 2004. The most aggressive mobilization effort ever mounted by Democrats failed to produce a base bigger than the GOP's. John Kerry won a majority of moderates and independents but was swamped by an outpouring of conservatives. For the first time in three decades, self-identified Republicans balanced self-identified Democrats at the polls.

The nature and magnitude of this defeat have broken the center-left stalemate. Chastened Democrats, including many liberals, are openly rethinking the party's positions on abortion, gay marriage, and national security.

3. It exposed and exacerbated the Democrats' geographic imbalance. Only one candidate in the 2004 Iowa Democratic caucuses, John Edwards of North Carolina, had ever won a statewide election in the South or Midwest. The two dominant candidates of 2003, Dean and Kerry, were products of New England, as was Joe Lieberman, the initial frontrunner. The party was doomed from the outset to nominate a candidate who would be perceived in battleground states largely as a domestic foreigner.

Where were the Southerners and Midwesterners? Erased from the top tier of senators and governors, thanks to four decades of Democratic decline in those regions. Edwards was criticized as unprepared for the presidency because he had served just one Senate term. Yet he decided not to seek re-election in 2004 largely because he recognized (and his replacement, Erskine Bowles, demonstrated) the near-impossibility of surviving as a Democratic nominee on the North Carolina ballot in a presidential election year. A first-term Democratic senator from North Carolina has to run for president, because there's no such thing as a second-term Democratic senator from North Carolina.

One of the most telling comments of 2004 was uttered by Kerry in what he thought was an off-the-record moment during the primaries. He said dismissively of Edwards, "He can't win his own state." Kerry thought—and convinced enough primary voters—that winning Massachusetts four times was better evidence of national viability than winning North Carolina once. This was a fatal misjudgment. Neither Kerry nor Dean had ever been tested in a difficult state. They dominated the race because they had avoided—not survived—natural selection.

In terms of statewide officeholders, the Democratic Party has been eaten out from the middle—the middle of the country and the middle of the ideological spectrum—leaving coastal liberals to vie for its presidential nomination. Worse, the cycle is self-perpetuating. The GOP's clean sweep in 2004 leaves Democrats with just four of the 26 Senate seats in the 13 Confederate states. There won't be any southern Democratic senators around to compete with Kerry or Hillary Clinton in 2008.

4. It was the dawn of commercial voter targeting and the national presidential caucus. The least appreciated factor of 2004 was a revolutionary decision by the Bush campaign. In a primary, a campaign's central task is persuasion, and its guiding objective is a plurality of the vote. In a caucus, the central task is turnout, and the guiding objective is an absolute number of votes. Kerry, like all presidential nominees before him, treated the election as a primary. Bush, unlike them all, treated it as a caucus.

Eight weeks after Kerry conceded, Thomas Edsall and James Grimaldi of the *Washington Post* detailed the ingenuity and impact of Bush's strategy. Instead of spending the usual 75 to 90 percent of their money on undecided voters, Republicans spent half of it on mobilizing sympathizers who had seldom or never voted. And instead of targeting these sympathizers through the usual methods—phone banks and direct mail in heavily Republican precincts—they used commercial databases to find Bush supporters beyond Republican bastions.

In previous elections, Republicans faced a big disadvantage: Only 15 percent of their voters—and even a smaller percentage of their soft voters—lived in heavily Republican precincts. Democrats could go into black neighborhoods and find reliable sympathizers; Republicans had to look harder. So Bush's strategists studied commercial databases for correlations between buying habits and political sympathies. They learned to target people who drank Coors, watched college football, or had caller ID. They analyzed this audience and tailored messages for each of 32 subgroups. This yielded a target audience four times bigger than normal, which they cultivated with tickets to Bush appearances and a huge volunteer get-out-the-vote operation on Election Day. The result was a jaw-dropping 23 percent increase in Bush's vote total from 2000 to 2004.

That's the good news for Republicans. The bad news is that it was probably a one-time trick. They'll be able to do the same thing next time, but Democrats will have caught up. The same commercial information that identifies Republican sympathizers in Democratic precincts can identify Democratic sympathizers in Republican precincts—and Democrats now have enough time to refine their own commercial targeting criteria for use in 2008.

5. It was the high-water mark of the antigay resistance. Most commentary in the election's immediate wake marveled at the success of religious conservatives in defeating gay marriage and re-electing Bush. All 13 states that considered ballot measures against gay marriage in 2004 passed them. Eleven of these referenda took place on Election Day and were widely credited with boosting Bush's turnout. In Ohio, pundits inferred that one such ballot measure had doubled Bush's share of the black vote and secured the state's 20 decisive electoral votes for the GOP.

In truth, the role of the ballot measures was overrated. As University of Virginia political scientist Paul Freedman demonstrated in an analysis of the election returns for *Slate*, "Putting gay marriage on the ballot actually reduced [relative to 2000] the degree to which Bush's vote share in the affected states exceeded his vote share elsewhere." But the larger story is that 2004 was an aberrational backlash year. The antigay ballot measures passed without a single defeat because the Massachusetts Supreme Court and the mayor of San Francisco, in authorizing gay marriages, had advanced too far ahead of the public. Nevertheless, the public is moving in the same direction.

A year before the election, the American Enterprise Institute compiled decades of polls on homosexuality. The numbers showed a pronounced, long-term leftward trend. From 1977 to 2003, the percentage of American adults who told Gallup that gays should have equal rights in job opportunities rose from 56 to 88, and the percentage who said gays should be hired as elementary school teachers rose from 27 to 61. In 1978, only 26 percent of adults told Gallup they would vote for a well-qualified gay presidential nominee of their own party. By 1999, that number had climbed to

59 percent. From 1986 to 2002, the percentage of college freshmen who told UCLA researchers it was important to have laws prohibiting gay relationships fell from 52 to 25. From 1991 to 2002, the percentage of adults who told the National Opinion Research Center that gay sex was always wrong fell from 76 to 53. Hostility to homosexuality is a short-term problem for Democrats but a long-term problem for Republicans.

6. **It was the crest of a cycle of moral conservatism.** Much ado was made of the 22 percent of voters who selected "moral values" as their top voting issue in 2004 exit polls. Democrats spent the ensuing months fretting about how to convey to the public their appreciation of values and religion. Subjectively, the problem was genuine: Dean and Kerry were uncomfortable talking about faith, and their discomfort was evident to many churchgoers. But objectively, the problem was overstated. As Freedman demonstrated, the percentage of values voters who cast ballots for Bush was no higher in 2004 than in 2000.

Moreover, 2004 was, in retrospect, the peak of a 20-year cycle of abortion politics. It was a replay of 1984, the midway point of the previous two-term Republican administration. In Ronald Reagan's first term, pro-lifers were riding high, and pro-choice politicians ran for the hills. The public didn't have to confront the serious possibility that abortion would be criminalized. But in Reagan's second term, two Supreme Court justices stepped down, and the balance of the court shifted enough to reopen *Roe v. Wade* in 1989. Millions of voters who had previously thought of abortion as a question of moral sentiment became alarmed at the increasing prospect of laws and cops meddling in family affairs. Not until the Court reaffirmed *Roe* in 1992 did pro-lifers begin to recover politically. Their support in polls grew from 1994 to 2004 precisely because *Roe* was safe and no more justices stepped down.

This was the history I recounted last year in *Bearing Right: How Conservatives Won the Abortion War* (www.bearingright.com). Now that history is on the verge of repeating itself. A conservative president is entering his second term. Several justices are likely to step down. An increasingly confident pro-life movement is pressing to overturn *Roe*, igniting a political war like the one that engulfed the nation in 1989 and 1990. Leading congressional Republicans are openly challenging the whole idea of a right to privacy. If they get that fight, the "values election" of 2004 could well be dwarfed by the "privacy election" of 2008.

7. **It was the debut of biotechnology as a campaign issue.** The completion of the Human Genome Project in 2003 and the death of President Reagan from Alzheimer's disease in June 2004 opened a new era not only in medicine but in politics. Human embryonic stem-cell research emerged as a potent issue for attracting and mobilizing millions of voters whose friends or relatives suffered from degenerative diseases. The public began to see biotechnology less as an arcane scientific topic or as a fringe moral concern and more as an issue of intense material self-interest.

John Kerry talked about stem-cell research routinely at campaign stops. In the general election, his campaign devoted two major speeches, a television ad, and two weekly radio addresses to the topic. Hillary Clinton and numerous other speakers raised the subject at the Democratic convention. Ron Reagan, son of the late president, talked about it for 20 minutes in the most watched hour of prime time. The Kerry campaign distributed internal polling that showed 69 percent of voters, including a majority of Republicans, supporting the research. Even the Republican governor of California, Arnold Schwarzenegger, endorsed a ballot measure to fund the research. It passed with 59 percent of the vote.

In the decades to come, there is every reason to expect steady expansion in the range of biotechnology issues and their impact in elections. As science advances toward applying this research to diseases, pressure will grow to loosen federal restrictions on funding. The California referendum is already prompting other states to bid more aggressively for biotech business. Democrats need a new issue to attract uncommitted voters, and this may be their most promising option.

8. It was the death of the 20-state campaign. Kerry began the 2004 general election with 10 states in the bag and aspirations to compete in 20 more. By late September, he had given up on seven of the targeted 20. By Election Day, he could count on only 13 states worth 186 electoral votes and was competing seriously in 10 others worth 126 electoral votes. Bush, meanwhile, had locked up 27 states worth 226 electoral votes. All Bush had to do was capture one-third of the contested electoral votes, which he achieved by taking Florida and Ohio. Kerry had left himself too few options and his opponent too many.

That was the mathematical problem. The political problem went deeper. By ceding whole regions of the country, Kerry allowed Bush to run up enormous margins, padding his lead in the popular vote. The theory of Kerry's 20-state campaign was that the popular vote didn't matter. After all, it hadn't saved Gore. But that view was mistaken. Gore's victory in the popular vote was what gave him the political credibility to challenge the outcome in 2000. And Kerry's defeat in the popular vote by three million ballots was what denied him the political credibility to challenge the outcome in 2004.

The increasing precision of campaign technology—specifically, the ability to calculate vote spreads in each state and to reallocate resources away from states that aren't close to those that are—suggests that the trend of the last two presidential elections will continue. More and more states will be too close to call on election night. In that situation, the popular vote will become a *de facto* arbiter of the apparent loser's ability to fight on in the courts. Candidates will have to compete nationwide because lawyers won't decide who gets a recount. Voters will.

William Saletan is the chief political correspondent for *Slate* and the author of *Bearing Right: How Conservatives Won the Abortion War* (Berkeley: University of California Press, 2004).

CHAPTER FOURTEEN

Conclusion

Charles E. Cook
Cook Political Report

After any American presidential election, a hundred analysts could reach at least a hundred different conclusions as to what were the key elements and turning points in that election, probably many more. National campaigns have many moving parts; ascertaining which ones were more decisive than others is obviously highly subjective. Unfortunately, too many contemporaneous analyses of elections these days are tinged by either personal ideological or partisan biases, are self-serving, or both. The University of Virginia's inimitable Larry Sabato has pulled together some of the best in this unique book, which undoubtedly will be a terrific resource for those who want to rehash this election sooner or for scholars later wanting to divine what the 2004 election was all about, who won, how, why, and what does it mean.

Some conservatives and Republicans are calling 2004 a transformational or realigning election, which indicates a seismic shift in American politics that will continue to be felt in future elections. Conversely, Democrats and liberals argue that Democratic nominee John Kerry and his campaign were solely to blame, that another nominee or better campaign would have carried Ohio, and very likely held onto Iowa and New Mexico, and emerged victorious with Electoral College votes to spare. A third point of view is that President Bush's enhanced stature and leadership dimension after the 9/11 tragedy and his handling of 9/11, led to a natural advantage on security issues that made a 2004 election result almost inevitable.

While there will always be questions about the outcome of the 2000 presidential election, only members of the political equivalent of the Flat Earth Society question who really won in 2004. A 51-percent to 48-percent popular vote outcome is hardly a landslide. Indeed, it is the narrowest victory margin for an elected incumbent President in history. Still, it is a decisive, measurable and unquestioned win. In terms of the Electoral College, where President Bush prevailed over Sen. John Kerry 271–266, the election effectively came down to 118,599 votes in the state of Ohio where 5,627,903 people voted, a very close race but not one for which reasonable people can question the outcome.

Although Republicans made small gains in the House, it was their four-seat pick-up in the U.S. Senate, taking them from 51 seats to 49 for Democrats before the election up to a 55 to 45 majority after, that underscored the overall Republican victory on November 2. The upset defeat of Senate Minority Leader Tom Daschle, the first Senate leader to lose re-election in 52 years, was the exclamation point.

A GREAT BUSH-CHENEY CAMPAIGN

There is rarely just one reason why one candidate wins or loses a competitive presidential election. In the case of this election, the first reason that President Bush won was that Bush-Cheney '04 was the best organized and executed presidential campaign in American history. They were focused, disciplined and relentless, thinking several moves ahead like a master chess player. While they did not end up having the financial advantage that just about everyone predicted, they still prevailed. It's hard to spot any serious mistakes or flaws in strategy or tactics. The few errors that were committed ended up being of no real consequence.

Equally important is that Bush campaign operatives believed that previous Republican presidential candidates "lost" about two percentage points on Election Day simply because Democrats usually have a superior "get-out-the-vote" operation. While Democrats, largely through the Americans Coming Together and state parties, fielded the best ground game in their history by a long shot, reaching their vote total goals in many key states such as Florida and Ohio, the GOP effort was every bit as good as the Democrats and very likely just a bit better.

But not to be underestimated is that as a result of the tragedy of the September 11, 2001 terrorist attacks and President Bush's subsequent handling of the terrorist attacks, Bush's political stature and the perception of a strong leadership soared, and even in the toughest of times during the two years of this election campaign, his stature advantage and that leadership dimension provided a foundation of support that never left him. This is not to say that President Bush could not have lost re-election because of 9/11, far from it, but that the political benefits that he enjoyed from his handling of it proved to be of incalculable benefit.

A TRANSFORMATIONAL OR REALIGNING ELECTION?

Generally speaking, when a party scores a big, meaningful win, they either pile up the states and electoral votes as Lyndon Johnson (1964), Richard Nixon (1972) and Ronald Reagan (1980 and 1984) did, or they enjoy big gains up and down the ballot and from coast to coast, as in the cases of Johnson and Reagan (1980). Such wins also occurred in the mid-term elections of 1958, 1974 and 1994, and to a lesser extent in 1982 and 1986. Big and broad victories are an indication that there was more substance to the win than just one side fielding a superior candidate, running a better campaign, or having greater financial resources. But if one looks at the 2004 results, it's hard to write this as a coast-to-coast, top-to-bottom victory for the GOP, let alone a mandate.

In the U.S. House of Representatives, Republicans scored a net gain of just three seats, out of 435 seats up for grabs. Republicans picked up five seats in Texas as a result of an extraordinary mid-decade redistricting, engineered by House Majority Leader Tom DeLay. If Texas had not been in the equation, the GOP would have actually suffered a net loss of two seats nationally. While a gain is a gain, it tends to undercut an argument that voters nationwide sent a strong, pro-Republican message on Election Day. Perhaps what is more impressive than the three-seat gain is the fact that after spending 40 years in the minority, Republicans have held onto control of the House for a decade. This is the first time that Republicans have held onto a House majority for ten years since 1932, when they lost a majority they had held for 16 years.

Republicans lost some ground in state legislative races, suffering a net loss of 59 of the 7,382 seats nationwide, giving Republicans a microscopic one-seat edge, 3,657(R) to 3,656(D) (from the National Conference of State Legislatures). Before the election, Republicans controlled both chambers of the state legislatures in 21 states, Democrats were in charge in 17, 11 were split (the remaining state, Nebraska, has a non-partisan, unicameral legislature). After the election, Republicans have majorities in 20 states, Democrats in 19, and 10 are split. If this were truly a transformational GOP election year, Republicans would have gained a substantial number of state legislative seats, perhaps several hundred, not lost five dozen seats. Plus, the narrow split suggests that our two major parties remain very evenly matched.

In the U.S. Senate, where the unexpected four-seat gain by Republicans is unquestionably impressive, it is important to note that it was essentially scored in the South and reflects a continuing realignment of that region from Democratic to Republican. The GOP gained five seats in the South (Florida, Georgia, Louisiana, North Carolina and South Carolina), but outside of the South, Republicans actually suffered a net loss of one seat, losing seats in Colorado and Illinois while gaining one in South Dakota. A big, regional victory for the GOP? Absolutely, Republicans were rocking and rolling in the South, but outside of the South, and South Dakota, it is impossible to interpret the Senate results as a sign of a pro-Republican or conservative trend.

Even on the presidential level, only three states voted differently in 2004 than they did in 2000. President Bush picked up two states that Democratic nominee Al Gore carried last time, Iowa and New Mexico, but he lost New Hampshire, which he had carried four years ago. The voting patterns were quite similar to four years ago, with the President doing a bit better here and there, a bit worse in a few others but the resemblance from four years ago is very high.

THE RED-BLUE VOTER TURNOUT DIFFERENTIAL

I do not know a single person who voted for John Kerry on November 2. Yet half of all the people I know voted against George W. Bush. It would appear that Kerry did not win a single state, demographic group or political subgroup that would not have gone for virtually any credible Democrat running against President Bush under those circumstances. Early on it was posited that Kerry might excel among military veterans, particularly fellow Vietnam War veterans, but in the end, that was not the case. Kerry simply won the default Democratic vote.

In part, the three-point popular vote gap between President Bush and Sen. Kerry can be partially explained by a disparity in voter turnout increases between the Bush "red" base states and Kerry "blue" base states. In the 12 "purple" swing states, voter turnout went up a whopping 17 percent over 2000. In the bright red states, those that were universally expected to vote Republican, turnout increased by 14 percent. In the bright blue states, those expected to go for Kerry, though, turnout only went up by 11 percent. It would be logical to assume then that in those states that were not "in play," Bush's supporters were more motivated than those voting against him. It's hard to find someone who was enthusiastically voting for Kerry, but not at all hard to find someone who was passionately voting against the President.

Four years ago, author Michael Barone accurately observed in his essay introducing the newest edition of *The Almanac of American Politics* that we were a 49–49 nation. While one can make the case that we are a 51–48 nation, pointing to the overall presidential popular vote (the popular vote for Congress was almost identical at 50–47), it's hard to make the case that the country is any less polarized than it was four years ago. No matter who won this election, roughly half of the electorate would be devastated, emotions ran so high.

A BIFURCATED ELECTION

One aspect about the 2004 presidential campaign that sets it apart from others is the extent to which it was a bifurcated election. While presidential campaigns have always focused more on swing states than those they were clearly going to win or lose, this has never been so obvious as it was last year. Voters in swing states were bombarded by television ads, mail and phone calls, while voters in other states were seeing the campaign only on the evening news, on cable, in the newspaper or on the Internet. One set of voters had 50-yard line, front row seats, while others were watching from the last row of the corner section of the stadium.

The irony is that candidates are judged to a large extent by their standing in national polls (though they actually just survey the 48 continental states) and by the national popular vote after the election even though the campaigns are only really waged in roughly a quarter of the states. Top strategists from previous presidential efforts like Ed Rollins (Reagan 1984) and Carter Eskew (Gore 2000) have noted that back in the late spring and early summer of 2004 when money was no object, the Kerry campaign would have been well advised to run some national advertising, rather than focusing so narrowly on the swing states, in an effort to define himself before the national surveys became part of the fabric of the race.

This was a campaign in which both parties mounted Herculean efforts to identify their voters and get them out. The Bush-Cheney campaign, in concert with the Republican National Committee and state parties, undertook an unprecedented effort to get out their vote. They got considerable assistance from the business community led by the U.S. Chamber of Commerce and Business-Industry Political Action Committee, and an impressive effort by social and religious conservative groups to motivate the estimated four million social conservatives who apparently did not vote in 2000. At the same time, the Democratic National Committee, the AFL-CIO, the environmental community and especially America Coming Together mounted the most sophisticated effort that Democrats had ever waged. They not only met but exceeded their vote total goals in key states such as Ohio and Florida, only to be edged out as turnout across the board surged and Republican efforts matched them vote for vote.

The two sides had the same objectives—identifying and turning out their supporters in the dozen key states—but they employed vastly different methods. Democrats relied more on paid workers, some from out-of-state, who walked door to door in key precincts carrying handheld personal desk assistants loaded with data on each household. Republicans relied more on the efforts of volunteers than paid workers, using rallies featuring President Bush to attract and identify campaign volunteers or to provide an incentive for volunteers to work harder by offering up VIP seating to those who knocked on more doors or made more calls or stuffed more envelopes. In the end, Republicans did a bit better job, but the grassroots efforts on both sides dwarfed previous efforts at the presidential level by leaps and bounds.

HOW THE CANDIDATES WERE DEFINED

Whenever an incumbent president is seeking re-election, the election is first and foremost a referendum on that president and how he has performed. In this election, just over 40 percent of the nation believed it was critical to re-elect President Bush and another 40 percent or so were adamant in their opposition, meaning that the campaign began with President Bush clearly at the pivot point regardless of who he ran against. But once Sen. John Kerry secured his party's nomination, the Bush-Cheney campaign set about making the election as much a referendum on Kerry as about the President. They effectively defined Kerry as an unacceptable alternative for voters unhappy with or ambivalent about President Bush's tenure.

The Bush-Cheney campaign used a two-prong strategy to attack Kerry. First, they sought to define Kerry as unacceptably liberal, and given that Kerry is a Democrat from Massachusetts, that wasn't too hard. Long before it was clear that Kerry would be the Democratic nominee, Bush campaign strategist Matthew Dowd was privately making the point that it was not coincidental that the last three Democrats to win the White House were all southerners: Lyndon Johnson (TX), Jimmy Carter (GA) and Bill Clinton (AR). Dowd made the point that among swing voters there is a presumption that a southern Democrat was relatively moderate until proven otherwise. There is also a presumption that any Massachusetts Democrat is a liberal until proven otherwise. When Democrats nominate a candidate from the Northeast, particularly New England and most specifically, Massachusetts, the party takes on a burden of proof, having to prove to the American people that their nominee is within the American mainstream. When Democrats nominate a candidate from the South, that burden is shifted to Republicans, who most prove that the Democratic nominee is outside that mainstream. Stereotypes are alive and well in American politics.

Using the *National Journal* congressional voting ratings, President Bush and his campaign charged that Kerry was the single most liberal member of the Senate, often saying that he was more liberal than "Teddy Kennedy or Hillary Clinton." While there is little doubt that Kerry is quite liberal, the charge was based on just one year's worth of votes out of Kerry's previous 19 years in the U.S. Senate. That year, 2003, Kerry participated in very few votes since he was on the campaign trail almost full time and only came back for a few key votes.

A more accurate and fair measurement of Kerry's liberalism is his lifetime *National Journal* voting rating, which ranked him the 11th most liberal Senator out of all current U.S. Senators. While 11th out of 100 is unquestionably liberal, there is a huge symbolic difference between being number 1 and number 11. Still, Kerry clearly lost the argument and was tagged as an unreconstructed liberal.

The second prong of the strategy, and one that ran somewhat contrary to the first charge was that Kerry was a "flip-flopper," one who would lick his finger and stick it up in the air to see which way the political winds were blowing at any given time. This is obviously something different from being an unreconstructed liberal. But Kerry's statement that he "voted for the $87 billion [in funding for the war in Iraq] before he voted against it," became "the gift that kept on giving," as Karl Rove said after the election. It was a devastating blow to anyone seeking to be entrusted with the presidency, particularly at a time when security was a top concern.

Thus, Kerry was plagued with the worst of both worlds. He was portrayed as a flip-flopper, which robbed him of any credit for having principled views while being tagged as a hopeless liberal who would be unable to deal with changing conditions and situations. It is very hard to win an election carrying these dual burdens.

At the same time, the September 11 tragedy and his position as a wartime President offered Bush opportunities to project strength and leadership that clearly gave him an advantage in this election. To be sure, the economy was simply not creating the number of jobs expected and desired, and a controversial war in Iraq that by just about any standard had not gone well, were real and serious problems for this President. Despite these problems, President Bush entered the race with the characteristics of strength and leadership clearly in his favor, something that did not change over the course of the campaign.

Apart from how the Bush campaign effectively positioned Kerry as both an unreconstructed liberal and a flip-flopper, the Democratic nominee was plagued by his inability to connect with rank-and-file voters. Voters sensed that Kerry was cut from a very different social and economic bolt of cloth than they. Few voters would likely believe that Kerry would have been comfortable at a barbecue in their backyard or that of anyone they knew. Democratic analyst Ruy Teixeira points out that in the exit polls, among working-class white voters (defined as whites without a four-year college degree), Kerry lost by 23 percentage points, six points worse than Gore fared four years ago. Among these working-class white voters, only 39 percent said that they would trust Kerry more to handle the economy, 55 percent said that they would more likely trust President Bush.

At the same time, while Kerry would undoubtedly get votes from those who were adamantly against the war in Iraq and would vote for just about anyone against President Bush, his ability to extend that base level of support and siphon off the support of independents or moderate Republican voters, or get a greater share of conservative and moderate Democrats, was undercut by this perception that he was aloof and unlikely to understand their lives and the issues that concerned them. President Bush's pedigree is quite similar to Kerry's (Ivy League education, economic status, etc.), yet Bush's speaking style and his personality are not consistent with his social and economic status, and therefore he is not plagued with this inability to connect to average Americans the way Kerry was.

Kerry's inability to connect was exacerbated by the public's perception of his wife Teresa and her Heinz fortune. Mrs. Heinz Kerry's off-hand remark during the campaign questioning that First Lady Laura Bush had never held a real job definitely hurt her husband's candidacy. Pollsters in both parties say that Mrs. Bush, a former librarian, enjoys perhaps the greatest popularity of any First Lady in history. Mrs. Kerry, meanwhile, is seen as one of the richest people in the country and one of the very few with her own private jet.

His impressive concession speech on November 3 notwith-standing, Kerry only seemed to be an interesting person for all of 15 minutes during his 20 years as a member of the U.S. Senate and 18 months on the campaign trail. Those 15 minutes came in July during the Democratic Convention in Boston when his two impressive and well-spoken daughters spoke about their father. They showed Kerry as a real person and revealed a side of him that had been absent until that point and would only resurface again during his concession speech. While Kerry was never going to be a charismatic or compelling figure, his campaign failed him by not more effectively portraying him as a real, interesting and caring person who could comfortably walk into any suburban living room to discuss voters' problems.

When people vote for president, they are deciding who to let into their living rooms for four years. As such, they want to feel some connection, some bond with whomever they support for President.

When incumbent Presidents have lost re-election over the course of the last 30 years, it has been when three circumstances have existed. First, the economy was either in, or perceived to be in, bad shape. Second, the challenger was an interesting, compelling or even charismatic person. Third, the challenger's message was perfectly matched for the circumstances and political climate of the election year.

In 1976, the U.S. economy was a mess when along came Jimmy Carter, a Naval Academy graduate, former nuclear submarine officer, former Georgia Governor and peanut farmer with a family that was straight out of the movie *Fried Green Tomatoes*. The public was angry and distrustful of politics and career Washington politicians in that first post-Watergate presidential election. They were looking for honesty and integrity and Carter's message that, "I will never lie to you," resonated perfectly. This message would not have worked four or eight years earlier and it obviously didn't work four years later.

In 1980, the economy was a mess again, and along came Ronald Reagan. Reagan, too, was a fascinating person with a message that was perfectly formulated for the year. American hostages were being held in Iran, the United States had bungled an effort to rescue them, Americans were frustrated with a government that had grown bloated and were upset with high taxes. Reagan's optimistic message about restoring America's place in the world as well as cutting the size of government was perfect for the year and he was able to beat President Carter.

In 1992, the economy was in a downturn once again and the public perceived President George H.W. Bush as inattentive to both economic and domestic problems and overly preoccupied with foreign policy. Along came Bill Clinton, yet another fascinating person, with a message that he was going to "focus on the economy like a laser beam," and was going to put domestic concerns at the top of his priority list. He beat President Bush.

Thinking back to those three elections, it's hard to describe John Kerry as an interesting person or someone who had a message that matched up in the same seamless way that Carter's, Reagan's and Clinton's did.

Furthermore, Kerry's message on the issues of importance like the economy, job creation and the war in Iraq were not clean or easily understood. In fact, Kerry did not come across as someone who truly understood the economic and pocketbook problems facing working people, and his position on Iraq was unintelligible at best.

THE KERRY CAMPAIGN

While there is much to criticize about the strategy, tactics and message of the Kerry campaign, there was much that they did do right. The campaign raised an unprecedented and unexpectedly large amount of money. They also used the internet very effectively, learning from Howard Dean's campaign and then taking the lesson several steps further. Finally, at least after the Labor Day arrival of several former high-ranking Clinton White House and campaign staffers, Kerry's message was sharper and his missteps became fewer and further in between.

Still, besides the fact that they failed to flesh out Kerry the person, the Kerry campaign also had a slow, cumbersome decision-making process that lacked clear lines of authority. Kerry seemed to want to consult with half the western world before making decisions. This was in stark contrast to the Bush campaign that had a small, tightly knit and nimble high command that could make decisions quickly and without too much outside interference.

While repeatedly saying that they had learned the lesson about failing to respond to attacks quickly and forcefully from the ill-fated 1988 Dukakis campaign, they managed to repeat history, particularly when it came to attacks from a group of fellow Navy Swift Boat veterans. Although the Kerry campaign was heavily focused on the Senator's four-month Navy tour in Vietnam, they failed to anticipate the damage that the attacks on his performance in the war by the Swift Boat veterans would cause. The campaign's decision not to answer the charges effectively for several weeks would keep the charges alive and cause Kerry's candidacy to hemorrhage at a critical juncture of the campaign.

Apart from putting too many eggs in his Vietnam service basket, the Kerry campaign squandered the opportunity provided by the Democratic National Convention. There are very few points in a presidential campaign when many Americans "check in" and really pay attention. One of those times is during the parties' national conventions. The Kerry high command's strategic decision to have an upbeat, positive convention that extolled Kerry's leadership and valor in Vietnam rather than shine the spotlight on President Bush and his actions on the economy and jobs, health care and drug costs was a colossal blunder.

After the election, Bush campaign strategists continued to be amazed that the Kerry campaign never honed a coherent and convincing message on the economy and specifically on jobs. One key player in the Bush campaign later conceded that had the Kerry campaign articulated a strong jobs message, Ohio would have unquestionably fallen into the Democratic column. Instead, jobs and economic concerns, even in places that had suffered horrific job losses like Ohio, were crowded out by other concerns, including social and cultural issues including "Amendment One," the gay marriage amendment in Ohio. While the issue of gay marriages, as opposed to civil unions, would undoubtedly have been a controversial and polarizing issue, a stronger economic message or perhaps a more convincing spokesman on the jobs issue would likely have muscled the jobs issue to the forefront.

In contrast, the Republican convention was brilliantly designed and executed. Every major moving part had a form and function that fit the needs of the campaign. The Bush campaign saw the need to talk about how September 11 changed the country, the world and the presidency while not opening itself up to charges of exploiting the tragedy. Their answer was to give the task to popular former New York City Mayor Rudy Giuliani, and he handled it very effectively.

Next, the Bush campaign wanted to reiterate the case for waging a war in Iraq, but needed it to come from an independent person with enormous credibility. So, they went to Sen. John McCain, a man with an impeccable military record who challenged Bush in the 2000 GOP primaries and who has never been shy about criticizing the President and his administration.

They also needed someone to talk about the President's economic philosophy and its focus on self-reliance and opportunity. Who better to do this than a successful immigrant, Austrian native and California Gov. Arnold Schwarzenegger?

Finally, the campaign needed someone to forcefully attack Kerry. Again, they wanted an unlikely suspect, so they got Zell Miller, a Democratic Senator, who viciously attacked the Democratic nominee. Miller's speech was extremely effective and more so as he was at least nominally one of Kerry's colleagues.

In addition to their inability to take advantage of the national convention spotlight, the Kerry campaign also stumbled by continuing to return their focus to the war in Iraq, despite the fact that it was winning them little additional support. Voters who were opposed to the war were already supporting Kerry, despite the fact that his own position on the war was nebulous.

It was obvious throughout the campaign that any day voters were focused on the economy and the slow growth in jobs, or on health care or prescription drug costs, was a bad day for President Bush. But, if the focus was on just about anything else, it was either a not-so-bad or even a good day for the President. In the closing days of the campaign, Kerry chased that rabbit down that trail again when he chose to talk about the missing arms cache in Iraq, rather than about the economy and health care. While certainly not under Kerry's control, the release of a new tape from Osama bin Laden right before the election further threw Kerry off-message at a critical juncture.

In thinking about Kerry's problems as a candidate and those of his campaign, the fact that he got 48 percent of the popular vote, the second largest number of popular votes in American history, took 266 Electoral College votes, and came within 118,599 of winning the presidency, tells us just how vulnerable President Bush was. This was a very winnable race for Democrats. Not just any Democrat could have won, but the outcome of this race was hardly a foregone conclusion, regardless of how impressive the Bush campaign was.

THE DEMOCRATIC PARTY

For all of Kerry and his campaign's problems, there are also significant problems within the Democratic Party that cannot be blamed on him. Even the most cursory look at the national county-level red-blue map of the 2000 and 2004 presidential election returns reveals the truth that Democrats have become the party of minorities and metropolitan areas. Cities and close-in suburbs, along with counties with very heavy minority populations are blue (Democratic), while the rest of the country is almost solidly red (Republican). Democrats do great among voters who watch "Friends" and "Will and Grace," sip Starbucks lattes and listen to National Public Radio. In the outer suburbs, exurbs, small towns and in rural areas where voters watch old reruns on TV Land, drink coffee from

Dunkin' Donuts and listen to country music, though, Democrats ring up "No Sale."

In the past, voting patterns have been driven to a large extent by income and education. Those voters with lower income and educational levels would vote more Democratic, while those with higher incomes and more education would vote more Republican. Over the last 20 years, however, we've seen social and cultural issues become more important in determining how Americans vote. Attitudes on abortion, gun control and, to a lesser extent, the environment have now become important. This explains how a heavily Democratic state like West Virginia can vote for George W. Bush in 2000 and re-elect him by an even higher margin in 2004, while heavily Republican suburban areas like Montgomery, Bucks and Delaware Counties just outside of Philadelphia voted for Al Gore four years ago and for Kerry by larger margins last year.

While this can get a Democrat up to 48 percent as Kerry won in 2004 or 48.4 percent, as Gore won in 2000, it doesn't quite get a Democrat to 50 percent, or more important, to the 270 Electoral College votes needed to win the White House. Over the last four elections, Democrats have won 19 states with a total of 248 electoral votes, suggesting that the party is not fundamentally broken, but needs to expand its appeal to win the presidency.

Much has been said about the role that values may have played in this election. The national exit poll suggested that moral values, named by 22 percent of those polled, was the biggest single issue cited by voters in their presidential election decision-making. Critics, including some of the pollsters involved in the formulation of the exit poll questionnaire, have suggested that this was a badly worded question and noted that *values* means different things to different people. But the fact that 80 percent of those who cited values as their key decision-making factor cast their ballots for Bush and only 18 percent for Kerry suggests that whatever values means to those voters, they clearly saw Bush as more aligned with their views than Kerry.

Interestingly, a majority of those values voters were not white, evangelical born-again Christians, as many believe. While they may be church-goers, these were not necessarily followers of conservatives like Rev. James Dobson or Pat Robertson. They were just heartland and middle Americans who believe that American society is changing too fast and who associate the Democratic Party with these unwelcome changes. The differences between the lifestyle and world view of urban and metropolitan America and those of small town/rural/outer suburban/exurban America are great. The worlds of Starbucks and of Wal-Mart are almost mutually exclusive. These are people who do not know each other and who do not share common attitudes about politics or policy.

Whether Americans fully agree with President Bush's set of values, they know he has them and what they are. No one had any clear idea whether Kerry had a set of values or what they were if he did. People are more likely to respect someone who clearly articulates his/her values, even if some are different than their own.

One small but telling factor in this campaign was that while the Bush-Cheney campaign spent millions on radio advertising, *Hotline* editor Chuck Todd points out that neither the Kerry-Edwards campaign nor the Media Fund, the primary independent pro-Democratic media group, spent much money on radio, except on minority radio stations. This is telling because Democrats knew they had problems with voters in small town and rural areas in places like Ohio and Iowa, yet they seemed unaware that reaching at least some of these people is better accomplished while they are in their cars and trucks than when they are sitting in their living rooms watching television. Television ads are easier (and more profitable) to buy, but some voters don't watch much television and must be reached in other ways. The Bush-Cheney campaign seemed to appreciate this, even airing ads on special television networks in health clubs to target young professionals who spend little time at home watching television.

Certainly it is unfair to label the side who took 51 percent as geniuses, and the side who took 48 percent as goats. But as the saying goes, "close only counts in horseshoes and hand grenades." For Democrats, the status quo means coming close, but not winning. This election was the product of a fabulous Bush-Cheney campaign apparatus and an incumbent who was helped immeasurably by his handling of the 9/11 tragedy on the one hand, and on the other, an aloof, distant candidate with a mediocre campaign that never measured up to the competition.

Charles E. Cook, Jr. is editor and publisher of the *Cook Political Report*, a weekly columnist for *National Journal* magazine and a political analyst for NBC News.